After Abolition

For the nameless ones

After Abolition

Britain and the Slave Trade Since 1807

MARIKA SHERWOOD

I.B. TAURIS

LONDON · NEW YORK

Published in 2007 by
I.B.Tauris & Co. Ltd
6 Salem Rd, London w2 4bu
175 Fifth Avenue, New York ny 10010
www.ibtauris.com

In the United States and Canada distributed by Palgrave Macmillan,
a division of St. Martin's Press, 175 Fifth Avenue, New York, ny 10010

isbn   978 1 84511 365 0

A full CIP record for this book is available from the British Library
A full CIP record for this book is available from the Library of Congress
Library of Congress catalog card: available

Typeset in Monotype Jansen by illuminati, Grosmont,
www.illuminatibooks.co.uk
Printed and bound in Great Britain by
TJ International Ltd, Padstow, Cornwall

Contents

List of illustrations

Acknowledgements

My thanks are due to many people and organisations.

First of all to the Royal Academy, for providing me with travel funds. Then to Liz Friend-Smith at I.B.Tauris for her careful and constructive criticism.

In the USA: librarians at the Library of Congress, Washington DC; Jessica Kratz, Legislative Archives, NARA, and Rod Ross, Congressional records, NARA; New York Historical Society librarians; University of North Carolina at Chapel Hill – Devon Lee of the library's manuscripts department. Ulrike Bernhardt and Susan Hauser, for offering me free beds. In Ghana: archivists at the National Archives, Accra and Tamale; librarians in the Palm Library, University of Ghana at Legon, and the George Padmore Research Library. In Spain: Publicaciones Periódicas.

In the UK: librarians at Birmingham (Peter Drake), British Library, Canterbury Cathedral Archives, Goldsmith's Library at the University of London, Institute of Commonwealth Studies, Liverpool Local History Library. And archivists Fiona Tait, Birmingham City Archives; Jane Bedford, Colchester Record Office; Alison Campbell, Cornwall Record Office; Alison Cable, East Kent Archives; Mairi Hunter, Ewart Library, Dumfries; James Turtle, Gloucestershire Record Office; Helena Smart and others, Liverpool Local Record Office; Sue Donnelly, London School of Economics and Political

Science; Richard Bond, Manchester Local History Library; Guy Grannum and others, National Archives, London; Lorna Hyland, National Maritime Museum, Merseyside; all the archivists, Rhodes House Library; William Meredith, Unilever Archives, Port Sunlight, Wirral; and to Mary Cunneen, chair, Anti-Slavery International; Steve Hartgroves, Historic Environment Service; and Tony Tibbles, Keeper, Merseyside Maritime Museum.

For encouragement, help and support, Russell Cartwright, Max Farrar, Peter Freshwater, Victor Gray, Avtar Jouhl, Malcolm Mc-Ronald, Takyiwaa Manuh, Shirley Meredeen, Ayodeji Olukoju, Colin Prescod, Tom Wareham. For help with editing, Andrew Fenyö, Craig Sherwood, Rosie Sherwood, Jenny Tarrant and Kim Sherwood (who also helped with research and gave invaluable stylistic suggestions).

Thank you all!

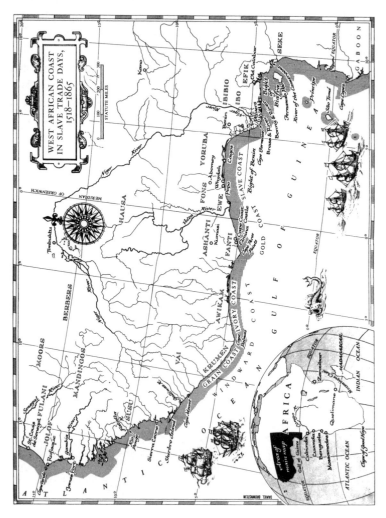

Map of the West African coast

Introduction

Britain, after much campaigning by Black and White residents and lengthy debates in Parliament, passed an Act in 1807 making it illegal to participate in the trade in enslaved African women, men and children. As the government recognised that various ways of avoiding this Act were found by traders, other Acts were passed in an attempt to close these loopholes. There were so many Acts that they were 'consolidated' twice, in 1824 and again in 1844.

Britain was *not* the first European country to make it illegal to trade in slaves. That honour goes to Denmark: in 1792 the Danish government declared that importing slaves into her Caribbean colonies would be illegal from 1803. Whether Denmark was permitted to supply slaves to any other colonies after this date I have not been able to discover.

Trading in slaves was a very lucrative business. Britain attempted to cajole, persuade, inveigle other trading countries to follow her example. Most European countries slowly acquiesced; some passed Acts that were obeyed, other Acts were circumvented. North Americans were probably the most robust traders from the 1840s onwards. Negotiations with independent Brazil frequently faltered and for a while led to ill feelings and a reduction in 'legitimate' trade.

In 1833 Britain passed an Act emancipating her slaves – in the Caribbean, Canada and Cape Town, not elsewhere in the then

Empire, and not immediately. Caribbean slaves were to serve an 'apprenticeship'. This period was curtailed and emancipation was announced in 1838. There was no compensation for the slaves. Their ex-owners received £20 million for their loss of unpaid labour. That would be just under £1 billion in 2005.

In 1842 there were estimates of between 5 and 10 million enslaved people in India, then ruled by the British East India Company on behalf of the British government. Some were Africans, others indigenous peoples. In this book I barely glance at India, and have omitted the trade in enslaved Africans across the Indian Ocean and to Arabia.[1]

Other European countries also freed their slaves. For example, the Dutch announced emancipation for their slaves in Surinam, in South America, in 1863 – after a ten-year apprenticeship. The last Act of Abolition in the British Empire was in 1928, in the Gold Coast.

Whether there had been a profit in the trade in slaves in the eighteenth century, and if so how much, has been much debated. However, why anyone would have continued to participate in a trade which did *not* make them rich is incomprehensible to me. What is even more difficult to understand is why so many of the historians engaged in this debate stop at 1807. Why have they created the notion that the passing of that very famous Act stopped Britain from profiting from the slave trade, and from slavery? Is it still not possible to look at British history critically? Thoroughly? And honestly?

There has been no thorough investigation of British involvement, though David Eltis, one of the leading historians of the slave trade, has written that

> The flow of British resources into the slave trade did not cease in 1807. After this date British subjects owned, managed, and manned slaving adventures; they purchased newly imported Africans in the Americas; they supplied ships, equipment, insurance, and most important of all trade goods and credit to foreign slave traders.[2]

Another leader in the field, Hugh Thomas, in his magisterial *The Slave Trade: The History of the Atlantic Slave Trade 1440–1870*, published in 1997, admitted that 'continuing English involvement in the trade is more difficult to analyse'. The admission is on page 570; there are another 250 pages in this book, but barely a mention of the involvement.

ANNO QUADRAGESIMO SEPTIMO

GEORGII III. REGIS.

****

C A P. XXXVI.

An Act for the Abolition of the Slave Trade.

[25th *March* 1807.]

WHEREAS the Two Houfes of Parliament did, by their Refolutions of the Tenth and Twenty-fourth Days of *June* One thoufand eight hundred and fix, feverally refolve, upon certain Grounds therein mentioned, that they would, with all practicable Expedition, take effectual Meafures for the Abolition of the *African* Slave Trade, in fuch Manner, and at fuch Period as might be deemed advifeable: And whereas it is fit upon all and each of the Grounds mentioned in the faid Refolutions, that the fame fhould be forthwith abolifhed and prohibited, and declared to be unlawful; be it therefore enacted by the King's moft Excellent Majefty, by and with the Advice and Confent of the Lords Spiritual and Temporal, and Commons, in this prefent Parliament affembled, and by the Authority of the fame, That from and after the Firft Day of *May* One thoufand eight hundred and feven, the *African* Slave Trade, and all manner of dealing and trading in the Purchafe, Sale, Barter, or Transfer of Slaves, or of Perfons intended to be fold, transferred, ufed, or dealt with as Slaves, practifed or carried on, in, at, to or from any Part of the

From May 1, 1807, the Slave Trade fhall be abolifhed.

4 L   Coaft

1807 Abolition Act

British merchants, shipbuilders, insurers, bankers, manufacturers and many workers as well as investors profited from this trade and the use of slaves on plantations, farms and mines until the final abolition of slavery, in 1880 in Cuba and in 1888 in Brazil.

A few of the many questions which have to be asked are: How was this illegal participation arranged and managed? What were the forms of participation? Which manufacturers, bankers, shippers participated? Were other businesses and workers involved? What happened in Liverpool after 1807 as it had been the prime British slaving port? Were Britons involved in the actual slave trade on the African coast? Did the government turn a blind eye? Who tried to influence government? Were the Parliamentary Acts too weak, too general, to deal with the issues? If so, were they 'watered down' in debate, and if so, by whom? How much profit was being made? How dependent was British manufacturing, banking and the export trade on slavery and the trade in slaves?

I must emphasise here that by 'involvement' I mean involvement and profiting both from the trade in slaves and from slavery. There is not much difference between the two, so far as I am concerned. It is very simple really: if no slavery, no slave trade.

This book will attempt to find *some* answers. To find all the answers, the full answers, would require a book for each question. The vast amount of information stored at the British national and some local archives, and those in the USA; in Africa, at least Nigeria and Ghana; and in Cuba and Brazil, as well as Portugal and Spain, would need to be thoroughly analysed. I just sampled the readily available evidence. There are what might seem like endless references, which I hope will make it easier for others to do more work in this area.

A long chapter focuses on Cuba and Brazil, as these countries, one a Spanish colony, the other first a colony of Portugal and then with some measure of independence, were dependent on slaves for their very existence. So, of course, was much of the southern United States. Therefore British involvement there can only be interpreted as supporting and profiting from the slave trade and slavery.

I am asking what are undoubtedly very uncomfortable questions for some people. But they need to be asked, not only because of the two-hundredth anniversary of the passing of the 1807 Act, but because of the ongoing debates about 'Britishness'. Were the British as generous, as selfless, as they have been led to believe they were? Are they to be misled again?

CHAPTER I

The slave trade and slavery

Slavery has existed since time immemorial. It existed in the UK and Britons themselves experienced enslavements and transportation by the Romans. In the sixteenth century captured British seamen were used as galley slaves by the Spaniards. In the seventeenth century the British government exported Irish women and men to the Americas in conditions very much akin to slavery.[1] What was different about the enslavement of Africans by Europeans was that they were treated as chattels, as non-human goods at the mercy of their owners. While the conditions experienced by enslaved Africans in Europe were often not quite so monstrous, in the Americas, where most were transported, they were treated as expendable subhuman labourers. As the Roman Catholic Church imposed some strictures on its adherents' behaviour, it is possible that the British owners were the most inhumane.

There was only one reason to enslave and transport African women, men and children to the Americas: to make money for emigrant Europeans establishing mines, plantations, farms, businesses. Except in the North American colonies, this money was generally repatriated to Europe. Slavery persisted in the European colonies, and in those that attained independence until the last Act of Emancipation in Brazil in 1888.[2] Britain passed the last anti-slavery Act in her African colonies in 1928.

The trade in enslaved Africans was started by Spain, which obtained a monopoly from the Pope. This was thwarted relatively quickly so that by the eighteenth century the Netherlands, Denmark, France and Britain were also shipping Africans to their 'New World', and British companies obtained contracts to ship slaves to Spanish colonies.[3] The vast majority until 1807 were shipped by British vessels. The European traders obtained their cargoes of human beings from African traders, who could not have imagined the conditions of slavery prevailing under pious Christian slave owners.

As in Europe in the sixteenth century, indigenous slavery existed in Africa – a form of slavery very different from that practised by Europeans in the Americas. In African countries slaves were often prisoners of war who had to serve a period of unwaged labour for their captors. They were not dehumanised or treated brutally. Even if enslaved for life, usually they could marry and become assimilated into their captors' families and villages, even if not always as equals. As the Chief Justice, Lord Denman, explained, 'slavery is universal among these [African] nations, but it is of mild character ... the right to treat human being as articles of trade was taught them ... by the sons of civilized, Christian Europe'.[4]

Africans exchanged their captives for what became known as 'trade goods' or 'coast goods' – these almost always, and throughout the period of the trade, included guns and gunpowder, as well as rum. Captives were usually obtained in the traditional way, by warfare; some were kidnapped. This was at times induced by European interventions. As the demand for slaves increased, coastal Africans began to raid inland, and march their enchained captives to the coast. Many, an untold number, died in the process of capture and during the long march to the coast. More died on the coast in the Europeans' grossly overcrowded barracoons (slave-holding prisons) while awaiting shipment. In the late eighteenth century it was estimated that 4.5 per cent of captives died on shore; 12.5 per cent on board ship and 33 per cent during 'seasoning' in the Americas.[5] When one adds the numbers killed in battle or in raids, it looks as if half those destined to be enslaved died before they commenced their often brief lives as unfree, dehumanised, labourers. This is surely a shocking indictment of nations and peoples supposedly practising Christian virtues and calling themselves civilised.

A convoy of captured negroes
(from Jenny Lovett Cameron's *Travels in Central Africa*, 1873)

This horrific death rate was not reduced: it has been estimated that death rates on slaving vessels reached as high as 25 per cent in the early to mid nineteenth century. Probably thousands lost their lives when they were thrown overboard by the captains of slavers approached by an Anti-Slave Trade Squadron vessel. This was to avoid the confiscation of the vessel, which was the penalty for being caught with slaves on board. For example, Peter Leonard in HMS *Dryad*, reported that 'the Spanish slavers ... *Regulo* and *Rapido* ... chased up river and throw slaves overboard, shackled ... 150 drown ... some manage to reach the banks ... 240 remain on the *Regulo*, out of 450, when boarded'. (It was only the evidence of two Africans, rescued by the *Dryad*, that eventually gained the conviction of the vessels in the Courts.[6])

Africans did not acquiesce to their fate: in Africa they fought back, fortified their villages, attempted to escape their captors. On board ship some committed suicide by jumping overboard. Others died in attempts to free themselves by attacking the seamen. On the islands of the Americas they ran away to the mountains and swamps, forming what became known as 'maroon' communities. On the mainland they were sometimes accepted by the indigenous peoples and became assimilated into these communities; others formed independent settlements.[7]

Once they had been unloaded in the Americas, the enslaved were put on display and sold to the highest bidders. Many more died in the process of 'seasoning'. How many died of demoralisation, of loneliness (there were many fewer women than men), of illness, and how many were beaten to death by their owners is not known. Most died young. Many tried to escape and some led slave revolts, only to be viciously put to death.

It has proved impossible to calculate just how many African women, children and men died in Africa prior to shipment. Estimates of the total number involved range from 11 to 20 million. A large proportion of those captured and sold were the young and the strong. The effects on Africa, which I believe are still there today, will be examined in a later chapter.

Britain and the slave trade until 1807

Africans, who first arrived in Britain as Roman troops, begin to appear in 'modern' records with the arrival of Catherine of Aragon in 1501 to marry Prince Arthur: she was accompanied by African attendants. What the status of these Africans was has not yet been researched. By the mid-sixteenth century resident Africans – not noted as slaves – begin to appear in parish and other local records.[8]

Britain's entry into what became known as the 'nefarious trade' began with Sir John Hawkins, who in 1562–63 transported about 300 Africans to Brazil and exchanged them for pearls, hides, ginger and sugar. Queen Elizabeth I was pleased and invested in Hawkins' subsequent voyages. It has been calculated that British vessels transported about two and a half million enslaved Africans between 1698 and 1807. How much these figures are an underestimate is a source of ongoing controversy among historians.[9]

The protestors against slavery, up to 1807

Organised opposition to slavery in England began with the Quakers in 1671. Not all Quakers were anti-slavery; some were involved in the lucrative trade. The protestors presented the first substantial anti-slavery petition to Parliament in 1783. One of the many effective voices in the eighteenth century was that of barrister Granville Sharp, who published a tract called *A Representation of the Injustice and Dangerous Tendency of Tolerating Slavery* in 1769. In 1772 he took the case of escaped slave James Somersett to court. The Chief Justice ruled that 'no master ever was allowed here to take a slave by force to be sold abroad because he had deserted his service, or for any reason whatsoever' and discharged Somersett.[10] Sharp went on to rescue at least another ten slaves, including one 'Indian'.[11] Another powerful voice was that of John Wesley, the founder of Methodism, whose *Thoughts upon Slavery* was published in 1774.

Granville Sharp worked with one of the most active Black British abolitionist campaigners, Olaudah Equiano. Probably of Ibo origin, Equiano had been enslaved, shipped to the Caribbean and sold and resold many times. His final owner permitted him to keep some of the money he earned in order to purchase his freedom. He came to England in 1767 as a free man, and worked in various capacities. In 1789 he published his *Narrative of the Life of Olaudah Equiano or Gustavus Vassa, the African*, which was reprinted in Britain eight times prior to his death in 1797. (It was also printed in the USA and translated into Dutch, German and Russian during his lifetime.) It has barely been out of print since. Equiano toured Britain and Ireland addressing large audiences in towns and cities and selling his book. He also sent copies to every member of Parliament.

While many Africans signed letters to the press protesting against the trade in enslaved Africans and slavery, so far as we know at present only one other published a book.[12] This was Ottobah Cugoano, a Fante born in what the British called the Gold Coast. He was set free by his owner in London. Cugoano also worked with Granville Sharp and published his *Thoughts and Sentiments on the Evil and Wicked Traffic of the Slavery and Commerce of the Human Species* in 1787.

Among the others who raised objections to the enslavement of Africans was the Vice-Chancellor of the University of Cambridge. In 1784 he announced that the dissertation competition for that year would be on the topic of 'Is it lawful to make slaves of others against their will?' The first prize was won by Thomas Clarkson for his *Essay on the Slavery and Commerce of the Human Species, Particularly the African*.[13] The young man decided that 'the time had come when some person should come forward and put an end to such demonical atrocities', and determined to devote his life to this. He immediately set about visiting the British slaving ports to collect information.[14] Quakers from his home town of Wisbech in Norfolk helped publish his *Essay* in 1786. It was very successful. He soon met the group of Quakers who had been actively campaigning against the slave trade. Naturally he also met Granville Sharp and was invited to meet William Wilberforce MP, who had read his essay.

Sharp, Clarkson and the Quakers decided to establish a non-sectarian committee; Wilberforce agreed to raise the issue in Parliament when 'he was better prepared to support it, by arguments drawn from facts'. Clarkson set to work to supply the facts. Due perhaps partly to the hiatus caused by the French Revolution, but mainly due to the objections of the West India planters and the slave traders, it took twenty years from the formation of the Committee for Wilberforce to get an Act through Parliament. The Act to abolish British participation in the trade in enslaved Africans was finally passed in March 1807, to be activated from 1 January 1808.

None of the books on Wilberforce and Clarkson and the White abolitionists mentions Olaudah Equiano. Were the abolitionists imbued with such racism that they could not envisage accepting a Black man as an equal? And as an equally powerful campaigner? Or is the omission due to the racism of historians? After all, Equiano's book was distributed with recommendations from Thomas Clarkson, John Wesley and Dr P. Peckard, Dean of Magdalene College at Cambridge, who had awarded Clarkson his prize. Granville Sharp was among the original 'subscribers', as was Clarkson, and William, the son of another black author, Ignatius Sancho.[15] Wilberforce's name is not on these lists, but that is hardly surprising. He held racist views, for example believing that 'negroes' minds are uninformed and their moral characters are debased ... their notions of morality extremely rude', while African kings had two great vices, 'personal avarice and sensuality'. Clearly, he was not a man with whom Equiano would have felt comfortable; or who would have entertained the idea of working with Equiano. Why haven't biographers and historians traced these relationships?

The profiteers

Just how much money was made by the firms engaged in the trade in slaves is difficult to estimate. Not many of their account books have been preserved. Furthermore, I think it safe to agree with author Derrick Knight that 'absolute credence cannot be given to 18th century account books any more than it can today.'[16] Of course, we would have to add to the profits of the actual traders in slaves the profits of those who built the ships and those who supplied the materials for them; and the profits of those who manufactured and supplied the rum and other 'coast goods' that were exchanged or traded for Africans. It would be unfair to exclude the wages of those who depended on the trade: the sailmakers, rope-makers, ship-builders, seamen, carters, the weavers of sailcloth, gun makers, iron workers making manacles...

The manufacturers

To cite just one example: during times of peace, stated John Whately, one the leading gun-manufacturers in Birmingham, 'the Manufacture of guns ... is chiefly supported by the African Trade ... [It is also] a market ... for all the arms deemed by Government to be unservice-able, which would not otherwise produce one fourth if one sixth of their present value.' John Galton, one of the other major gun manufacturers in Birmingham, was also a slave trader. He invested part of his fortune in various canals, the East India Company and the Bank of England. His fortune was assessed at £300,000 (c. £15 million in 2005) when he died in 1832.[17]

Some of the merchant and bankers

The merchants or merchant-houses also thrived and many became highly influential. As the Heywoods, Leylands and many others are listed in Appendix 2; here are just a few as an indication of the range of interests – and rewards – of merchants and bankers:

- The Cunliffe family of Liverpool, who traded in slaves and in rum and sugar: Foster was mayor of Liverpool many times in the first half of the eighteenth century; Ellis represented Liverpool in Parliament in 1761 and imported slave-grown cotton from the southern United States. He was created a baronet in 1759. The ninth Baronet was living not immodestly in Herefordshire in the 1970s.

- Francis Baring, the founder of Baring Bros & Co., the banking firm which lasted until a few years ago, also started in the slaving business. He served as an MP for eighteen years. His son Thomas and grandson Francis were also MPs, and held various government posts such as Lord of the Admiralty, Chancellor of the Exchequer. Francis was an MP for 39 years; Thomas was an MP for 19 years and, like his father, was a director of the Bank of England.

  The Barings supported the trade in slaves. For example, Alexander Baring, MP from 1806 until 1835, opposed the Bill introduced in 1815 to prohibit 'lending capital or doing other acts … to assist the carrying on of the Slave Trade'. Eight years later in Parliament he was adamant that the 'condition of the Slaves [was] undoubtedly … superior to that of most of the English peasantry. They are well clothed, well fed and … generally treated with justice and kindness.' He was against the emancipation of slaves, as 'the inevitable consequence will be that the whole of the islands will be gone from this country; there will be an end to our colonial system'. Is it surprising that Baring was created Baron Ashburton in 1835?[18]

- David and Alexander Barclay, though Quakers, were slave traders in the mid-eighteenth century. David also owned plantations, but emancipated his slaves. James Barclay set up a bank with Joseph Freame, his brother-in-law, in 1756, called Barclay Bevan & Company. Their bank, Barclays, is hugely prosperous and very well known today both nationally and internationally.

Some of the planters

Some planters made fortunes and retired to Britain. One of the wealthiest was the Beckford family. Young Thomas had emigrated to Jamaica in 1660. He became a wine merchant and used the profits to establish plantations and became so powerful that he even served as Acting Governor and as the Custos of Port Royal. By the mid-eighteenth century Peter Beckford was the wealthiest planter in

Jamaica: owner of nine plantations 'employing' 1,737 slaves and part-owner of another seven using 577 slaves. His son William Beckford bought a 4–5000 acre estate in Wiltshire, served as London's Lord Mayor in 1762 and 1769; he was MP for Shaftesbury and then for London (1754–70). Of his brothers, Richard was MP for Bristol, and Julines for Salisbury. William's illegitimate son Richard was MP for Bridport 1780–84 and Leominster 1791–99, while his legitimate son William was MP for Wells and Hindon until 1820. All owned slave-worked plantations in Jamaica. Just one of the Beckfords mentioned above received £15,160 for his 770 slaves as compensation for losing his unpaid labourers. Naturally in Parliament they all fought on the side of the 'West India interest'.[19]

It would be very interesting to compile a list of Members of Parliament who were, one way or another, involved in the trade in slaves, or slavery, and assess their influence in and out of Parliament on issues relating to slavery, the slave trade, import and export duties and colonisation.

Britain and the slave trade after 1807

To deal with the whole spectrum of the trade after 1807 is not possible in one book, and one chapter. I shall concentrate on the trade in slaves on the West Coast of Africa and only on the activities of the Anti-Slave Trade Squadron there.

The campaigners

After the victory of 1807 Clarkson, Wilberforce and others continued the fight. It is not possible to list here the names of all the MPs who fought with them. Millions of Englishmen and -women signed petitions to Parliament. Clarkson's deep commitment continued: for example, in the 1820s, now in his sixties, he travelled 3000 miles around Britain to address public meetings and get petitions against slavery signed.[20]

In 1815 a bill was presented to proscribe investment in the ongoing slave trade; 722 petitions, bearing nearly 1 million signatures (this was around 13 per cent of the total population) were presented to Parliament demanding universal proscription.[21] Among those who objected to the bill was Alexander Baring, a descendant of the slaving family, MP for Taunton, Governor of the Bank of England and later President of the Board of Trade. The bill was thrown out by the House of Lords.

Wilberforce retired in 1825 so the struggle to get the Emancipation Bill (to end slavery) through Parliament was left in the capable hands of Thomas Fowell Buxton, the newly elected Quaker-related MP for Weymouth. Other men who fought staunchly on abolition issues and have not yet been credited appropriately by historians are Henry Brougham, who struggled resolutely in both houses of Parliament, and barrister George Stephen, who took on the case against Pedro de Zulueta (see Chapter 3) and published innumerable abolitionist pamphlets.

Again after much opposition, in August 1833 the bill for the emancipation of slaves was passed by Parliament.[22] Slaves were to be apprenticed and their owners were to receive compensation for their loss of free labour. A total of £20 million (£1 billion in 2005) was borrowed by the government for this − a vast sum, almost 40 per cent of the government's annual revenue! The loan was arranged by the banking house of Nathan Rothschild.[23] Apprenticeship was ended by 1838, but the freed women, children and men received no compensation for the dehumanisation and many brutalities they had suffered.

This vast sum demonstrates the influence of the West India lobby, which had campaigned so hard against the Emancipation Bill. But were there other considerations? I have found no fully satisfactory explanation for the size of this massive grant to plantation owners, most of whom were absentee landlords, living luxurious lives in the UK. So much so that by 1791, 177 plantations in Jamaica had been sold to repay debts, 92 had been seized by mortgagors and 55 had been abandoned. This proved, according to the Secretary to the Governor of Barbados, 'that bought slaves, who keep not up their numbers by births, do not nearly refund their purchase money and that the planter's true resource is to rear his slaves.' That the slave population did not reproduce itself is stark evidence of the horrific conditions under which the enslaved were kept.[24]

As the campaigners soon learned, traders, merchants, bankers, shipbuilders and others soon found ways to avoid or circumvent the strictures of new laws. Parliament considered the new petitions and new bills, and took evidence. For example, the indefatigable Henry Brougham presented a British & Foreign Anti-Slavery Society petition to the House of Lords on 20 September 1841. This focused on British-owned mining companies using slaves; on bankers loaning money to slave traders; on the export of shackles and manacles to Cuba and Brazil; and on 'vessels being built in this country which ... could leave no doubt that they were intended for the slave trade'. He asked for a committee to be appointed to investigate these allegations so that effective measures could be taken. No effective Act was ever passed to deal with these issues.

Acts of Parliament

Most of the Acts passed by Parliament regarding slavery are listed in Appendix 1. But it is important here to given an indication of the nature of the Acts that were passed.

Both Britain and the USA made it illegal to trade in slaves in 1807. As the British 1807 Act did not stipulate that carrying slaving equipment indicated the intent to trade in slaves, Henry Brougham convinced Parliament to pass another Act 'for rendering more effectual the 1807 Act'. Passed in 1811, the Act declared slave trading to be a felony and stipulated 14 years' transportation for any British citizen found guilty.

In 1819 'Courts of Mixed Commission' were set up, staffed with judges representing the countries which had agreed to prohibit slave trading. There were courts in Freetown (all nations); Rio de Janeiro (Anglo-Portuguese judges); Havana (Anglo-Spanish); Surinam (Anglo-Dutch) to adjudicate cases involving captured slave vessels.[25]

To prevent the movement of slaves between British colonies, and any further importations, the Slave Registration Act was passed by Parliament in 1820. Four years later, participation in slave trading was declared an act of piracy. In 1824 the Consolidating Act was passed, which brought all the legislation together, supposedly to make it easier for people to obey the laws. There is no evidence that this had any effect.

After years of campaigning, as explained above, the Emancipation Act was finally passed in 1833. It did not apply throughout the then British empire: slaves in India were not freed until 1848 and it was not until 1862 that owning a slave there became 'an offence'.[26] In some of the colonies established by Britain in West and East Africa, slavery remained legal well into the twentieth century.

In 1839 a new Act permitted the British Vice-Admiralty Courts to try vessels without registration papers; in 1845 this was extended to Brazilian vessels.

In 1842 Foreign Secretary Palmerston advised his consuls that it was illegal for British 'functionaries' to hold slaves. Can it be taken as indicative of the attitudes of the bureaucrats posted abroad that Palmerston had to issue this directive?

Some of the treaties with other countries

Naturally, Britain did not want other countries to continue to profit from the slave trade. Much effort was expanded by the government to persuade European countries and the USA to follow Britain's generous example. By 1840, 42 treaties on the slave trade had been signed with various countries. (See Appendix 1 for some of these.) That the trade in slaves actually increased indicates that most of the signatories ignored the papers to which they had put their names. The USA certainly did, becoming one of the most active slave traders from the middle of the nineteenth century.

The Netherlands agreed to prohibit slave trading in 1814, and France in the following year. In 1817 Britain was successful – when it agreed to pay compensation for the projected loss of trade – in also persuading Spain and Portugal to prohibit trading in slaves north of the Equator. But Brazil declared its independence in 1822 and thus did not have to (pretend to) conform to this agreement. A treaty with Brazil, making all Brazilian trade illegal, was ratified in 1827. It was ignored by most Brazilians and their British financiers.[27]

In 1818 these countries, as well as the United States, signed agreements with Britain which permitted the search of vessels suspected of having slaves on board. However, it was mainly Britain that made warships available for such duties.

Beginning in the early 1820s Britain began to persuade other countries to accept what came to be called the 'equipment clause'. This stipulated that vessels equipped for slave trading could be 'arrested', without there being any slaves on board. France, for example, accepted this in 1833, but insisted that such vessels should be tried by French courts.

At first the condemned vessels and their cargoes were auctioned – the purchasers were often agents of slave traders who returned the vessels to slave trading. The 1835 stricture to stop such sales was generally ignored.[28] The liberated slaves were handed over to the government of the territory where the vessel had been condemned, supposedly to be employed as free or 'apprenticed' labourers. In Cuba and Brazil they were often re-enslaved. In Freetown, they became the responsibility of the Liberated African Department, which registered about 65,000 as British citizens.

In 1839 Portugal agreed to ban slaving south of the Equator but not to condemn equipped ships or to break up those that were condemned. Three years later the Portuguese government decreed the trade to be a piracy. The British government responded by authorizing the Squadron to take Portuguese slaving vessels to the Vice-Admiralty Courts and to break up the condemned vessels. The main result of this was more and more vessels sailing without documentation or flags.

The effects of the Acts and treaties

No-one has tried to investigate how the £20 million (£1 billion today) compensation to the slave owners in Britain's West Indian colonies was invested. How much of it was used to aid the 'industrial revolution' in Britain? It would not be impossible to find the links between the beneficiaries and at least the major investors in railways, canals, road, manufacturing, shipping... Why have historians focused on the profitability of the trade in slaves prior to 1807 and ignored this huge sum of money?

Two examples of the use of profits and compensation payments are:

- George Hibbert received £13,120 compensation (c. £663,000 in 2005), some of which he invested in London's West India Docks; he served as MP for Seaford 1806–12.
- John Gladstone and his sons, including future Prime Minister William, received £85,600 (c. £4.3 million in 2005) for his 2183 slaves in Jamaica and British Guiana. Some of this was invested in the railway constructed between Liverpool and Manchester. He served as an MP for nine years and was very influential with

merchants and governments. (See Chapter 2 for more on Glad-stone's influence.) He was made a baronet in 1846.[29]

The trade in enslaved Africans certainly did not stop; it almost reached the same annual numbers as were exported prior to 1807. Historians calculate that during the 110 years from 1701 to 1810, over 6 million enslaved Africans were exported. The latest calculations for the 60 years from 1811 to 1870 give numbers between 2.5 million and 2.7 million. These figures do not take into account those who died in Africa or during the 'middle passage' to the Americas. One historian has calculated deaths on board in the nineteenth century to be between 4.4 per cent and 22 per cent, partly depending on the length of the voyage.[30]

These numbers would have been even higher had the British West African Anti-Slave Trade Squadron not operated with as much efficiency as it could muster, given that almost always its vessels were old and the most inefficient the Navy possessed. The numbers allocated to this task varied from 2 to 7 until 1841, when the fleet was increased to 13; it reached 30 in 1847. The percentage of vessels captured, Capt. Matson of the Squadron stated, varied from 13 per cent in the years 1837–38 to over 50 per cent in 1841–42.[31] Between 1842 and 1861, when much of the Squadron was relocated to blockade duties off the North American coast, it had captured 595 ships and freed 45,612 Africans. The total cost of suppression (the Courts and the Squadron) between 1816 and 1865 was about £12.4 million.[32]

The Squadron's crew were offered prize money for each slave captured and liberated. This was done in order to compensate them for the discomforts and dangers of the service. However, much of this prize money was used by the colonial governors and other officials. Whether this was legal or illegal has not been researched. When the 'equipment clause' permitted the Squadron to 'arrest' vessels equipped for slaving but not containing slaves, a 'tonnage' bounty was paid. The system was eventually revised to one of 'discretionary payments for meritorious services', to be voted on by Parliament.[33]

The Squadron learned to use local seamen, especially the Kru, originating from the Liberian coast, to help with navigation along the coast and rivers. These temporary members of the Royal Navy were usually discharged when the vessel returned to the UK. Merchant vessels also employed local seamen, but on a more permanent basis, sailing back to Britain with them as part of the crew.[34]

How Britain participated in the ongoing trade and in slavery

Most historians of British involvement in the trade in slaves and in slavery laud the Acts of 1807 and 1833, mentioned above, and do not ask the obvious question: were the Acts obeyed? Doesn't the very fact that more and more Acts dealing with slavery and the trade in slaves were passed indicate that there were attempts by Britons to avoid the strictures supposedly imposed? Why has no one thoroughly examined what efforts were made, other than by the Anti-Slave Trade Squadron, to enforce these laws? Is it possible that the work of the Squadron was seen as worthwhile because it demonstrated internationally that Britain meant what it said? But that passing legislation, or enforcing legislation, which affected the mercantile community was seen as too damaging to Britain's prosperity?

The slave traders

Slave traders found many ways to avoid the strictures of the Acts; naturally these varied according to the attempts to enforce the laws. But not all such evasions worked: between 1808 and 1816 (i.e., prior to the establishment of the Courts of Mixed Commission) the Vice-Admiralty Courts condemned a total of 130 ships, of which 22 were either owned or insured or fitted out in England.[35]

Some slave trade issues were avoided by Parliament. One was the ongoing importation of slaves by the newly acquired Crown Colony of Mauritius. It was estimated that this illegal importation of slaves amounted to at least 30,000 Africans, but the numbers were probably much higher. The issue was persistently raised in Parliament by Fowell Buxton and Henry Brougham. It was not ended until Britain finally abolished slavery on the island in 1835.[36]

Clearly the inspection of ships sailing from British ports was somewhat lax. How else could one account for the *John Campbell* sailing from Liverpool on 21 October 1843, fully equipped for carrying slaves? And with a cargo of 'coast goods', consisting mainly of gunpowder, cutlasses, coarse cloth and rum? When the ship's captain died (conveniently?) in Madeira, the supercargo – that is, the man in charge of the cargo – took command of the ship! William Laidlaw's account of the subsequent events when the ship arrived in Old Calabar is somewhat confusing, but the swapping of crews with other slave traders is clearly described.[37] (Some other examples will be given in subsequent chapters.) How many more slaving vessels were built in Britain? Why was inspection so very lax?

And what are we to make of the slaving vessel wrecked off the Essex Coast? I found it first mentioned in the *Anti-Slavery Reporter* of 16 December 1840: 'Two vessels wrecked in gale … Bucksea Sands, 10 miles for Brightlingsea … abandoned by crew … one with hidden equipment for the slave trade … the other a collier' (p. 316). Was it equipped on the Thames?, the *Reporter* queried. The next issue of the *Reporter* (30 December, p. 322) carried a letter from a Mr T.H. Lewis, saying he had talked to fishermen near Brightlingsea, and had been given some of the chains and manacles that had been found on board. I found Mr Lewis's letter preserved in the archives of the Anti-Slavery Society. He believes the vessel was Spanish, but the crew had deserted. Fitted with ring bolts for the enslaved men's chains, the ship was in ballast. As Mr Lewis states that 'part of the vessel is now lying in Mr. Jas. Aldous' shipyard', we have to presume that the gale had been so severe that the ship had broken up. Naturally, I asked the Essex Record Office if there was anything in the archives there regarding this vessel. Sadly, all they could find were advertisements in the local papers for mid-August for the auction sale of stores 'salved from the Brig "Guadalope" of Cadiz … lately wrecked on the Buxey Sand … on a voyage from Bremen to Cadiz'.[38] No mention of chains or manacles, but a vessel with a name, so not the nameless vessel reported by Mr Lewis. Did Spanish slavers find it easy to purchase manacles and chains from London traders?[39]

Some of the traders on the West African coast were British. Some are listed in Appendix 2; here are another three examples:

- *John Kearney* was the main trader on the River Gallinas until the 1830s;
- *Joseph Peters* and *William Tuft* were convicted of slave trading in Freetown in 1814.[40]

- *Richard Willing*, using the name Ricardo Villeno, was the main trader on the river Bassa. As related by his nephew, if any of Willing/Villeno's vessels were 'boarded by a British cruiser, my uncle or his captains could always show papers corresponding to the flag carried';
- *Benjamin Campbell* supplied the Lightburn slave-trading family on the Rio Pongas.[41] .

Some of the methods of evasion used by slave traders were:

- Vessels were sold fictitiously so their names could be changed and Spanish and Portuguese papers thus obtained. For example, the *Prince William Henry* became the *Marquis de la Romana* and the *Hercules* became *Gerona*. Examples of the use of Spanish and Portuguese flags by British vessels are noted in the annual reports of the Committee of the African Institution beginning in 1807.[42]
- Seamen of various nationalities were embarked on each vessel, who could then claim to be the captain, should the vessel be stopped. For example, between 1819 and 1829 the Anglo-Dutch Courts condemned 22 ships; of these the *Hoop* was an English vessel, but the nationality of her captain could not determined. Whether the *De Bay* and her captain were English or American the court could not decide. The *Eliza* was either French of English, but her captain was deemed English. The Parliamentary Slave Trade Committee of 1848 was told that many of the vessels arriving in Brazil had no known owners and claimed to be Sardinian![43]
- Most vessels cleared out from British ports for Spanish or Portuguese ports, or for Brazil or Cuba, carrying 'trade goods'. They then picked up manacles and the necessities for conversion into a slaver, such as timber for slave decks and water casks, from places such as the Canary Islands and Cape Verde and sailed on to the African coast.[44]
- Some vessels were built for the slave trade but began their life masquerading as innocent merchant vessels. For example, a vessel named *Elvira* was built in Glasgow for James McLintock. She was loaded with coal in Cardiff, from where she sailed 'under British colours' to Cadiz. The Foreign Office discovered that she had probably been built expressly for the slave trade. This could have been initiated by a man named Ysasi, the agent of premier

Cuban slave trader Julian de Zulueta, who is featured in Chapter 4. In Cadiz she was sold to Don Servando del Rio, who was either an agent or a partner of Zulueta. The inattentive (or well-paid?) British Consul in Cadiz signed the transfer papers. Renamed the *Ciceron*, she cleared for Matamoras, Mexico. But in fact she steamed to Africa, where she embarked 1000 slaves and transported them to Havana.[45]

- Another method used was described by the US Consul in Rio: as 'no English vessel [was] permitted to carry to Africa such a cargo', the merchants had to find another method. So British traders sold 'coast goods' to 'the commercial marine of the United States', which would then 'supply the Brazilian factories' on the Coast with these 'British manufactures and other products'.[46]
- Captain Fair of HMS *Champion* was so angered by his experiences that he published an open letter to the Foreign Office. He claimed that he had witnessed that the British-owned Bahama Islands were used by Cuban slavers 'for procuring supplies, often to receive information about our cruisers.... The slave dealers and the insurance companies in Cuba send vessels to rendezvous off certain Bahama Islands.'[47]
- Another ploy was for the colluding traders to send out the 'coast goods' and have the cargo landed prior to the arrival of the slaving vessel. The goods were exchanged for slaves in advance of the arrival of the slaver. When this vessel arrived the waiting slaves could be loaded in a few hours, thus making capture by the Squadron less likely.[48]

Investment in slavery and the trade in slaves

With the increase in the efficacy of the Anti-Slave Trade Squadron, British merchants had to find new ways of profiting from the trade in slaves – and, of course, from slavery.

As Brazil and Cuba (which remained a Spanish colony) were more heavily dependent on the labour of slaves than the other South American countries, I shall concentrate on them. (About one and a half million enslaved Africans were imported into Brazil after 1811, well over half a million into Cuba.) It has been estimated that about half the population of Brazil and at least one-third of the population of Cuba in the first half of the nineteenth century were enslaved

Africans. There is no information available on British investment in the southern, slave-worked states in the USA. However, I shall investigate the importation of slave-grown cotton from those states in Chapter 2.

The issue of supporting or investing in slave-worked economies was only questioned in Britain when Parliament discussed equalising the rates of import duty on free- and slave-grown sugar. This will be discussed in other chapters. Generally such investment was seen as anything but reprehensible: 'Spanish America is free and if we do not mismanage our affairs badly she is English' exulted Foreign Secretary George Canning in 1824. Spain had just lost most of her colonies in the Americas, and Brazil had become quasi-independent of Portugal.[49] Canning had recognised that imperialism need not be accomplished by settlement or warfare: trade and investment would serve just as well, if not better, as it required little investment by government.

Historian David Eltis believes that the 'Brazilian coastal and interior trade, as well as the slave trade depended on British credit.' He also accepts the 1849 estimate of the British Consul in Rio that Britain was financing half the Brazilian slave trade. And he believes this was true also for the Cuban trade.[50] Brazil was seen to be so lucrative that a special bank was established: the London Brazilian Bank, set up in 1862. Brazil was also a regular customer of the Rothschild bank.[51]

As these two countries were dependent on slavery for their very existence, it is not unfair to include what is called 'portfolio' investment in this accounting of British involvement. Both the Cuban and the Brazilian governments floated bonds in the UK for public works, which of course used slave labour. Cuban planters also raised mortgage funds from British banks.[52]

British exports to Brazil

Export trade with Brazil increased from just over £2 million in 1821 to just under £5.3 million in 1832.[53] It is likely that a considerable proportion of this was used to purchase slaves in Africa. A much smaller proportion was probably used to clothe and feed the enslaved in Brazil. Another proportion, the luxury goods, would have been sold to those Brazilians who were growing rich on the profits from slave-grown produce and products. In 1865, just to take one year as an example, Britain exported over £5.6 million worth of manufactures to Brazil; imports were valued at £6.8 million. The corresponding figures for Cuba and Puerto Rico (another Spanish slave-worked colony) were £2.2 million exports and £5 million worth of imports.[54]

Supplying 'coast' goods for the trade in slaves

As Foreign Secretaries Lords Palmerston and Aberdeen well knew, having been informed by their own consuls, ambassadors, Royal Navy officers and the US government, British manufactured goods were widely used in exchange for slaves on the African coast. While some were sold to US traders, as described above, the US Consul in Rio also told his government that 'of the vast amount of capital invested, and the great number of English houses supported and enriched by the African trade, this city furnishes abundant proof ... goods ... sent here [are] sold by English agents to notorious slave dealers.'

The reports of the US consuls in Brazil appeared in the British Parliament's printed *Slave Trade Papers*. Just to quote another example, the 1838–39 *Papers* included the Consul's 14 July 1837 report stating that 'the commission houses here [in Rio] of Liverpool, Leeds, Manchester and Birmingham sell their goods intended for the African market on conditional terms; the debt to be acquitted in part or in whole, according as the adventure may ultimately prove successful or otherwise'.[55] Captain Matson, affirmed this exposition in his statement to the 1848 Parliamentary Committee on the slave trade.[56] As traders aren't fools, it is safe to presume that the risk they were taking was relatively small: that is, that most slave trading ventures were successful and the goods were paid for.

Fowell Buxton mentioned this in his 1840 publication, *The African Slave Trade and its Remedy* (pp. 54–5). The issue was raised in Parliament many times. But nothing was done. Historian David Eltis has calculated that British goods accounted for 80 per cent of the purchase price of slaves imported into Rio de Janeiro. These goods included spirits, gunpowder, muskets and cloth from Manchester.[57]

In order not to be found with 'coast goods' should they be stopped by the Anti-Slave Trade Squadron, from the late 1830s slave vessels began to carry bullion with which to purchase goods from British and Hamburg vessels lying off the coast of Africa.

Slavers revenging their losses
(from *Life and Explorations of David Livingstone*, 1874)

Conclusion

The appalled British and Foreign Anti-Slavery Society summed up British involvement at its 1840 convention:

> This Convention learns with profound regret that there are British subjects who render immediate support to the slave trade and slavery ... [S]ome by supplying the articles necessary for conducting it, some by furnishing, as bankers, the capital employed in it, some by holding shares in mining associations, the purchasers of the victims of the traffic, and some even by the actual manufacture and exportation of the arms and manacles employed in the abduction of these victims.
>
> That the employment of British subjects, and British capital, directly or indirectly, in support of slavery or the slave trade, is ... a flagrant dishonour to the British name and an outrageous inconsistency with the avowed desire, the strenuous endeavours, and the costly sacrifices of Great Britain for the suppression thereof.[58]

Yet the outrage was all to no avail. Petitions regarding British ownership of slaves and slave-worked estates and mines drew no meaningful response from the government. British consulates were asked to display the latest anti-slavery Acts and to report their suspicions of involvement in the slave trade (not in slavery), but no action was ever taken. Lord Brougham in the House of Lords stated on 2 August 1841 that 'This very important subject (the employment of British capital in the slave trade) has been strenuously urged on the attention of Her Majesty's Government from various quarters, and there is reason to hope that some further measures of prevention will be devised to remedy so crying an evil'.[59] Lord Brougham's hopes were unfulfilled.

My outrage remains. The public face of Britain hid an omnivorous attitude by the rising merchant class. It seems clear to me that far too much money was being made by the bankers, insurers, merchants and manufacturers for any meaningful action to be taken by the government to stop British involvement in the slave trade and slavery. These omnivores had become too powerful, as Members of Parliament and as the moneymakers who fuelled British prosperity.

In 1847 Lord Denman wrote that 'the people of England are becoming indifferent' to issues related to slavery and the slave trade. I want to extend this to historians writing a century later. Why have the actions and issues outlined above not been thoroughly researched? Can British historians still not confront the possibility that Britain was not being magnanimous, but making huge profits from slavery and the slave trade after 1807?

CHAPTER 2

The tale of two cities built on slavery: Liverpool and Manchester

Before 1807 the trade in slaves was conducted from many British ports. After 1807 even more cities were involved in slavery. By this I mean that their business was, one way or another, dependent on slave-grown produce either in the Americas or in Africa. Those involved were not only manufacturers but also banks and insurance companies, shipbuilders and dockers, railwaymen and factory workers, seamen and sugar refiners. (There must also be many villages which grew from the 'beneficence' of the 'lord of the manor' who derived some or all of his wealth from the profits of slavery.) Liverpool is a prime example of a city that grew from both the 'nefarious' trade and from the profits of slavery. Manchester and the surrounding towns would not, I believe, have developed to more than a small fraction of their size had it not been for slave-grown cotton. The two towns became interdependent by the end of the 1820s.

Of course, other towns and cities could be, and should be, investigated from the same perspective. Glasgow, Bristol, Birmingham, London... There has been no thorough investigation of these cities' histories from the perspective of their dependence on slavery. Nor has anyone, as far as I have been able to ascertain asked: *what would Britain have become without the profits and the employment provided by cotton?* This chapter will begin to investigate how Manchester and Liverpool became prosperous from dealing with slave-grown produce and

supporting the illegal trade in slaves. Hopefully the cities' historians will elaborate on my explorations.

Liverpool before 1807

Liverpool, a large fishing village of fewer than 5000 inhabitants in 1700, had grown to a city of 34,000 by 1773. This was due partly to its involvement in the trade in slaves. In 1795 about a quarter of Liverpool's ships were engaged in the trade in enslaved African women, men and children. It has been calculated that Liverpool vessels carried 40 per cent of the entire European trade in slaves and controlled 60 per cent of the British trade. How many doomed Africans did the city's vessels carry? For example, in just two years, 1805–07, 70,294 enslaved Africans were carried to the Americas in 402 slaving voyages from Liverpool.[1] How many were killed in the process of enslavement, while awaiting shipment on the African coast, in the pestilential ships' holds or soon after arrival in the Americas, is not known.

Liverpool imported such quantities of slave-grown sugar from the British colonies in the West Indies that its first sugar refinery was built in 1668. By 1774 there were eight.[2] Slave-grown tobacco from the British plantations in Virginia on the American mainland was also imported by Liverpool's merchants. Since among the 72 members of the Liverpool Company of Merchants Trading to Africa there is a 'William Woodville, Havanna', it is likely that these imports included slave-grown tobacco from Cuba.[3]

The trade in slaves and with the plantations greatly aided local manufacturing and provided employment for thousands in and around Liverpool. Slaving vessels had to be built and manned; the goods exchanged for the enslaved; and the fetters, manacles and chains used on the coast, on the vessels and on the plantations in the Americas, had to be manufactured. Food and water containers were also required, as were tools for plantation use. The enslaved labourer also required a minimum of clothing, while the plantation owners and supervisors demanded all the fineries they would have enjoyed in Britain. Thus manufacturing and trade in Liverpool and its hinterland increased vastly. As the local merchants explained to Parliament in 1726:

The manufacture of cotton, woollen, copper, pewter, etc., spread particularly all over the County of Lancashire, so much influenced by this trade, are now put into the most flourishing circumstances.

A book on Liverpool published in 1796 noted that the export of Manchester cloth 'brought out the great burst of prosperity in both Liverpool and Manchester'.[4]

So a question has to be asked: *How many people in Liverpool and its hinterland were directly and indirectly employed in the slave trade?* How many sailmakers, gunpowder workers, ironworkers, sugar refiners, carters, rope-makers, seamen and shipwrights, barrel-makers and coppersmiths made their living from the trade in, and the labour of, enslaved African women, children and men?

The merchants' profits were generally vast: 'Dicky Sam', the chronicler of the Liverpool slave trade, calculated that the annual profits on the 303,737 slaves carried by Liverpool vessels between 1783 and 1793 was £214,677 (c. £13 million in 2005). I have been unable to find any estimates of the profits of the manufacturers, the ship-builders, the insurers or the bankers. The government also reaped profits: it collected £640,684 (c. £39 million in 2005) in duties from the port of Liverpool in 1784 alone.[5] The proportion of this collected from vessels employed in the slave trade and slavery is not known. But if the assessment of a quarter of Liverpool's vessels being in this trade is correct, then the figure would be over £160,000.

Liverpool's extensive involvement with Africa and Africans naturally resulted in an ever-growing population of Africans in the city and its hinterland. As recounted by Liverpool historian Ray Costello,

African students were educated in Britain ... during the 1780s ... it was thought that there were generally from fifty to seventy African children at school in Liverpool ... During the last quarter of the eighteenth century, black settlers, either as slaves, servants, students of noble descent or the dual heritage children of white plantation owners ... were both visiting or settling all over Liverpool and the surrounding district.[6]

Manchester must also have had a large black population: in 1787 when asked to preach in the city's Collegiate Church, abolitionist Thomas Clarkson found that 'the church was packed and some fifty black people were clustered around the pulpit'.[7]

Liverpool after the 1807 Abolition Act

Contrary to the expectations of some, Liverpool continued to expand after the abolition of the slave trade by Parliament. Its population grew from about 80,000 in 1807 to 286,487 in 1841. By 1824 the duties collected rose to over one and a half million pounds.[8] In 1845, Liverpool was the second busiest port in the UK after London. How did Liverpool accomplish this? Can the trade in slave-grown produce account for this growth? Did perhaps Liverpool also continue to reap profits from the ongoing trade in enslaved Africans?

It took about twenty years for the Abolition Bill to be passed by Parliament. These years gave Liverpool's experienced merchants and shipowners ample time to ensure not only their survival but their prosperity by diversifying their trade, should the abolitionists succeed in Parliament. By the nineteenth century Liverpool was entrenched not only in the trade in slaves, but also in the Americas, from where slave-produced raw materials were imported and to where manufactures were exported. Many of the slaving vessels after Abolition were redeployed to the West Indies and to North and South America.[9] On the African coast the (ex-?) slave-traders' intimate knowledge of trade and traders ensured participation in 'legitimate' – and other – trade.

It would be very interesting indeed to see an estimation of exactly how much the development of Liverpool had been dependent not only on the direct trade in slaves but also on slavery. I must emphasise here that had there been no market for slave-grown produce, the trade in enslaved Africans would have died a 'natural death'. Thus any merchant, any manufacturer, dealing in slave-grown produce was a de facto supporter of the 'nefarious', murderous trade.

Trade in the products of slave labour

It is clear that trade in slave-grown produce increased vastly after 1807. The Caribbean territories captured from the French during the Napoleonic Wars provided new markets and sources of produce.[10] Trade with slave-worked Spanish colonies in the Caribbean also increased: for example, in 1851, 63 vessels were 'cleared' Liverpool for Cuba. By 1810 sugar imports arriving in Liverpool amounted to 46,000 tons; in 1852 approximately 22 per cent of sugar imports were slave-grown. By the early 1850s, of the total annual tobacco imports of about 28 million lb, over 6 million lb was unloaded in Liverpool. About 2 per cent of this came from the labour of slaves in Cuba and the rest from slave-worked plantations in the USA. The government collected about £4.5 million annually from import duty on tobacco. Almost all this tobacco was slave-grown.[11]

But it was cotton that was most important to Liverpool. By 1830 Liverpool's share of Britain's raw cotton imports had risen to 90 per cent of the total imported. The amount imported kept growing: for example, by 1838 220 million lb of slave-grown cotton was unloaded in Liverpool – this was 96 per cent of the total imported.[12] The city became the 'chief port for the counties of Lancashire, Cheshire and Yorkshire'; for example, in 1851, 61 per cent of British textile and other cotton exports were shipped from Liverpool. Some of the export trade in manufactured cotton cloth was also with slave-worked areas: in the same year £18.2 million-worth of these textiles were sent to the slave-worked states in the southern United States, from where much of the cotton had been imported in the first place.[13]

In the mid-1840s, cotton exports were 64 per cent of total cloth exports; cloth exports were 43 per cent of total exports. By the 1850s, textiles were 60 per cent of Britain's total exports.[14] Two-thirds of these exports were produced from slave-grown cottons. That was a very good reason not to ask questions, to look the other way. Certainly the abolitionist William Rathbone had no problems importing cotton from the southern USA.[15] After all, this slave-grown produce was responsible for a large proportion of Britain's merchant wealth, and gave employment to hundreds of thousands of people! So why should he shy away from it?[16]

Cotton was so important, and so many related political issues had to be dealt with, that in 1841 the 90 cotton merchants formed the Cotton Brokers Association. Locally the Association was interested in projects such as extending the warehousing facilities in Liverpool. Nationally their concerns included the duties payable on cotton imports.[17]

Trade with Brazil and other South American slave-worked countries and colonies also increased. By 1812 Brazil supplied about 20 per cent of the raw cotton unloaded in Liverpool's docks. Brazil had little shipping of its own: building ships for the Brazil trade provided more work and profits for Liverpool's merchants, shipbuilders, et al. In a pamphlet published in 1833, entitled *Some remarks and observations on a Petition to Parliament from the merchants and shipowners of Liverpool praying for the admission ... of the products of Brazil, by a member of the Brazilian Association of Liverpool,* the unnamed author notes that 'the petitioners carry on extensive commerce with Brazil in the produce and manufactures of the United Kingdom ... export value is Three million Sterling.' The imports listed are sugar, coffee, cocoa and rum. The value of British exports to Brazil in 1850 was £2.5 million.[18]

Local directories list the Brazilian Association and its office-holders, but, as the Association's papers have not been preserved, I have been unable to find much information about its activities. The 1842 directory also lists a resident Brazilian consul, which indicates the importance of this trade.[19] In the 1840s, when President Tyler of the USA had publicly accused British traders of supplying the 'trade' or 'coast goods' used to pay for slaves, the Association declared it would send a petition to the government disputing any action against traders.[20] The Brazilian Association's protest, I believe, indicates the importance to Liverpool merchants of supplying 'trade goods' to slave traders.

A cursory glance through the Liverpool Customs Bills of Entry and *Lloyd's Lists* shows regular sailings to many Brazilian ports; for example, four ships left for Brazil in just one week in March 1844! Liverpool-based steam vessels were introduced in 1846 by the Pacific Steam Navigation Co. This company was replaced in 1865 by the Liverpool firm of Lamport & Holt, founders of the Liverpool, Brazil and River Plate Steamship Co.[21] This company also took over the carriage of mail from the UK to Brazil. That there was a need for a subsidised official carrier of mail of course also indicates the importance of trade with Brazil – that is, trade in slave-grown produce.

'Legitimate' trade with Africa

British, including 'foreign and colonial', goods exported to Africa in 1805 amounted to only 3 per cent of all exports from Britain while the 'official value' of goods imported from Africa was only £106,839 (c. £4 million in 2005). Twenty years later the 44 ships which sailed to West Africa from Liverpool still only brought back £154,755 (c. £6 million in 2005) worth of goods. Palm oil was the major product imported, followed by timber and 'gum senegal'. Most of the vessels used in the early years of this expanded trade had been slavers and were owned by merchants previously connected with trading in enslaved Africans.

Palm oil was, until the 1860s, enormously lucrative: a ton bought for between £10 and £20 in Lagos was sold in Liverpool for £40.[22]

Though the profits were vast, the amount of trade was low. How did the merchants, such as Matthew Forster of London (see Chapter 3), and the ex-slavers, such as Liverpool's Tobin clan, grow so rich? Could they have been involved in the ongoing 'nefarious trade'?

What were the goods exported to Africa? Some were sent in response to demands by traders in 'legitimate goods' on the Coast. But 'Liverpool entrepreneurs', according to historian Barry Drake, 'also supplied trade goods to factors in West Africa that were eventually used in the purchase of slaves'. This was admitted in Parliament in May 1848:

> goods which are employed for the payment of slaves either go to Brazil and are thence conveyed to the coast of Africa, or in some cases are sent direct to Africa, not to the persons who exchange them for slaves, but are consigned to persons who act for other individuals in other countries, who are concerned in the slave trade.[23]

When questioned, the Liverpool merchants naturally claimed that who their agents sold their goods to was none of their business. Among the longest lasting – and hence obviously profit-making – 'legitimate' traders were those who had been slave traders: I.O. Bold; John and Thomas Tobin, who also traded with the West Indies and India; the Aspinalls; the Horsfall clan under various company names and partnerships, such as Horsfall & Tobin, who also traded with the East and West Indies and North America. One of the large Tobin family, Thomas, owned gunpowder works in Ireland and supplied the huge demand for this in Africa.

Merchandise exported from Britain to the west coast of Africa included textiles, which gravely affected local weaving industries; by 1850 17 million yards was exported. Similarly, the export of salt from Cheshire ruined African salt manufacturing. Then – as now – arms and ammunition were the most popular of exports: in 1840 Liverpool ships carried 81 per cent of the over 3 million lb of gunpowder shipped to Africa, as well as an unknown proportion of the 89,653 guns. In the 1860s it has been estimated that over 100,000 guns, 'made from iron unfit to make firearms and horribly dangerous', had been shipped to Africa. Liverpool vessels also transported 55 per cent of the 2.8 million lb of iron bars. (Iron had also been manufactured in West Africa prior to the import of the cheaper European bars, which ruined the local manufacturers.) Among the other items listed in the Customs Bills of Entry are glassware, hats, wine, stone jars, rum and (probably slave-grown) tobacco and cocoa.[24]

Palm oil, the main import, was used to lubricate machinery and on the railways. The main ingredient in soap – for the newly cleanliness-conscious Britons – was also palm oil. This new industry provided employment – 'Palmolive' soap became a household necessity and an article of export, bringing more wealth into the city and the merchants' coffers. The volume imported rose from 112 tons in 1807 to over 10,000 tons in 1830 and 50,000 tons in 1860.[25] The traders ignored the fact that much of the palm oil was grown by enslaved Africans and that it was transported to the coast on the heads of slaves, some of whom were sold once they had delivered the oil.[26] Between half and three-quarters of the oil imported into the UK was in the hands of Liverpool traders, who thus profited, yet again, from slavery. *Tenuous weak.*

Ongoing participation in the trade in enslaved Africans

Historian Hugh Thomas admits that

> Continuing English involvement in the trade is more difficult to analyse. A few dealers established in West Africa … continued to play a part. Some English captains sailed under United States flags, and later under Swedish, Danish, and even French ones. More important, probably, several prominent firms participated in the trade after 1807 by investing in or even owning theoretically Spanish- or Portuguese-owned ships…. Many English firms still supplied the 'trade goods' for slave voyages.[27]

Liverpool traders had to find ways around the strictures imposed by the Abolition Act of 1807. Thomas Clarkson, who continued to work in the interests of Africans, now concentrated on discovering and documenting who was involved and how they avoided indictment. He visited Liverpool in 1809 and reported that while he was there three English ships, the *Flying Fish*, the *Susan* and the *Neptune*, left Liverpool, 'going as tenders to collect slaves'. He had also been told by two seamen who had just returned on the *Neptune* that her captain had bought 13 slaves and taken 2 'pawns'[28] while picking up wood and produce on the River Gaboon, and had 'sold them to a

Thomas Clarkson by C. Turner Mansell

Portuguese vessel ... other [vessels] have gone and are going, under Portuguese Papers and Colours ... some are English with a mixture of English and Portuguese officers, others really Portuguese ... now and then with an English agent on board. Thus for example, the *George*, Capt. R.P. Jackson and the *Venus* ... both sailed for Africa the first week in May with Portuguese Papers and with a mixture of Portuguese and English officers.'

Clarkson then illustrated another tactic of avoidance: 'The *Ferrula* renamed *Perrula* [*sic*], Capt. Miguel de Salva, now fitting out in Liverpool with a cargo of muskets and gunpowder ... for Africa and the Brazils'. Another Liverpool vessel, the *George*, was suspected of having carried out some of the goods exchanged for slaves on the coast by the *Perula* (*sic*). Clarkson believed that 'by the Act it is seizable if provable that it is actually going to Africa for slaves. To get this proof is very difficult. All we can do is send information to the cruisers.'[29]

Such 'sham sales' were conducted in British, Spanish, Brazilian and other ports, where Spanish-named captains were put on board, while the real English 'master' continued on the voyage as the 'supercargo'. For example, William Roscoe reported that the *Maria Dolous* carried 'three persons on board' – an American, a Spaniard and an Englishman, 'who are probably captains alternately'. The *8th Report of the Directors of the African Institution* lists 17 prizes taken by the Anti-Slave Trade Squadron whose masters' names were English. One master bore a name which often appeared in the lists of Liverpool slaver traders: Backhouse. The name of the ship is given as *Maria Dolores* – presumably the *Maria Dolous*.

The volumes of *Lloyd's Register* list some, but not all sales: for example, the Liverpool-registered *Hercules* changed owners seven times between 1809 and 1813.[30] Could there have been reasons for this other than the desire to avoid traceability and the possibility of indictment for slave trading?

We do not know how many ships sailed from Liverpool on slaving voyages once these became illegal after 1 January 1808. Abolitionist activist Zachary Macaulay asked his Liverpool colleague William Roscoe to report suspect vessels in Liverpool.[31] Between December 1809 and February 1812, 14 vessels are named in their correspondence as having sailed on slaving voyages from Liverpool. According to the E. Chambré Archive, in 1809 Macaulay 'listed thirty-six vessels which were suspected of having sailed from Liverpool on a slaving voyage since 1807'.[32] Macaulay could not 'see on what grounds the officers of the Customs should hesitate to detain and prosecute the vessel'.[33] I have to ask: could the 'retired' slave traders on the Liverpool Common Council perhaps have had some influence with the Customs?

Clearly the dealers/traders had figured out various means of avoiding detection. How much officials turned the proverbial 'blind eye' to what was going on in Liverpool docks we shall probably never know. A few Liverpool ships were among those captured by the inadequate Anti-Slave Trade Squadron (see Chapter 5). I have not read through the records of the Mixed Commission Courts or the Vice-Admiralty Courts, to which captured vessels were taken, but the impression I get is that most British vessels were exonerated. Is it because condemnation was so rare, or because the capture of Liverpool ships was so rare that only one case was reported in the *Liverpool Mercury* on 18 September 1840? I know some would argue that it is the Liverpool involvement that was rare, but this I do not believe. The *Mercury* had received

> a communication from a gentleman long resident in Sierra Leone, but recently returned.... Several vessels condemned ... the English brig *Guyana*, belonging to Mr Logan, a merchant, of Liverpool, was condemned on 12 August for aiding and abetting in the slave trade. It appears this vessel sailed from Liverpool on 18 October 1839, with a general cargo to Bahia (Brazil), to Edwards & Co, and was there chartered through the agency of the same house with the sanction of the British Consul (Mr Wheatley) to carry a cargo of merchandise to the coast of Africa, touching at various places for the purpose of trading. That on the 26 March.... HM schooner *Viper* ... brought her to by firing a shot. After overhauling her a prize crew were put on board ... to Sierra Leone where she lay 102 days before she was condemned. The cargo is not yet disposed of (and much is ruined). The merchants complain very much of the frequent sales of the slave cargoes brought into Sierra Leone, ruining their business.[34]

This must refer to the *Guiana*, whose registered owners in 1839 were James Logan and John Moore of Liverpool; the master was George Nickel. The cargo, consigned to J. Edwards & Co., was insured for $60,000 'by a company in Liverpool'. She sailed to Bahia (Brazil), where it was first thought that she was chartered by Manuel Lopez, a trader in enslaved Africans, to take a cargo to his trading partners on the African coast. However, documents subsequently found indicated that it had been George Nickel who 'had engaged the vessel in taking goods on freight for delivery in Lagos'. (*Lloyd's Daily Lists* describes the *Guiana* as a whaler. Three captains are listed: Nicholls, Hogg and McKellan.) She was captured by the Anti-Slave Trade Squadron and eventually condemned for 'aiding and abetting the slave trade'.[35] The official report by the Commissioners on the *Guiana* noted the 'connexion with the Slave Trade for some time past of the alleged charterer of the *Guiana* and nearly all the shippers and consignees of goods embarked... [W]e have proof'.[36]

Another example of Customs' and other officials' 'blind eye' is the *Duoro*, wrecked off the Isles of Scilly in January 1843, two days after she had left Liverpool. She was found to be carrying manillas (used exclusively for purchasing slaves), chains, and cannon mounted in the centre of the ship, 'which swivelled so it could be used on revolting slaves'? Why did Liverpool customs clear a ship carrying slave-trade goods, even if she was ostensibly bound for Oporto in Portugal? And who owned the *Duoro*? In 1840 her master was listed in *Lloyd's Daily List* as Capt. Ball; in 1842 as Capt. DeHaas Smith – obviously not Portuguese names![37] (The vessel is not listed in *Lloyd's Register.*)

I shall give just two examples of somewhat dubious exonerations by the Courts of Liverpool vessels. The first is the *Maid of Islay*. She had been trading on the coast for two years, seemingly innocuously. But she was intercepted in 1848 at the Gallinas, a well-known slaving area. The intention, its captors believed, 'was either to ship slaves or sell the vessel to one of the Spanish slavers at Gallinas ... the slave trade is almost the *only* [sic] trade at Gallinas ... [The *Maid*] was equipped for and engaged in, the Slave Trade, or otherwise aiding and abetting that traffic.' The master of the *Maid* was William Cunningham Townley of Liverpool. It could not be determined whether he was also the owner or if the ship had been sold to Hartung & Co. of Hamburg. Taken to the Courts at Sierra Leone, Captain Townley was found innocent and the *Maid* was restored to her owners. The Adjudicator in the case had been the Acting Chief Justice Charles Heddle, who was in the same line of business! Acting Commission Judge James Hook advised the government that it should 'appeal to a higher court at home'.[38]

The second example of a manoeuvre is from the files of the Treasury. Thomas Crowther, a Liverpool merchant, had written to the officials regarding the unauthorised sale of his vessel, the *Lady Combermere*, by the captain. The vessel had been sold on the African coast to a Brazilian slave trader for $6000. The case was taken to court, but the Treasury Solicitors decided that 'no prosecution can be maintained against him [the ship's officer] under the Slave Trade Prohibition Act'.[39] One can be sure that the 'message' contained in this decision was well noted by shipowners in Liverpool. As were all the other non-prosecutions and non-interventions by the government.

The 'message' that the British government and its agents in Liverpool were not very concerned about enforcing laws regarding the port's ongoing participation in the trade is exemplified by the case of the *Nightingale,* an American vessel. In 1860, 53 years after the British abolition of the trade, and almost 20 after the above cases, the *Nightingale* was caught trading in enslaved Africans off the Angolan coast. It had been outfitted for the voyage in Liverpool. That the ship had been outfitted for the illegal trade was well known in the city, as was the outfitting of the *Harbinger,* the *Propontus* and a steamer, the *City of Norwich,* in 1864.[40] If these, how many others? Lord Russell had promised 'the closest investigations [of the *Nightingale*] ... and all the powers of the law shall be put in motion with a view to prosecute to conviction the perpetrators of this odious crime.' But I can find no evidence of such action, then or at any other time.

Ongoing abolitionist struggles

Two years after the passing of the Abolition Act, Thomas Clarkson recognised the inadequacies of the law and its implementation. He believed that there was a need for a 'new Act regarding the evasion'. For example, he advocated that it should be made a 'misdemeanour for English subjects to be found knowingly in English or Foreign ships, trading for slaves'. The following year he told William Roscoe that he was planning on 'bringing in a Bill next session regarding all the known Evasions ... to prevent effectually not only the Evasions of Englishmen but of Foreigners'. In 1811 Macaulay believed that Roscoe needed professional – that is, legal – assistance in Liverpool to investigate Customs documents. He and Lord Brougham, another very active member of the British and Foreign Anti-Slavery Society, were going to see the Attorney General regarding the various limitations in the Abolition Act. However, Roscoe felt that 'penalties and punishments' would be useless while the British slave traders 'sent out Agents, capital and goods to fit out vessels in foreign ports'. When Brougham presented a bill in Parliament to proscribe investment in the trade in slaves, the resistance was led by A. Baring MP, a member of the Baring clan, who feature in many of the chapters of this book.[41]

As the 'tricks of the trade' were well publicised by abolitionists, including captains of many of the Anti-Slave Trade Squadron, many questions have to be asked. *Why did the government not take firm action?* Would the government have enforced more stringent Acts if Parliament could have been persuaded to pass them? How could Liverpool Customs turn the proverbial 'blind eye' to vessels fitting out for slaving voyages in Liverpool? Why did central government do so little to enforce the laws? Was British prosperity so dependent on the trade in slaves, and on slave produce (which in turn depended on the trade), that it was inconceivable to pass meaningful Acts?

An interesting, and for once positive, light is thrown on Liverpool and slave traders by the actions taken by William Roscoe in 1809 to free the imprisoned 'Negro' crew of the *Monte de Casino.* The vessel's captain, José A. Cardozo, had the men arrested and jailed on the ground that he had lent them money which they had not repaid. Thomas Clarkson, then in town, heard of this, contacted a lawyer and obtained discharge papers for the men. But the crew refused to leave the jail. The jailer then notified Roscoe, who obtained bail for the men. A magistrate freed them. Roscoe arranged for eight of them to enter the Royal Navy. The ninth had 'an infirmity', so Roscoe had a friend give him a job on one of his vessels. In his deposition, Ioze, one of the freed men, explained that they had all been slaves of Cardozo.[42]

Regrettably, there is no compilation of British vessels captured by the Anti-Slave Trade cruisers and taken to the Mixed Commission or the Vice-Admiralty Courts. An analysis of these and the Treasury Solicitor's papers would clarify ongoing British involvement and perhaps the politics behind the frequent decisions not to indict these vessels. An investigation of the carriage of multiple flags and non-registration of vessels could also, of course, lead to greater understanding of the mechanisms of the illegal trade.

Slave and 'legitimate' traders' influence

Many of the wealthiest slave traders became prominent and influential citizens of Liverpool. As described by one historian, 'Liverpool was dominated by a strong, almost hereditary caste of merchants and shipowners.' Their experience and attitudes became not only unquestioned but respected – and widespread.[43] Some have already been listed in Chapter 1. Another prime example is John Gladstone, who was deeply involved in slavery, and in Liverpool, and in the national government. Here I shall only detail those aspects of his life that are pertinent to slavery. Information on some other prominent Liverpudlians can be found in Appendix 2. How many of these merchants were involved in supplying slave traders on the African coast or in the Americas, and how many traded in slave-grown produce and supplied goods to slave owners, has not been researched.

But before we glance at Liverpool's rich men, it is important to note that the city also housed the poor and the transient, most of whom were seamen Black and White. Frederick Engels in the 1840s found that 'a full one fifth of the population live in narrow, dark, damp, badly ventilated dwellings'. Oxford's Professor John Melville, on his visit, found that

> of all seaports in the world, Liverpool, perhaps, most abounds in all the variety of land-sharks, land-rats and other vermin, which makes the hapless mariner their prey. In the shape of landlords, bar-keepers, clothiers, crimps, and boarding house-loungers, the land-sharks devour him limb-by-limb.... In Liverpool ... the negro steps with a prouder pace and lifts his head like a man; for here, no such exaggerated feeling exists in respect to him, as in America.[44]

But about twenty years later, when Charles Dickens visited and noted the 'negro' residents, the police superintended who acted as his guide said that they 'generally kept together, because they are at a disadvantage singly and liable to slights in neighbouring streets'. They were also 'too often underpaid', according to Henry Mayhew.[45]

John Gladstone (1764–1851), already mentioned in Chapter 1, was probably the most influential of the Liverpool merchants at the national level. He had begun his long career as a partner of Corrie & Co, suppliers of goods to slave-worked West Indian plantations. By the 1820s he had acquired a number of sugar and coffee plantations of his own – and 2183 slaves – in Demerara (now part of Guyana) and Jamaica. After the Abolition Act, Gladstone expanded his trading ventures to India and China,[46] and also imported slave-produced goods from Brazil. (Gladstone took a very active role in destroying the power of the East India Company and in setting up a banking system for India.)

What sort of attitudes towards Africans did John Gladstone attempt to inculcate in his son William, who was elected to Parliament in 1832, served as Colonial Secretary twice and became Prime Minister in 1868? On Monday, 13 October 1823 *The Times* reported that slaves in Demerara had taken over some of the plantations, claiming that the freedom promised them by the King in England was being withheld from them. They placed the plantation managers in stocks and demanded to talk with the Governor. The Governor refused to grant them their freedom and proclaimed martial law. The revolt spread. Two White men – missionaries – were arrested on the basis that they had helped the slaves.[47] The man who presented the written demands to the Governor was named Jack Gladstone. The man who was probably the main leader was named Quamina Gladstone. Obviously both were slaves on John Gladstone's plantations.

The frenzy of the 'civilised' colonists was unbounded: about a hundred of the slaves were killed by the military and 47 were hanged. Some were 'literally torn to shreds under the whip': slaves were still being whipped – up to 1000 lashes – months after the revolt had been put down. Some of those who survived the whipping were then given prison sentences, to be followed by labour in heavy chains for the rest of their lives. Quamina was hunted down, and his bullet-ridden body was displayed in chains in front of the plantation. Others had been strung on gibbets.[48]

There was fury in and out of Parliament in London, not so much about the treatment of the slaves or the conditions under which they were forced to labour, but regarding the death sentence pronounced on missionary Smith. John Gladstone naturally spoke vehemently, upholding the justice of the colonial authorities. In 1824 when events in Demerara were debated in Parliament, the city of Liverpool presented Gladstone with £1400 and a 'dinner table service, plates excepted, of twenty-eight pieces: two candalebra, two ice pails, two tureens ... to mark their high sense of his successful exertions for the promotion of trade and commerce and in acknowledgement of his most important services to the town of Liverpool.'[49] The defence of slavery was clearly much appreciated by all those who had contributed to the 'voluntary subscription' for the gifts to slave owner (killer?) John Gladstone.

John Gladstone appears to have owned at least three plantations in Demerara: the Vreed-en-Hoop, Belle Vue and Vriedenstein. Two years after the Emancipation Act was passed in 1833, unable to flog his slaves into obedience any longer, Gladstone persuaded the Secretary of State for the Colonies to let him import Indians to labour on his plantations. (This proved to be the inauguration of the general scheme of indentured labour recruitment in India for the Caribbean.) He was assured by his recruiters that the Indians 'have no religion, no education and in their present state, no wants beyond eating, drinking and sleeping'. And, as 'the natives [were] perfectly ignorant of the place they agree to go to, or the length of the voyage they are undertaking', there will be no difficulties, the Calcutta-based company promised. Nor did Gladstone consider that the Indian men might want the companionship of Indian women, as at first he asked for one woman per ten men 'for cooking and washing', then for one per twenty-five.[50] When 'it was discovered that [they] were being flogged like slaves on the Gladstone estates, there was an abolitionist outcry in Britain', according to historian Robin Blackburn.[51]

The outcry, led by the Anti-Slavery Society, resulted in an official investigation. This found that the flogging of 'coolies' with a cat-o'-nine-tails and then rubbing salt into their wounds had apparently been such common practice on Gladstone's Vreed-en-Hoop plantation that 9 of the 65 labourers imported died within 18 months of their arrival there. The state of the plantation hospitals might have contributed to this appalling death rate: one of the investigators found 'such unalleviated wretchedness, such hopeless misery ... never before had he seen'.[52] Perhaps frustrated with his inability to flog his workers with impunity, Gladstone sold this plantation for £35,000 in 1841. He got another £2000 for 'the services of the coolies for two years'.[53] Is this tantamount to selling them?

What was John Gladstone other than a racist, rich man? In 1811 he was honoured with the 'freedom' of Liverpool, perhaps for his leadership of the Liverpool West India Association, which passed resolutions against slave emancipation at his behest. He had also been in the forefront of the agitation for the Liverpool-to-Manchester railway, which was needed to facilitate speedy transport of raw and manufactured cotton, and served on its Liverpool Committee. The bill permitting construction was passed in 1826, the lead in the House of Lords having been taken by Lord Derby, a Gladstone friend. John's son Robertson became one of the directors of the completed railway.

Gladstone was also part-owner of the *Liverpool Courier*, which naturally proved a forum for his views and politics. He was also quite a prolific author, signing his letters to the *Courier* as 'Mercator', but publishing pamphlets and tracts in his full name. A number of these were on the trade in slaves; others were on cotton, trade issues, Liverpool docks and the Corn Laws. Those on slavery explained his views very clearly. For example, in *Letters Concerning the Abolition of the Slave Trade* (1807), he explained that the reason why slaves in the British colonies in the West Indies did not reproduce themselves was because

> negroes yield to the ardent and uncontroled [*sic*] influence of the passions, where a promiscuous intercourse of the sexes takes place, there consequently fewer children are born ... So constant supply of negroes from Africa is requisite.

'The slave was born a slave, without political rights, and is ignorant of the meaning of the term', Gladstone believed. Naturally, his views regarding 'negroes' had not changed when emancipation was being debated. In Africa there was only a

> state of savage life ... despotic form of government ... disposition to indolence.... In the colonies their labour is moderate ... all their wants ... are fully provided for them by their owners.... When negroes understand the obligations as well as the advantages of being their own masters, then steps towards emancipation can be taken with due and just regard to the lives, the property and the interests of their masters.

The legislators in the colonies would effect whatever changes were necessary; they did not need interference from Parliament in London, he advised. That 'negroes' might also have 'interests' clearly did not cross the mental horizon of John Gladstone. But then he had argued that 'the loss which has been suffered by the insurrection [in Demerara] should, and must, be made good by the public here'. Flogging and murdering the slaves was clearly necessary as they, Gladstone maintained, wanted the unthinkable – 'immediate freedom'.[154]

Gladstone's attitude towards the colonies' White settlers (as the 'negroes' are not mentioned) is clearly stated in his *Letter addressed to ... the Rt. Hon. W. Ewart Gladstone, MP for the University of Oxford*. Son William had spoken in Parliament favouring the repeal of the Navigation Laws and his father chose to rebuke him in public in this *c.* 1848 pamphlet. The existing Laws limited the transport of British produce and manufactures to British shipping. The colonies which had been 'earned at the cost of British blood and treasure', would be 'rendered valueless to us' with this measure, Sir John warned. They had been settled at 'great expense [and we] have given them privileges, protection and admission to our markets for their produce on conditions advantageous to them'. The Laws provide 'important advantages to Britain and British shipowners ... [there would be] 'no real benefit to the colonists', even if 'cheaper ship rates' became available to them. Had Gladstone, I wonder, sold all his plantations by 1848? How many ships did he own?

With support from the Duke of Marlborough, John Gladstone served as MP for Woodstock and Lancaster for nine years. Both Gladstone and his son participated in the debates on emancipation and both advocated that very gradual steps should be taken. John Gladstone, with considerable interest in the issue, was a vocal contributor to the debates regarding the tactics to be used in the compensation of slave owners.

John Gladstone was created a baronet in 1846, despite having been unseated from Parliament for bribery in 1827. He died in 1851, worth some £600,000 (c. £36 million in 2005). He had given £100,000 to each of his four sons prior to his death.

John's eldest son Thomas also served as an MP from 1830 until 1842 in various constituencies; he was 'unseated on petition' at Ipswich. Second son Robertson (married into the Heywood banking family) continued the businesses on his father's death in 1851; he served on Liverpool Council for many years and was elected mayor in 1852.[55]

To determine the extent of Liverpool's dependence on the slave trade after 1807 – that is, on importing slave-grown produce and exporting to slave-worked societies – much more work needs to be done on the trading companies, the banks, the insurance companies. To get at least a glimmer of understanding of the trade with slave traders, an analysis of the ships sailing to intermediate ports, where goods intended for the trade were offloaded in order to be reloaded on to the slavers themselves, would be a good beginning. These activities and the ports used are delineated in the many reports of the Anti-Slave Trade Squadron.

Manchester

Manchester's involvement with the trade in slaves and slavery was of long standing. The 1788 'Account of the Trade of Manchester to Africa', prepared for the Privy Council, states that

The value of goods annually supplied from Manchester and the
neighbourhood for Africa is about £200,000 [c. £11.4 million in 2005] ...
This manufacture employs immediately about 18,000 men, women and
children. This manufacture employs a capital of at least £300,000 ...
Besides [this] the manufactures of Manchester ... equally furnish for
the West India trade upwards of £300,000 a year worth of manufactures
in the making of which still greater number of hands are employed.[56]

It is not surprising, therefore, to discover that to expedite the transport
of goods to Liverpool, the nearest port, a canal was dug in 1758. The
Sankey Brook Canal was partly financed by Liverpool slave trader
John Ashton. This was followed by other canals, linking the manufacturing towns of the Midlands and the North West with Liverpool.
The expensive and relatively inefficient canals were soon outpaced
by the Liverpool and Manchester railway, which began to carry passengers and freight in 1830.[57] I do not know who provided the finance
for the railway, but it would certainly be interesting to know!

The wealth of the area is demonstrated by the county of Lancashire, which included Manchester, paying the second highest amount
of tax to central government in 1841.[58] Again, this is not surprising, as
'Lancashire [had been] the outstanding case of a region of unceasing
expansion ... from the 1720s onwards.' Expansion at least partly based
on slavery and the trade in slaves. Professor Herman Melville was
quite explicit about this, writing that the cities of Manchester and
Liverpool owed their 'opulence to the exchange of their produce with
that raised by the American slaves'.[59]

The cotton industry

The growth of Manchester was based on the cotton industry. Most
of the 1,261 million lb of raw cotton unloaded in Liverpool in 1861
would have been forwarded to Lancashire's 2109 cotton mills.[60] The
proportion of slave-grown raw cotton imports from the USA rose from
c. 48 per cent in 1811 to 78 per cent in 1851; dropping to 55 per cent in
1871. The proportion imported from Brazil, also slave-grown, varied
between 6 per cent and 33 per cent, while that of possibly free-grown
cotton from India only rose to over 20 per cent from the 1860s.[61]

The numbers employed

By 1861 the number of workers *directly* employed in the cotton industry
had risen to over half a million, from the 1835 figure of 219,286. In 1838,

of the 255,478 employees in the 'cotton factories', 56 per cent were women. The proportion of children under 13 was between 9 and 10.4 per cent. A survey conducted in the 1830s found widespread use of laudanum (opium) by women workers to assuage the hunger of their children while they were working 14-hour days in the mills. It was also found that many young children died from accidents attributable to lack of supervision.[62] Among the popular 'Infants' Quietness' syrups was Atkinson's Infants' Preservative, made in Manchester, a mixture of chalk and laudanum which sold around 70,000 bottles a year.[63]

In 1841, 22 per cent of Lancashire's population was directly employed in the cotton industry. If half the population was too young or too old to be working, then that is 44 per cent of the total population of 1.67 million people.[64] Twenty years later *The Times* in January 1861 estimated that the number of people in the UK 'dependent' on cotton manufacturing was about 4 million, of whom over 1 million were Lancastrians. The paper reported that about a fifth of the British population (of *c.* 20 million) was estimated to be directly or indirectly dependent on cotton.[65] Other workers involved in the industry included bleachers, printers, packers and other storeroom workers, and the manufacturers of machinery, as well as the coal miners producing the fuel for the looms and spinners, the canal and railway workers, the seamen, and those producing food for the workers.[66]

Merchants' and national income from cotton

Cotton exports, as indicated, formed a very large proportion of British exports. The 'official value' of 'cotton manufactures' exported was over £40 million (*c.* £1822 million in 2005) in the 1860s according to one author. Others give higher totals, for example £79.8 million (£4078 million in 2005) in the mid-1840s and £132.8 million in the 1850s (£6640 million in 2005).[67] Cotton cloth was, of course, also exported to the slave states of Brazil and Cuba, and to the slave traders in Africa. In 1853, for example, 5 per cent of total exports, valued at £1,788,366 (*c.* £90 million in 2005) went to Brazil and just under 2 per cent to Cuba.[68]

In 1831, 9.4 per cent of the 'national income' was derived from the cotton industry. Thirty years later the proportion was 11.5 per cent. In 1834 almost half of British exports were cotton 'manufactures'; by 1864 it was only 34 per cent. By the 1860s Manchester had become 'the centre of that commercial and credit organization which was so important a factor not only in the development of the Lancashire cotton trade, but in making England the clearing house of the Continental cotton trade'.[69]

The cotton merchants

Many Manchester and Liverpool cotton merchants and processors were closely linked with the southern, slave-worked states in the United States of America. Nathaniel Evans, for example, an Irishman who owned the Oakland Plantations in Louisiana, was 'involved in commercial ventures as far afield as Liverpool'. Richard Singleton, son of an immigrant from the Isle of Wight, owned cotton plantations in South Carolina and traded with William Forde & Co., of Liverpool. Washington Jackson, a cotton, sugar and tobacco merchant of Philadelphia, had a branch in Liverpool.[70] The firm's New Orleans office, selling cotton from Mississippi, was in partnership with Todd, Jackson & Co. of Liverpool. James Hewitt & Co., also of Liverpool, had a branch, Hewitt, Norton & Co. in New Orleans.[71] Correspondence between cotton exporters Brown Bros & Co. and their partner Brown Shipley & Co. of Liverpool, and the firm of Paul A. Oliver and its trading partners in Liverpool and Manchester, have been preserved by the New York Historical Society.

Among those who had invested in this industry, and thus supported and profited from slavery, was Baring Bros, who had opened a Liverpool office in 1832 and by the following year were 'number five in the list of receivers of cotton'. Barings had its own 'factors' (agents) in Charleston, Mobile, Savannah, and well as in southern ports and the cotton markets of the northern states.[72]

The discovery of these trading links led me to wonder whether there were Britons who owned slave-worked plantations in the South. Unfortunately no one seems to have investigated this topic. However, the University of North Carolina at Chapel Hill searched their Southern Historical Collection for me and sent me details of the 'James Amedee Gaudet' and 'George Scarborough Barnsley' collections. The Gaudet papers include information on two British subjects, John Burnside and Nelson McStea, who had acquired Gaudet's plantations in 1858. Burnside (and McStea?) owned a total of 14 sugar and cotton slave-worked plantations. Scarborough Barnsley, also a British subject, owned cotton plantations and exported cotton from Savannah and New Orleans. After the Civil War he emigrated to Brazil, where he owned a gold mine. His children married British 'business associates' John Kelso Reid and Thomas Gilmour.[73]

How many other Britons, I wonder, owned slave-worked plantations, or were in partnership with plantation owners and cotton (and tobacco) merchants? How many thus grew rich on the labour of slaves when British subjects were no longer supposed to hold slaves? Another question that needs to be asked is, who were the people who campaigned for and won the reduction of duty on foreign-grown (i.e., slave-grown) cotton, from 5 shillings and 10 pence per 112 lb in 1831, to 2 shillings and 11 pence in 1833, while cotton from 'British possessions' paid 4 pence? And who obtained the complete elimination of import duty in 1845?

From the Barnsley papers it is clear that many southerners emigrated to Brazil after slavery was ended in the United States. This indicated that other questions, to which I could find no answers, should be asked: did plantation owners from the British West Indies emigrate with their slaves to the USA as emancipation approached in 1833? Or to Brazil?

Other questions I want to ask are about the millionaires who profited from slave-grown cotton or other enterprises profiting from slavery or the slave trade. What did they do with their vast wealth? How did they contribute to the Industrial Revolution and Britain's growing wealth? How many British workers were dependent on (and exploited by) them? Some of these men were:

- *Sir Robert Peel* (like John Gladstone, the father of a future prime minister), who left over £1 million in 1830 (£50 million in 2005); he was a cotton manufacturer.
- Cotton manufacturer *Richard Arkwright* left 'above £1 million' in 1843.
- *James Morrison*, who left between £4 and £6 million in 1857, owned textile warehouses and banks in America.
- *Thomas Fielden*, a cotton manufacturer, left £1.3 million in 1869.
- *Thomas Baring*, a member of the banking clan, left £1.4 million in 1873.
- *Edward Langworthy*, a cotton manufacturer, died in 1874, leaving £1.2 million.[74]

These men would clearly not have supported the exposition in a 1846 pamphlet by an anonymous Mancunian, entitled *Reasons for Withdrawing from our Trading Connection with the American Slave Holder: and a plan for doing so suggested*. The author coupled the increase in the export of raw cotton between 1790 and 1843 with the increase in the numbers of slaves in America from 657,000 to 2,847,810. He advised that

> if you buy stolen goods, you become a 'participator in the crime'.... [I]f
> we purchase American cotton, knowing that wretched system under
> which it is produced, we become aiders and abettors of the American
> slaveholder and participators with him in the criminality of the system
> of American Slavery. And in consequence of this criminality, not only
> the merchant, the spinner and the manufacturer must participate,
> but our whole manufacturing community – and so indeed, the nation
> itself.... [W]e may indeed be said to share its profits ... [withdrawal] is
> a question which has passed without regard for more than fifty years.[75]

The author advocated the purchase of cotton from other sources, for example from India.

Sir George Stephens wrote in 1854: 'Manchester and Birmingham manufacturers lived by it', meaning the slave trade and slavery.[76]

Lobbying governments

By the 1820s one-third of Britain's (i.e. mainly Manchester's) raw cotton imports came from slave-worked plantations in Brazil – and was largely paid for by the export of manufactured cotton there. As one would expect, the city's Chamber of Commerce was continually petitioning the government in its own interests – for example, to open consulates in South America, to support the independence of the Spanish and Portuguese colonies there, and the separation of Uruguay from Brazil. These attempts to influence or intervene in foreign policy increased with the rise in the export of cotton 'piece goods' to Brazil.[77]

The manufacturers and merchants of Manchester were not supporters of attempts to curb the trade in slaves. For example, in 1849 the Chamber of Commerce, together with the Liverpool Brazilian Association and the Glasgow Chamber of Commerce, petitioned the Foreign Office to repeal what came to be known as Lord Aberdeen's Act, which gave the Anti-Slave Trade cruisers the right to seize any

vessel found engaged in the slave trade. This 'hampered trade and fos-
ters ill-feeling', the merchants claimed.[78] Without slave-grown cotton,
what would have been the fate of the Lancashire mills and workforce?
And of the British economy? In the early 1840s the Chamber corre-
sponded with the government attempting to ensure that the response
to US President Tyler's accusation of Britons supplying trade goods
to slave traders would not result in any trade restrictions.[79]

Though Liverpool's interest in West Africa was naturally manifested much earlier than Manchester's, the 'cottonopolis' soon caught
up. The Huttons, a Manchester-based merchant family who had
traded with West Africa for over a hundred years, and Matthew
Forster of Forster & Smith (see Chapter 3) had petitioned and lobbied
the government for years on many issues regarding trade with West
Africa.[80] (Most revealingly, in the 1842 *Parliamentary Papers on the Slave
Trade*, vol. 12, p. 495, there is an allegation that W.B. Hutton & Sons
fitted out their vessels for the trade in slaves on the African coast.)
The steady increase in the export of cotton cloth alerted Manchester
merchants to the rising importance of this trade. The Huttons did
their best to create a myth of the possibility of untapped markets
in West Africa. The result was a petition and a delegation to the
government in 1872, asking for a voice in the government of newly
conquered Lagos. French expansionism led to more vigorous lobbying
for the protection of their trade. In 1892 the merchants succeeded in
convincing the Manchester Chamber of Commerce to establish an
African Committee. J.A. Hutton, who had been elected Member of
Parliament for Manchester North in 1885, was a member of this committee. Huttons had no problem dealing with slave traders: they sold
200 guns to the notorious Pedro Blanco in the early 1840s. It is not
surprising – but it is sad – to discover that J.A. Hutton was known to
be a good friend of King Leopold of Belgium, in whose Congo colony
the atrocities perpetrated against the Africans exceeded even those
on Gladstone's plantations.[81]

Liverpool, Manchester and the American Civil War

Naturally Britain, and the cotton industry, were very concerned as
the USA headed towards civil war. Though some had turned to Brazil
as a source of raw cotton, the 'Liverpool merchants', according to

historian Stanley Broadbridge, 'were eager to retain their slave-grown cotton and set on foot a vigorous agitation for armed intervention on behalf of the South'.[82]

The Civil War broke out in April 1861. The South had much to defend: in the eight 'cotton states' in 1850 there were 1.8 million slaves and only 2.1 million Whites. In 1860, this 60 per cent of the total enslaved population of the USA produced 66 per cent of the total exports of the country.[83] The North sought to blockade the Southern ports in order to starve the rebels of imports and armaments and, more importantly, to starve them of funds by preventing the export of cotton.

Given British dependence on cotton from the American slave states, did the cotton industry take steps to avoid disintegration? There was no crisis in the first few months as there had been an overproduction of cloth, so production was reduced. This should have resulted in a drop in the price of raw cotton, but the imminence of war pushed the price up. In turn this led to a hoarding of raw cotton by the importers. Speculation in cotton in the Liverpool Exchange 'became a continued round of animation.... The multiplicity of trans-actions afforded lucrative employment for nearly double the number of brokers ... all operators made money ... an investor [could] gain £1,000 a day'.[84] The Cotton Supply Association of Manchester stepped up its investigations of other sources of cotton, such as India, Brazil, Egypt and the West Indies, and eventually West Africa. But, as will be detailed below, ways of continuing importation from the Southern states were found.

The causes of the Civil War are much debated to this day. Was it fought to retain slavery? To advance the industrialising North? Was it Southern free trade against Northern protectionism? These and other suggestions for its cause are not of direct importance to the issue of British relations with the slave-owning, cotton- and tobacco-growing South. Despite pressure from the cotton importers and manufacturers, including Liverpool merchants and the chairman of the Liverpool Chamber of Commerce, in May 1861 the British gov-ernment proclaimed neutrality.[85] No Briton was permitted to serve in the armed forces of either side, or in either's merchant marine. British ports were forbidden to fit out the vessels of the North or the South, armaments for them were not to be carried by British ships, and blockades imposed by either side were to be respected. The Foreign Enlistment Act, also in force, imposed a penalty for equipping or arming a vessel whose intention was to 'commit hostilities against a friendly State'.

Were these regulations enforced? They were not. As explained by Thomas E. Taylor, a Liverpool merchant, the regulations

> awakened no respect whatever ... It was a piece of international courtesy ... Firm after firm, with an entirely free conscience, set about endeavouring to recoup itself for the loss of legitimate trade.... In Liverpool was awakened a spirit the like of which had not been known since the palmy days of the slave trade.[86]

It was pointed out at a meeting of the Union and Emancipation Society of Manchester in 1863 that the 'English port of Nassau is a permanent rendezvous for steamers watching to break the blockade in order to deliver goods, including arms, to the South'. A loan of £3 million had been raised in London to pay for the war vessels being illegally built in Britain for the Confederates. At another meeting, a resolution was passed asking the government 'to put an effectual stop to the nefarious proceedings of certain persons in England, including MPs, [who] are engaged in the illegal enterprise of providing and furnishing war ships and otherwise aiding the ... Confederacy.'[87] *But the government did nothing.*

Trade and an armed navy were hugely important to both the North and the South. This led both sides to attempt to destroy each other's vessels and ports, and then to blockade the ports to prevent merchant vessels getting through. British shipbuilding and trading expertise thus became of great importance to both sides. But British companies were not supposed to aid either combatant.

Naturally the Confederates did all they could to enlist British aid: Capt. James Dunwoody Bulloch was despatched to Britain as their secret agent. He worked with the 'house' of Fraser Trenholm & Co. John Fraser of Liverpool was in the shipping business between Liverpool and Charleston; George Trenholm was a hugely wealthy Southerner who 'enjoyed almost unlimited credit in the United Kingdom'. New branches of the firm were opened in the Bahamas and Bermuda to aid the blockade-running enterprise they engaged in. Bulloch and the company were also instrumental in raising the £3 million loan for the Confederates. According to Bulloch's memoirs, 'five times that amount was subscribed'.[88]

'Blockade runners' – small, very fast vessels – were built on the Mersey and elsewhere in the UK. Historian George Chandler notes that 'many merchants sent blockade runners to the Southern States'. As the merchants ignored the government regulations, so did the shipbuilders and owners of these vessels. 'Blockade running was not regarded as either unlawful or dishonourable, but rather as a bold and daring enterprise', recorded one trader involved. Norman Longmate has estimated that at least 36 blockade runners were built on Merseyside: 'a great many were built and the war ... brought a minor boom to the shipyards of Merseyside and the Clyde'. According to historian Malcolm McRonald, the Liverpool firm of Fawcett, Preston had been facing a decline in business and 'were probably very pleased to find a new (and very profitable) source of business by supplying engines to the blockade runners ... Many fast coastal and cross-channel ships were sold for this purpose, and there were new ships owned/built at other ports.' The total number of ships which ran the blockade was 588 and the 'majority of these ships sailed from Liverpool and it was on her docks that the valuable cargoes (well over a million bales of cotton) were ... unloaded'.[89]

Great Britain served as the '"arsenal and treasury" of the Confederate Government', according to Capt. Bulloch. But Britain also acted in the same role for the North. While not supporting slavery, this was as illegal as trading with the South. It was Baring Brothers who acted as agents for the shipment of arms to the North: they charged 1 per cent commission and 5 per cent interest on loans to the US Navy Department.[90]

It was not only merchants and shipbuilders who ignored the regulations. So did officers of the Royal Navy. Under pseudonyms, they went in search of excitement and undoubtedly much higher pay, captaining the runners through the North's blockades. 'Captain Roberts', for example, a retired officer, was in fact Augustus Charles Hobart-Hampden, the younger son of an earl. Two blockade-runner captains went on to become admirals in the Royal Navy.[91]

Some of the tactics which had been used in the illegal participation in the slave trade after 1807 were now employed in the new illegal trade. For example, warships built or refitted for the Confederacy were never, or very seldom, equipped with arms before they left Liverpool. Armaments were shipped out in another vessel and then fitted at a convenient port – such as the ports in the British colonies in the West Indies or even off the French coast. For example, the *Japan*, built on the Clyde in 1853 and renamed the *Georgia*, met with the *Alar* off the French coast. The *Alar* had been despatched from Liverpool with the guns and ammunition to turn the *Georgia* into a warship.

The firm of Laird Brothers built:

- the *Florida* (also known as the *Oreto*), which sailed to the Bahamas in March 1862 where she was outfitted with armaments and other war equipment, which had been shipped there on another vessel, the *Prince Alfred*;
- the *Alabama*, also built by Laird Brothers, similarly sailed from Liverpool as an 'innocent' vessel, and was also outfitted for war in the Bahamas;
- the *Georgina* was outfitted in Nassau;
- the *Shenandoah*, which proved as successful as the *Alabama* in destroying Northern vessels;
- two vessels supposedly built for the Chinese naval service, the steamers *Tiensin* and *Kwang Tung*.[92]

(Liverpool was not the only port to support the Confederates – without any reprimand or punitive actions taken by the government. To give an example of another port: Southampton permitted the Confederate privateer *Nashville* to take refuge there in November 1861.[93] An example of an arm of the government breaking its own proclaimed neutrality was the Royal Navy: in 1863 the Navy sold its steam sloop, the *Victor*, to a Confederate agent. She was renamed the *Scylla* and sailed to Sheerness, for refitting 'under the direction of persons connected to the Royal Dockyard'. She was next seen in Calais, as a Confederate war ship, with a new name, *Rappahannock*. Whether three other vessels sold by the Admiralty, the *Amphion*, *Cyclops* and *Phoenix*, also ended up serving the Confederates I have not been able to discover.[94])

But neither the blockade runners nor the alternative sources of cotton could prevent what eventually came to be known as the 'cotton famine' and consequent massive unemployment. That the numbers recorded as seeking relief in Lancashire in December 1862 were just under half a million men, women and children indicates the fundamental importance of slave-grown cotton to the county's economy.[95]

One has also to question the accepted version of the workers' attitudes towards the enslaved working on the plantations. It has become generally accepted that the relatively well-paid British workers supported their unpaid, enslaved counterparts in the cotton industry of the USA. But this is a myth, 'born of propaganda [which] survived because, like all myths that endure, it told people what they wanted to believe'. The only cotton town which was unequivocally pro-North was Rochdale, the home of the radical politician John Bright. Manchester people were of mixed opinions, and in most of the cotton towns the number of pro-South meetings grossly exceeded the numbers pro-North. In Ashton, for example, 14 pro-South meetings were held and five petitions supporting it were sent to Parliament. The total number of pro-South petitions from the cotton towns was 40, while between 8000 and 10,000 people voted for the recognition of the South at an Oldham meeting. As one would expect, Liverpool's business class, as well as 'public opinion', supported the South.[96]

Karl Marx explained the cotton situation like this:

> The second pivot [on which English modern industry relied] was the slave-grown cotton of the United States. The present American Crisis forces them to enlarge their field of supply and emancipate cotton from slave-breeding and slave-consuming oligarchies. As long as the English cotton manufacturers depended on slave-grown cotton, it could be truthfully asserted that they rested on a twofold slavery, the indirect slavery of the white man in England and the direct slavery of the black men on the other side of the Atlantic.[97]

Conclusion

What is curious, or remarkable, or dishonest, or all three, is that there has been no thorough investigation of the basis of the wealth of British cities, or Britain itself. How much of it was based on dealing in slaves and on dealing in slave-grown produce?

Cities profited in many ways. Liverpool's dock revenue, for example, rose from just over £100,000 in 1822 to £867,756 in 1871.[98] How much of this was from shipping involved in slavery? In the 1850s there were about 700 voyages annually from Liverpool, to the USA; in 1851 there were 63 to Cuba. What proportion of these carried slave-grown produce or manufactures? In 1851, 144,000 British seamen sailed from Liverpool: what proportion were on the vessels that were carrying slave-grown produce – over 40 per cent of Britain's exports? How many of Liverpool's expanding population were dependent on the port's seamen? How many dockworkers? How many of the almost 19,000 shipwrights, and others involved in the shipping business?[99]

Liverpool was the 'chief port for the counties of Lancashire, Cheshire and Yorkshire in 1851'. The total number in these counties employed in manufacturing in 1844 was just over half a million, or about 20 per cent of the total population of the three counties. Of these men and women 295,348 were employed in cotton manufacturing. How many of these workers and their dependants would have been manufacturing either slave-grown raw materials or for the trade in slaves directly? And how many more were what we could call 'ancillary workers'? Workers such as those on the railways and in other forms of transport, and agricultural workers growing the food for the factory workers?[100]

There were about 378,000 employed in cotton manufacturing in Great Britain – that is, about 26 per cent of all those involved in manufacturing.[101] Let us say that four people (two too old to work and two too young) were dependent on each of these workers, then *about 1,890,000 people were directly dependent on cotton manufacturing alone.* That is 10 per cent of the total population! So how many altogether – 20 per cent? 25 per cent?

What would these figures be for that other major manufacturing town, Birmingham? Or for the other ports? After all, only 3610 vessels entered Liverpool in 1844 while 6885 entered London, 2473 entered Hull and 1674 entered Newcastle.[102] How many of those were directly or indirectly involved in slavery? And what proportion of the profits of London's banking and insurance worlds depended on slavery?

Historians have avoided investigating these involvements, these profits, these dependencies on slavery since they began arguing over profits and losses of the slave trade prior to 1807.

CHAPTER 3

Some British companies
and slavery

There must have been many companies involved in slavery, companies which, on the surface, appear far removed from the 'nefarious trade'. There were merchants who declared themselves to be exclusively in the 'legitimate' trade with Africa – which I find somewhat doubtful. There were merchants who traded in slave-grown produce. There were manufacturers using slave-grown produce. Then there were those with established connections to slave-worked economies. Then there were shipbuilders of the vessels carrying slave-grown produce and the manufactured goods to slave-worked economies. Finally there were the bankers and insurers who were, it appears, wholly uninterested in how they made their fortunes.

As far as I'm aware, there has been no research to unpick the tangled webs of commerce and banking in order to discover who profited by how much from slavery and the slave trade. I am sure that books could be written on those involved – for example, in the cotton and tobacco trades.[1] I would like to know how much of the shipping business – building, manning, insuring, provisioning, unloading, storing – was dependent on slave-grown produce and on shipping goods directly or indirectly to slave traders? And how much of the improvement for example in transport within the UK was dependent on, or financed by, this trade?

As previously, all I can do is give some indications of the realities behind the well-promoted image of an altruistic and anti-slavery Britain. It is a very sad reflection on British historiography that I can find no discussion of these issues in the many books published on the slave trade and slavery.

Perhaps it is again necessary to emphasise that without slave-worked economies there would have been no need for the ongoing trade in enslaved Africans.

In this chapter I shall give just three examples of these generally unacknowledged involvements in slavery. And if these companies, how many more? Then I shall look at two banks, *not* the one generally acknowledged as being involved in slavery, Barclay's, whose rise to power began as a member of the Company of Merchants Trading to Africa.

Some merchants

Rabone Bros

The first time I came across Rabone Bros of Birmingham was when I was reading through a book by the Kingston Committee, entitled *The Jamaican Movement for Promoting the Enforcement of Slave Trade Treaties.* This mentioned Rabone Bros, whom it describes as a

> Great house of business in Birmingham ... agents and representatives of one of the most notorious houses at the Havannah, who have acquired immense wealth by large transactions in slave-trading ... [W]holesale ironmongers and bankers ... Built in a distant English seaport under the order of Sr. Menguago, an experienced Spanish navigator, sent to England for that purpose from the *Havannah*, a vessel of such doubtful character that the shipbuilders, Moore of Plymouth, on hearing that it was clearing from Liverpool for *Havannah*,

warned the British Consul in Havana to watch the *Antonio* as it could be adapted for the slave trade. The *Antonio* was under the command of Capt. Wallen and was registered as being owned by the firm of Rabone Bros of Birmingham. Menguago was listed as the supercargo.

The Consul investigated and found that 'a bill of sale had been executed in Liverpool', in the name of the Havana firm of Fernandez Pozo & Co. The Consul contacted the firm. Yes, it was involved in slave trading, but would not be using the *Antonio* in this trade, though

it was unsuitable for the Liverpool trade. The Consul refused to register the transfer of ownership and sent the *Antonio* back to Liverpool for the British government to decide on ownership and use.

It seems that the government or the Liverpool authorities upheld Consul Turnbull's refusal of the sale. The following year, 1840, the *Antonio* returned to Havana, with a Mr Lloyd, a partner of Rabone Bros, among the passengers. Mr Lloyd, on arrival in Havana, stayed with the slave-trading firm of Pozo & Co. Consul Turnbull arranged for an audience with Viceroy Valdez, the governor of the colony. The Viceroy informed Mr Lloyd that his government in Spain had – for this once – also refused to sanction the transfer of registry.

A furious Mr Lloyd now sailed to Jamaica. What his connection was with Jamaica I have not been able to discover. (Did he own, or had he owned, plantations there? Was he involved in financing slave-worked sugar estates?) In the meanwhile, the British government had moved the abolitionist Consul Turnbull from Cuba to Jamaica, to the Mixed Commission Court about to be established there. Lloyd wrote to Turnbull demanding indemnity. He refused. Lloyd wrote again. And again. His requests were refused each time.

The Kingston Committee also mentions that rumours had reached it that the captain on the *Antonio*'s second voyage from Liverpool to Havana had been a Maltese named Babbe. That after this the *Antonio* was 'not heard of again'. But a vessel which resembled the *Antonio*, but named the *Triumphante*, had sailed from Liverpool to Havana under Hanse Town flags.[2]

I decided to investigate and found that the firm had been established in 1765 by Joseph and Samuel Rabone. It imported wine from Spain and Portugal, for which it exchanged 'metal articles such as toys' produced by the firm. Another Rabone set up John Rabone & Son in 1784 as 'rule makers and wood turners'.[3] In 1790 Joseph Rabone was a member of the Birmingham Commercial Committee. The 1839 *Wrightson's Directory of Birmingham* lists Rabone Bros as merchants, as do all the other directories. There are no indications whatsoever of any involvement with South America or the West Indies. Mr Lloyd is not listed as anything other than a banker. Yet, by 1815, according to a pamphlet recently discovered in Birmingham Archives, the firm had extended its business to South America, which seemed to have included some sort of involvement in the sugar business.[4]

So I tried to find out about the shipbuilder, Mr Moore. Unfortunately, the West Devon Record Office could only tell me that there had been a shipbuilder named William Moore in Plymouth. No other information has been preserved.[5]

Having received some information from Fiona Tait, archivist at Birmingham Central Library, I searched the archives there. In the 'Archives of Soho' I found that in the 1770s one of the Rabones had been in partnership with a man named Lewis Crinsoz. In 1778 Crinsoz had given some evidence to Parliament regarding cotton manufacturing – is that what their firm was involved in? If so, was it purchasing cotton grown by enslaved Africans? In 1781 the company also had another line of business: providing the Royal Navy with brandy.[6] The source of this is unknown, but I also wonder if the company might have been providing rum as well, a by-product of slave-grown sugar, to the seamen.

In the same collection I found that Boulton & Watt, a local firm, was 'prepar[ing] drawings for an 8 horse engine and sugar mill' for Rabone Bros in 1841. So did the Rabones own plantations? And if so, when had they acquired them? The files list a number of plantations, but not their owners. Or were they only supplying plantations? If so, for how long had they been doing this – prior to Emancipation and the end of apprenticeship in 1838? That Mr Lloyd sailed to Jamaica after his contretemps in Cuba certainly indicates a long-standing relationship with that island.

My next discovery was a publication at the British Library: *A Letter to Lord Viscount Palmerston by Thomas Lloyd Esq.*, dated 'Birmingham, 4 August 1850'. This was the 'Mr Lloyd' mentioned by the Kingston Committee! He told the Foreign Secretary that

Rabone Bros. & Co. of which firm I am a member, are the correspondents of at least twenty parties, who purchase hardware goods and utensils for the manufacture of sugar in Cuba ... [W]ith Pozo & Co. we have had extensive dealings for ... 30 years ... [I]f we heard their names, in common with many others, as occasionally engaged in what is now held to be the nefarious traffic in slaves, it would have been as much out of our place to call them to account for the proceedings ... as it would be to consign to obloquy many most excellent and patriotic Englishmen now living who were formerly slave traders.

Lloyd then advises that Mr Moore of Plymouth denies having written to the Havana Consul and states that the vessel was 'built for and is ... a burdensome merchantman, with a flat floor'. Purchasing this vessel was not out of 'our line of business as we are largely connected with shipping', Mr Lloyd maintained.[7] He had had permission from the Liverpool authorities to cancel the English registration of the *Antonio*. Once the *Antonio* had returned to Liverpool, the 'Danish consul receive[d] her as a legal transfer'. She was renamed the *Copenhagen* and sailed to Havana, where he 'assisted [Pozo & Co.] in a regular re-purchase ... vessel now called *Triumfant* ... trader between Liverpool and Havannah'.

In an appendix, Lloyd enclosed a letter he had addressed to the government in 1842. I presume that this might have been in response to some communication from Foreign Secretary Lord Aberdeen, who had been informed about the sale and re-sales of the *Antonio* by David Turnbull, the Consul at Havana. In this he had explained that 'Rabone Bros. & Co. are considerable shippers ... of machinery and iron manufactures.' (Manacles and chains, perhaps?) F. Pozo & Co., their correspondents had asked them to 'purchase a vessel suited to this trade'. It had been Capt. Wallen, 'having some supposed complaint against his employer and denounced the vessel to H.M. Consul ... as being intended for the slave trade'. The *Antonio* had been registered to Edward Rabone, Abram Dixon and Lloyd himself.[8]

This account contradicts that sent by Consul Turnbull, who maintained that Captain Wallen had told him that while in Plymouth 'the appearance of the vessel had excited the suspicion of the Admiralty Superintendent, the Magistrates of Plymouth, and many naval officers'.[9]

So we now have confirmation of the long involvement of Rabone Bros with slave traders and indications that, as well as purchasing slave-grown produce (including coffee and sugar) from Cuba, from where little else could be bought, the company might well have been supplying 'hardware' – such as chains, manacles, and so on, for the trade in slaves. Could 'hardware' also have included guns, often used to barter for slaves? Samuel Rabone was a manufacturer of guns.[10] It certainly included 'railway materials', as Rabone was 'largely responsible for the supply of materials' for Cuba's railways. But there is no mention of this branch of their trade in the listing for the Rabones in the various commercial directories for Birmingham.[11]

Mr Lloyd became Mayor of Birmingham in 1859 and served as an alderman for many years. He was also a county magistrate and chairman of the Board of Guardians. He was clearly a man who did not expect to be trifled with. He and the brothers George and Abraham Dixon had become partners of Rabone Bros in 1839. Dixon's brother George was Member of Parliament for Birmingham.[12] Who was Tomás H. Stevens, whose 'Rabone Bros & Co.' business card is held in Birmingham Library?[13] Tomás is a Spanish name; Stevens, English. Was he one of the Rabone employees stationed in the countries with which the company traded – including, from *c.* 1898, South Africa?

Thomas Lloyd's letter raises the question of British attitudes towards ongoing involvement in the slave trade. I have found nothing else for the nineteenth century, but some evidence from the previous century reveals much about what can perhaps be termed 'split minds'. Or 'profit above all else'? Matthew Boulton of the firm of Boulton & Watt, mentioned above, had been among those who had welcomed Black abolitionist Olaudah Equiano on his visit to Birmingham in 1789. The following year Boulton & Watt were corresponding with 'the slave trader John Dawson of Liverpool about supplying engines for Trinidad'.

Who, around the mid-nineteenth century, manufactured the '"Manillas" [coins], once made by the ton, the circulating medium of exchange of the natives of the Gold Coast'? Who made the 'rings and ornaments of brass, sent out in immense quantities, the chief decorations of the *belles* [*sic*] on the banks of the distant Zambesi'?[14] Other Birmingham companies involved in the slave trade were the gun manufacturers, for example Samuel Galton and his son, Samuel Jr. Both men were Quakers, and the Quakers were firm abolitionists. Thus the Galtons were advised to undertake a 'very serious consideration' of their 'supplying slightly proved guns to the Merchants on the coast of Guinea' and 'making thousands of pounds [from] the 40 years' commerce in these articles'. Samuel Galton Jr replied in 1795 that

> The censure and the laws of the Society against slavery are as strict and decisive as against war. Now, those who use the produce of the labour of slaves, such as Tobacco, Rum, Sugar, Rice, Indigo and Cotton, are more intimately and directly the promoters of the slave trade, than

the vendor of arms is the promoter of war, because the consumption of
these articles is the very ground and cause of slavery.[15]

I wholeheartedly agree with Galton's statement, though of course it
does not excuse his sale of guns to slave traders.

There has been no account by historians relating the prosperity of
the gun manufacturers of Birmingham to the slave trade and slavery.
About 7000 men, women and children and an unknown number of
'home workers' were employed in this industry. The amount of gunpowder shipped from Britain to Africa reached a peak of 2 million
lb in 1790. Between *c*. 1845 and 1865, according to one estimate, up to
150,000 'Africa guns' were exported to Africa. Lord Shelburne thought
that 'half of them, from the manner in which they are finished in,
are sure to burst in the first hand that fires them'. Three-quarters of
a million rifles, probably not quite so substandard, went to America
during the American Civil War, when Britain was not supposed to
be supporting either side. What proportion went to the slave states
is not known.[16]

Forster & Smith

Forster & Smith was a company involved in 'legitimate' trade in
West Africa from about 1817. The company was eventually merged
with others to form the United Africa Company. The family, from
Berwick-upon-Tweed, was in the shipping business in London from
perhaps the last years of the eighteenth century, and traded with
the Baltic coast and Russia. It is argued that it was the blockades
imposed by Napoleon that led Matthew Forster to look further afield
– to West Africa. William, Matthew's brother, was sent to trade in
Senegal, a colony seized from France during these wars. When the
colony was returned to France, William moved on to the Gambia
river, from where he traded in gum.[17] At least one of their methods
of trading there reveal strategies probably practised later: British
Customs regulations only permitted the sale of hides to British traders, so the Forsters shipped hides north, to Cape Verde, where they
could sell them to American traders.[18]

In 1826 the brothers merged their business with Smith & Sons,
a rival 'house' trading in West Africa, to form Forster & Smith.
The 'house' became the leading British merchant on the West Coast
until the advent of F.&.A Swanzy, with whom they then shared

pre-eminence. Forsters attained their position partly through their control of shipping: they could charge exorbitant rates to competitors, both European and African.[19]

By the 1840s, Forster & Smith had at least 14, if not 17 vessels involved in this trade, importing palm oil, hides, gum, gold dust, timber, coffee, rice, ivory and groundnuts into Britain and shipping out 'trade goods'. In 1845 the company imported 2.5 per cent of the palm oil coming into Britain; their share in 1850 was 4.5 per cent but dropped to 1.5 per cent in 1855.[20] By mid-century the company had agents ensconced all along the West African coast, from Bathurst in Gambia to Whydah in Dahomey, to the East of the Gold Coast.

The company flourished. On 'legitimate' trade, it claimed. But historian Edward Reynolds believes that 'Forster & Smith were known to have traded with slave dealers on the Slave Coast'.[21] That is what my research also indicates. How else could the company have grown rich enough to own (at Cape Coast)

> Government House, a very large and handsome building, bought for their representatives ... [They] had got it by bankruptcy of its last owner ... and Gothic House, an enormous edifice, reached their hands the same way ... When Forster and Smith retired from business, they left to their successors for collection a sum of debt ... not less than half a million sterling.[22]

How much of this debt-to-be-collected was paid to Forsters by the company's purchaser I do not know.

The biographer of Matthew Forster states that 'there is no indication in any of the records, that Forsters ever trafficked in the "abominable trade"'. In fact, Roderick Braithwaite asserts that they 'kept up a flow of information to the British Government about the continuance of the slavers'.[23] For example, in 1817 Matthew passed on his brother William's report on the revival of French slave trading to the Secretary of State for Colonies.[24] But is that the whole story? Forster constantly pressed the British government for protection against other traders and the need for Britain to acquire more territory in West Africa. Was he supplying information on *foreign* slave traders in order to divert attention away from himself? To create an image of himself as a man of innocence and righteous indignation?

By searching *The Times* I found that Matthew Forster was involved in much else besides trade with Africa. Had he made the money for these other financial involvements from African trade? How much money had he invested in the Liverpool and London Insurance Company, the York and London Assurance Co. and the South-Eastern Railway Co., as he was on the board of all three and chaired two?[25] He was also on the Committee of Portuguese Bondholders, who petitioned the government to help them 'obtain redress for the grievances and continued injustices inflicted by Portugal on her long-suffering foreign creditors'. Forster must have had an 'interest' in Portugal. What was this based on? Portugal was trading in slaves, despite having signed various treaties to cease doing so.

Forster's investments included the Berwick Salmon Fisheries and 'a considerable partner[ship] in the South Hetton Colliery and shares in Hartlepool Docks'.[26] (Could he have been involved in, or at least known about the construction of, at least one slaving vessel in Hartlepool, as mentioned in Chapter 4?) Forster's wealth was displayed in his Hampstead mansion: in 1852 his butler was jailed for having stolen 'plate' worth between £200 and £300 (between £12,800 and £17,600 in 2005), as well as some articles from the 'Museum-room' in the house.[27]

Clearly Forster felt that his membership of the Steamship Owners Association,[28] and his ever-broadening business connections, did not permit him to exert sufficient influence on the government. Would it be beneficial to his interests to become a Member of Parliament? In 1841 he was elected to represent the constituency of Berwick-upon-Tweed. The *Newcastle Journal* noted that Forster had won with 'the grossest system of bribery and corruption practised by the liberal agents.... [T]he price of Whig Votes ranged during the day from £20–£30 each.'[29]

As one would expect, Forster's main concern in Parliament was with trade with Africa and with import and export duties.[30] A glance through some House of Commons debates often finds him not speaking for the whole parliamentary session. Whether he actually attended, but did not speak, is not possible to ascertain.

Forster & Smith in Africa

How was Forster & Smith involved in West Africa? In many ways. Forster was almost from the beginning of his trade there involved in the government of the settlements. Either he or his agents were members of the governing committees or had enormous influence with them. For example, in 1824, when the British government handed over the government of its Gold Coast forts to a committee of merchants, Forster was nominated for membership.[31] Presumably supplying arms to the government for its 1848 'expedition' against the Chief of Ahanta in the south-east of the Gold Coast was not the first time the company dealt in arms.[32]

Forster's trade was along the whole coast, or at least as far as Whydah (Ouidah). The company owned its own vessels, which, according to George Brooks, 'denied transport to [African] trading firms in order to monopolize commerce between Britain and the Gold Coast'.[33] Some of their activities were anything but 'straightforward' trading. For example, one of Forster & Smith's vessels, the *George and James*, was sold at Whydah by its captain to his first mate, a man names Ramsay, who then sailed it to Bahia (Brazil). He returned and sold the cargo to vessels on the coast 'trading for slaves'. When the ship was detained by the Anti-Slave Trade Squadron in 1825 it was alleged that the money for the purchase had been provided by the Whydah slave trader Da Souza. Why would the company have sold the ship unless it stood to make good money – better money than continuing to use it for their 'legitimate' business? Could the sale have been a sham? Or a new partnership? And was it protests by Forster & Smith that led to questioning of the 'arrest' of the vessel by the Foreign Secretary?[34]

Among Forster & Smith's employees and subsequently business partners was the firm of F. & A. Swanzy. This company had grown into one of the main traders on the Coast and also owned plantations worked by 'pawns' – the 'polite' name for indigenous slave labour. The firm was also said to be involved in the trade in slaves.[35] Matthew Forster's relationship with both F. & A. Swanzy and the Gold Coast government is amply demonstrated by their being assigned to handle the Krobos. The Krobo people, in eastern Gold Coast, refused to pay the newly imposed Poll Tax. The Gold Coast government exchanged the right to collect taxes in the form of palm oil, for the actual amount of taxes owing. The recipient of this largesse was F. & A. Swanzy, who shared it with Forster & Smith. The companies set up their own militia to collect the dues, now payable in palm oil. The Krobos held out and made deals with exporters paying higher prices.[36]

Another somewhat dubious, but on the surface very respectable, example of Forster & Smith's 'correspondents' along the Coast was Heddle & Co., Sierra Leone. Heddle was known to buy condemned slaving vessels and their contents at the auctions in Freetown.[37] Did Heddle also trade in slaves? Did he sell the vessels to slave traders? And with whom did Forster & Smith do business on the Gambia? It has been suggested that it was with one of the firms supplying goods to the slave 'factories' on the Cacheu river near Gambia. According to Hugh Thomas, 'evidence for legitimate trade is missing' for the area, which was 'not far from Forster & Smith's Gambian trading station'.[38] Was Forster & Smith among those traders who submitted false customs statements, decried by the governors? Did Forster's vessels avoid British ports, as 'customs duties were always heavier in formal colonies than in nominally independent states'?[39]

Forster & Smith and the Americas

I had absolutely no idea, and still know nothing, about the company's interest in Cuba. But as in the correspondence files of Thomas Fowell Buxton I found a letter from John Forster to his father Matthew, dated 'Havana 24 January 1839', there must have been some involvement. Why else would John Forster have been in slave-worked Cuba?[40] I am equally ignorant of the extent of Forster & Smith's involvement with the United States. All I know is that from 1844 the company was purchasing tobacco from Kentucky, undoubtedly slave-grown, via the merchant/banking 'house' of N.M. Rothschild & Sons.[41] Some of the tobacco was then shipped to West Africa.

Matthew Forster and the British government

Forster was an assiduous correspondent and unsolicited adviser to the government.[42] There are hundreds of pages of correspondence from him preserved at the National Archives, some regarding trade issues, others regarding the government of the West Coast settlements.[43] For example, in 1832 he criticised the efficacy of Governor Randall, and suggested that the government should set up a Committee of Commerce in Gambia to aid him. The list of his nominees for the Committee included his brother William. In the same year, in a pamphlet addressed to Viscount Goderich, Secretary of State for Colonies, he admonished the government for not appreciating the existing and future value of trade with Africa. This, he argued, profited not only the merchants, but the state as well, in the form of import and export duties and by providing work for many in Britain. While all this was true, as in the same long submission he argues that the merchants in Africa should not be asked to contribute to the cost of the Anti-Slave Trade Squadron, one has to question his anti-slavery beliefs.[44]

Matthew Forster was always the chief spokesperson representing the interests of the coast merchants to the British government. For example, in his 1832 plea for Britain to retain the 'West Africa settlements', he detailed the principal export items: machinery and cotton piece goods. By 'machinery' he must have meant the £122,729 worth of guns and gunpowder as well as the £22,762 worth of 'iron' exported. What was this iron used for? Making chains and manacles, or local tools? He advocated the 'suppression of the trade in slaves, [which] cannot fail to produce effects as favourable to the trade and civilization of Africa ... [E]very article imported from Africa is in exchange for goods ... Europe owes to Africa a heavy debt for the crimes that have been committed under the slave trade.'[45] A public avowal of guilt, and endorsement of 'legitimate' trade! But how did the Africans produce those 'legitimate' goods, if not with slave labour? And did Forster & Smith ensure that the traders with whom they dealt did not exchange the goods for slaves? They did not.

From 1836 until 1838 Forster tried to convince Parliament that he should be permitted to import coffee grown on the River Nunez by a man named Michael Proctor at the low rate of duty charged for produce from British 'possessions'. After two years of correspondence he lost his argument with Treasury officials.[46] Proctor, I discovered, was an agent of Forster & Smith! In fact, Matthew Forster's involvement with the River Nunez, north of Freetown, was more extensive. His partners, George Martin and Joseph Braithwaite owned 'factories' there. What they dealt in is not known, though the river was an old slaving area. The French and Belgian fleets bombarded the 'factories' in 1849. Matthew Forster demanded – for four years – that the British government should seek compensation from the French and the Belgians. It was not until 25 August 1853 that the Foreign Secretary, Lord Clarendon, ended this colossal expenditure of government time, informing Forster that 'Her Majesty's Government [will] not take any further steps in the matter'.[47]

Why had Forster decided to spend such a lot of his money precisely in 1841 to win a seat in Parliament? (I don't know if he had made previous attempts to win a seat.) Could he have been worried because the issue of the ongoing slave trade and possible British participation in it was raised at the 1840 Anti-Slavery Convention? Articles about it had appeared in the Society's *Reporter*. The issue was also raised in a number of publications, for example by Sir George Stephen, a very active member of the Anti-Slavery Society and brother of Sir James, the equally pro-abolition Colonial Under-Secretary.[48] There was such pressure that Lord John Russell, the Colonial Secretary, decided to investigate and sent Dr Richard Madden to West Africa. The choice was excellent: Dr Madden, a very critical and outspoken abolitionist, had already served as a Special Magistrate overseeing emancipation in Jamaica, and then as 'Protector of Liberated Africans' in Cuba (see Chapter 4). His appointment could not have been welcome news to Matthew Forster. Did he think – was he advised by equally apprehensive colleagues – that he could best deal with Dr Madden by becoming a Member of Parliament?

Lord Russell intended publishing Dr Madden's findings, but the elections at which Forster won his seat also brought a new Secretary to the Colonial Office. Lord Stanley refused to publish the report, 'say[ing]', according to the Anti-Slavery Society, that 'it is too confidential ... it seems ... clear that the reasons for withholding it are derived ... from a wish to screen certain individuals from exposure.' But something had to be done. Nothing too hasty, Matthew Forster beseeched Lord Stanley within days of the new government taking office. He pleaded that 'no hasty measures may be resorted to on the evidence or recommendations of parties imperfectly acquainted with the subject'.[49] The new government decided to set up a Select Committee on the West Coast of Africa to take evidence. Dr Madden's report was eventually published in an appendix to the Committee's report. 'But some material was omitted ... and interspersed with commentaries by others', stated the Anti-Slavery Society.[50] Was all this the result of manipulations by Matthew Forster MP and his colleagues?

Naturally – or so it would appear – this new Member of Parliament was appointed to the new Select Committee. He had the highest attendance rate at its meetings. The chair of the Committee was Viscount Sandon, the MP for Liverpool, a city much involved in slavery, as described in Chapter 2. The Committee minutes indicate that Forster used his (biased?) expertise regarding the Coast to nominate some of those asked to give evidence. The others – his opponents – he questioned assiduously and closely, and often rudely. He was especially harsh towards Dr Madden, whose report confirmed British involvement in the 'nefarious' trade.[51] To counteract any support for Dr Madden, Forster also attacked him in the press, calling him a liar.

It is impossible even to summarise all of Forster's correspondence – it is so voluminous that it would provide substance for a book looking at the influence of such traders on the government. An incidence in 1841 demonstrates some of this. Captain Tucker in charge of HM schooner *Wolverine* of the Anti-Slave Trade Squadron searched a vessel, the *Robert Heddle*, owned by Forster's partner. It had been trading with Da Souza, the most notorious slave trader at Whydah.[52] The vessel, though not equipped for carrying slaves, was carrying wooden planks. These were often part of cargoes intended to convert innocuous vessels into slavers by the construction of 'intermediate slave decks'. Captain Groves, the *Heddle*'s master, admitted that he had had a 'factory' at Whydah for twelve years and employed one of Da Souza's sons to run it. But all Captain Tucker could do was make Groves sign a promise not to carry goods to Da Souza or any other slave trader.

Forster was outraged, and for months virtually bombarded both the Colonial Office and the Foreign Office with very lengthy if not exhaustive diatribes.[53] The government, he demanded, would have to furnish merchants with information on which traders along the coast were slave traders. This was needed because

> on no other ground could it be considered reasonable to impose upon British traders the obligation of distinguishing them, nor on any other ground would it be just to threaten them with penalties and the seizure of their property.... It was no part of Capt. Groves' duty to sit in judgement on his customers.... The result of such proceedings will be that the trade of Whydah and other places will be entirely given over into the hands of foreigners.[54]

Many government departments dithered over how to respond to
the tirade. The influence of Forster is revealed in their internal
memoranda. For example, the Foreign Office officials believed that
any reply they sent would be used by Forster 'most unscrupulously
... in attempts to press for compensation'.[55] In the end the government
decided that 'if the Owner or the Master are not aware [that they
are dealing with a slave trader] they had not committed an offence',
and decided to 'suspend any further directions on the subject'.[56] Was
this decision based on the influence exerted by all those supplying
goods to slave dealers? And – or – on British recognition of the
growing income derived from this trade? It is simply not believable
that those trading with the Coast and on the Coast did not know who
the slave traders were. The merchants, including Matthew Forster,
and the Squadron knew them well. So did the well-informed British
government.

Forster repeated his understanding of the trade to a House of
Lords Committee in 1843:

> it was painful to hear the twaddle that is talked on the subject of the
> sale of goods to slave dealers on the coast of Africa. People forget that
> there is scarcely a British merchant of any eminence who is not proud
> and eager to deal as largely as possible with slave importers in Cuba
> and Brazil, and slave buyers and sellers in the United States.

He did not exempt himself from the 'merchants of eminence'.[57]

Forster repeated the threat of a takeover by foreign traders again
and again, for years and years, both in Parliament and in his endless
correspondence with the government. It was on this basis that Forster
successfully urged the government to purchase the Danish colonies
on the Gold Coast.[58] In Parliament, when the import duty on non-
British sugar was lowered, he argued that this should be extended to
other non-British-sourced imports – some of which he was supplying
from the River Nunez, as indicated above.

From the 1820s Matthew Forster had advocated the replacement
of the slave trade by legitimate trade, by encouraging the exploration
of the hinterland by Europeans, and new agricultural production. He
was against the operations of the Anti-Slave Trade Squadron and
vociferously opposed their burning of barracoons (holding prisons)
at the slaving ports along the coast. He believed that 'the promotion

of English commerce [was] the greatest medium of civilizing the Natives and destroying the slave trade'.[59] Forster also admitted that 'slavers ... interrupt our operations as the natives neglect the produce trade to attend to the Slave Trade'.[60] Wasn't he tempted to participate in this easier and more lucrative trade? Just as importantly, did he ever consider offering a higher price for the palm oil and other legitimate goods he bought, in order to make these as profitable for the African merchants as trading in their brethren? Did he simply turn a blind eye to the slave-workers on the plantations producing the palm oil?

So what were Matthew Forster's attitudes towards Africa and Africans? I imagine he would have agreed with the sentiments expressed in a letter by Brodie Cruickshank, his agent in Cape Coast, in September 1849:

> there are still tens of thousands of hands in this Colony ... who seldom do a day's work and only pass their time in idleness and riot ... I am convinced that coffee, cotton and sugar ... cannot be profitably produced ... without slave labour being sanctioned ... I proposed in my Report ... to legalise the Slave Trade to a certain extent.[61]

What do we learn of Matthew Forster the man, and Matthew Forster the MP, from his being indicted for not paying his fare on public transport? He had refused to pay his fare on the 'omnibus' he rode from City Road to Broad Street in the city of London. Taken to court, he was made to pay the sixpenny fare, and three shillings in costs as well as four shillings to the conductor 'for two days' loss of time'.[62] Again, was it arrogance that made his bribery of voters at the 1857 elections so conspicuous that he was taken before a Select Committee at Berwick-upon-Tweed? The Committee declared that he was 'found guilty of bribery at the last election for the town, and borough' and was thus 'not duly elected a burgess to serve in this present Parliament'. An investigation in 1860 found that 'the election had cost him [about] £3,000' (c. £134,000 in 2005).[63] Not a paltry sum, by any means. Had he spent as much on the previous elections? One can only conclude that not only was Forster rich, but that serving as an MP was financially remunerative, and gave him the power and influence he needed to protect himself and other merchants.

Matthew Forster died in 1869, leaving £120,000 (c. £5.5 million in 2005) in his will as well as his mansion Belsize Court (also known as Bellsise Villa) in Hampstead set amidst 16 acres.

Zulueta & Co.

The Napoleonic wars led to a period of unrest in Spain; civil war erupted. Among those who fled Spain and settled in Britain was Juan Pedro de Zulueta. A Basque merchant, he had been living in Cadiz, Spain's chief slave-trading port.[64] Whether Juan Pedro was personally involved is not yet known. On the restoration of the monarchy he returned to Spain and was created Conde de Torre Diaz. Today the museum and library of the Basque people is housed in the Zulueta Palace.

One member of the Zulueta family, Julian, emigrated to Cuba in the late 1820s to join an uncle, Tiburcio, an established coffee planter there. Whether Tiburcio had fled from Spain in 1823, the same year as Juan Pedro, is not known.

Julian became the agent of his cousin Pedro, the London-based son of Juan Pedro. Julian also became, as described in Chapter 4, the leading slave-trader in Cuba. In London, Pedro joined his father's business, became a British citizen and married the daughter of Brodie Wilcox, one of the founders of the Peninsular and Oriental Steamship Co. Pedro himself was a shareholder and founder director of the company from its inception in 1834.[65] The firm of Zulueta & Co had 'connexions to a large extent in Spain, and in the Havannah, and in South America, and several other places'. Contemporary commercial directories list the firm in the 1860s as dealing in rice and general merchandise to the West Coast of Africa from the Liverpool office; and in colonial produce (Cuban? slave-grown?), cottons and woollens to Mauritius, the Mediterranean and Spanish and Portuguese settlements, from London.[66]

Zulueta was asked to give evidence to the 1842 House of Commons Select Committee on West Africa. It must be emphasised that the most attentive Committee member, and the most vocal, was none other than Matthew Forster MP, whom Dr Madden had named as being involved in the slave trade. Forster himself had also given evidence to the Committee! At the hearings, Captain Hill[67] of the Anti-Slave Trade Squadron and Henry W. Macaulay, a retired judge of the Sierra Leone Court of Mixed Commission, had both named Zulueta & Co. as being involved in the trade in slaves. They also repeated Dr Madden's assertions regarding British involvements with slave traders on the West Coast of Africa. Both also emphasised that the only trade on the Gallinas was in human beings.[68]

Zulueta gave lengthy evidence on one day, but returned the next to correct a 'mis-statement' he had made: his company's business with Pedro Blanco at the Gallinas and with Martinez had not been to the value of £100,000, but £400,000 (c. £20 million in 2005). He knew from general reports that Martinez dealt in slaves, but he did not know if the goods his firm shipped on behalf of Martinez to Blanco and others on the coast were destined to be used in exchange for enslaved Africans.[69] Though he bought and sold vessels, it was quite untrue that he regularly bought vessels in England and sent them to Cadiz from where they sailed to Havana and re-entered the slave trade.

In spite of being well protected by Matthew Forster MP, an empathetic and assiduous member of the Committee, Zulueta had to face some probing questioning. Queried about a vessel named *Augusta*, Zulueta acknowledged that the company had acted as agent for Martinez in all transactions connected with her. Yes, they had lent money for her purchase on behalf of Martinez. It was then chartered by Martinez and loaded with goods on behalf of Martinez, by Zulueta & Co in Liverpool. The *Augusta* then set sail for the Gallinas.[70]

Though

(a) the Colonial Office had known since at least 1835 of the banking connection between Zulueta & Co. and Pedro Blanco;

(b) the government had received a report from Governor George Maclean of the Cape Coast in August 1839, in which he stated that the British merchants knew that the Spanish, Portuguese and Brazilian vessels trading on the coast – of which he had 'seen hundreds' – were engaged in trading in slaves. 'But the merchants have always considered themselves fully justified in selling their merchandize to any person who might come to their warehouses prepared to pay them money, or other equivalent, for their goods, nor have I ever imagined that I could legally interfere with such traffic';[71]

(c) Dr Madden had reported that both Zulueta & Co. and Forster & Smith were participating in the slave trade;

(d) a few years earlier the British Consul in Havana had linked Zulueta with another slaver, the *Arrogante*, and with the slave trader Martinez;[72]

(e) Zulueta was named in another case involving the *Cazador*, a slave vessel in 1837;[73]

(f) the evidence regarding the *Augusta* was pretty damning;

(g) the Gallinas had been described by Governor Doherty of Sierra Leone in 1841 as 'the most celebrated mart and stronghold of the Spanish Slave Trade on the whole line of the African coast';[74]

(h) 'Correspondence relative to the slave trade at the Gallinas', which fully described the trade in enslaved Africans as the sole trade on the river, had been 'ordered to lie on the table' at the House of Lords in 1841;[75]

the government did *nothing*.[76]

It was up to a private individual, Sir George Stephen, a barrister and staunch abolitionist, to attempt to bring Zulueta to justice. A few days before Zulueta was forced to appear in court, the *Anti-Slavery Reporter* warned its readers that 'there has been a very suspicious reluctance manifested in certain quarters to take any measures to bring to light hidden things of darkness'.[77] How right they were.

There had been innumerable delays as Zulueta attempted to avoid being taken to court. But Sir George succeeded in indicting him on the charge of 'fitting out a ship with the object of dealing in slaves, and for shipping a cargo on board the said ship to be used for the said purpose'. The trial began on 27 October 1843 and lasted three days.[78] The court was 'crowded by personal friends and eminent city merchants, who appeared to take the greatest interest in the proceedings'.[79] Among the many bankers and merchants and consuls who spoke up for Zulueta was Baron Lionel de Rothschild.[80] The jury found Zulueta innocent. The reason for this was simple: there was 'insufficient evidence to lead to a conviction'. The verdict was 'greeted with a loud burst of cheers and the cheers were renewed by people outside as Zulueta left the Court'.[81] Cadiz also cheered, according to the *Anti-Slavery Reporter* of 13 December 1843 (p. 232), which stated that the trial had caused a sensation there. But then

Cadiz had a lot to lose as it had been serving as a port for exchanging crews and as an entrepôt for 'trade goods' being shipped to West Africa to be exchanged for enslaved Africans. And, of course, Pedro's father was a count.

Was Zulueta found innocent because of his wealth and his position in society, or because some of the evidence against him had been withheld? Probably not: he was a public and important figure. In 1839, the Peninsular & Oriental Steamship Co., of which Zulueta was a director, had been awarded the government contract to carry mail to Egypt![82] Was Zulueta's fellow P & O director J.C. Ewart, who was to become MP for Liverpool in 1855, among those who cheered for him in court? Given the support for Zulueta, a guilty verdict might have proved embarrassing to the government. Were the jurors 'advised' about this?

That the case might indeed prove embarrassing was discussed in *Herepath's Journal* and reprinted in the *Anti-Slavery Reporter* on 18 October 1843:

> That Zulueta will be acquitted we have already said – there is no doubt of it. Governments too often wink at offences committed by the power-ful and wealthy.… The stir that is now made is conceived to be a feint, a mere pretence. If it was not, there are other parties besides Zulueta … that could be arraigned. It is a fact, we believe, that this trade has been carried on for years, and large sums made by it. It was but the other day that a vessel was pointed out in the docks as having cleared 30,000 dollars in six months by this inhuman traffic. It is commonly reported that Zulueta bought the vessels through others (whose names we have) who fitted them out – and received a commission. (p. 190)

The judge's closing words, after he had granted costs to Sir George, were: 'I think it is a very proper case for an enquiry.'

There was – I am tempted to say 'of course' – no enquiry. The Corporation of London refused to pay Sir Stephen's costs.[83] Zulueta was certainly not damaged by the court case, to judge by the number of times he is listed as attending social functions at another court – that of Queen Victoria. An examination of his appearances at legal courts, some listed in *The Times* (one of which is against a Cuban mining company) and others at the National Archives, might throw further light on Pedro de Zulueta's involvements in slavery, the trade in slaves and Cuba.[84]

Some bankers

Without bankers and insurers, the slave trade would have collapsed. I have not investigated insurance companies, but there is some readily available information on bankers. I have focused on activities with colonies and countries dependent on slave labour in these brief accounts of two banks.

Baring Bros

Johann Baring had emigrated to Exeter from Bremen in the early eighteenth century and established himself as a merchant and banker there. His sons John and Francis expanded the company and moved it to London.[85] John, who retired from active participation in the family firm in 1777, invested heavily in land, became a Devon 'country squire' and served as the MP for Exeter from 1776 until 1802. His election is said to have cost him about £40,000.

Francis Baring served as a director of the East India Company from 1779, and chaired its Board 1792–3; he was a Member of Parliament from 1794 to 1806. By 1783 Francis was so wealthy that he purchased a residence near Blackheath for £27,000; in 1800 he moved to an estate near Winchester, purchased from the Duke of Bedford for about £150,000 (c. £5 million in 2005) – a paltry sum, given his annual income of about £80,000.

How was this vast wealth accumulated? By the late eighteenth century the firm was heavily involved in North America, with 'correspondents' in Philadelphia: it was in the import/export business, owned land, financed American trade to Europe and became an agent of the US national bank. The company 'floated' (i.e. marketed) loans for the USA, for example to purchase Louisiana and the Mississippi basin from the French colonizers there. It became the 'pre-eminent London agent for US markets, banks and government institutions'.[86] Not surprisingly Francis Baring served as an unofficial adviser to the British government on commercial matters in general, and particularly in the USA and India. From at least 1805 there was a Baring serving on the Board of the Bank of England.

Louisiana and Mississippi joined America's slave states. This did not bother Baring Bros, who also issued bonds for the states of Alabama and Virginia (to raise funds for their 'development'). Baring Bros also sold bonds for the Association of Louisiana Planters, from whom it also purchased cotton. By 1837 cotton had become so lucrative that Barings set up their own purchasing agent in Natchez and New Orleans. A Barings branch was established in Liverpool in 1833, to deal with their American – that is, mainly their cotton – business. For example, in 1837 the company received around £225,000 worth of cotton from New Orleans. Other imports from slave-worked US states were tobacco and sugar.

Baring Bros also dealt with Jamaica, where they had a 'correspondent, Atkinson & Hosier'. The contact was fairly minimal, probably because Francis's son Alexander (created Lord Ashburton in 1835) believed little money could be made there: he believed that 'every man there is needy for no men of any fortune and consequently *credit* live there'.[87] However, even this indicates that Baring Bros were involved with Britain's West Indian colonies prior to emancipation. The company was much more involved with Cuba, from where, for example, it bought sugar until about 1846. More credit was extended to Brazilian merchants, especially to Naylor Bros & Co., partner of Todd, Naylor & Co. of Liverpool. Barings also traded directly with Brazil in coffee. But Barings had yet another link with Brazil: they were the bankers of Caetano José Nozzolini, the slave trader on the Cacheu river (Gambia) who supplied Brazil as well as Cuba with slaves in the 1830s and 1840s.[88]

In 1846 Baring Bros obtained the contract to supply tobacco to the Spanish and French government monopolies. From which slave-worked plantations did they obtain this large quantity of tobacco? It is also possible that Baring Bros was involved in the manufacture of cotton in Lancashire, as from 1848 the company was involved in the export of cotton cloth from Manchester to China.[89]

Just how little the source of its profits bothered the company was demonstrated by Alexander Baring MP, who assured the House of Commons in 1828 that 'the misfortune of slaves is much exaggerated … they are in reality well fed and housed and generally treated with justice and kindness.'[90] According to evidence presented to the Parliamentary Committee on the West Coast of Africa in 1842, Barings acted as bankers to Pedro Blanco, one of the most successful – and well-known – slave traders on the Coast. Unsurprisingly, when Lord Brougham's bill to curtail the use of British capital in the slave trade was debated in Parliament, Baring opposed it.[91]

N.M. Rothschild & Co.

This Jewish family business was started by Mayer Amschel Rothschild in Frankfurt in the latter half of the eighteenth century. Successful, despite the manifold restrictions imposed on Jews, in 1798 Mayer sent his son Nathan to England with £20,000 to start a business. He first settled in Manchester and traded mainly in textiles and perhaps also in tea, sugar and coffee. He was so successful that in 1808, the year after he had become a naturalised British citizen, he moved to London and established a firm which on his death in 1836 became known as N.M. Rothschild & Sons. (Rothschild in London and four continental cities had — and have — multifold dealings with governments and businesses.) The outline below is on the aspects of the British firm's entanglements with slavery and hence the trade in enslaved Africans.[92]

From London, Nathan continued his trading ventures, and also went into the banking business in bullion, exchange and securities. He seized opportunities to support the British government: for example, in 1811 he 'provided specie' to the value of £800,000, at an agreed rate of interest, for the Duke of Wellington's campaign in Portugal.[93] This debt escalated to well over £1 million by 1812. In the 1830s Rothschild 'floated' the loan for the £20 million the government had promised West Indian plantation owners as compensation for the loss of their slaves.[94] (I have not been able to discover the rate of interest on this loan and Rothschild's motives for giving it.) In about 1847 Rothschild & Sons shared with Baring Bros the marketing of an £8 million loan for the government for the relief of the 'potato famine' in Ireland. Also with Barings they floated the bonds for the Manchester Ship Canal.[95] In the 1850s, Rothschild raised a £9 million loan to cover the government's costs in the Crimean War.

Rothschild were also involved in founding at least two insurance companies — Alliance British and Foreign Life and Fire Assurance Co. and the Alliance Marine Assurance Co. Whether these companies insured slave-trading ventures, slave-worked enterprises or development projects such as railways in slave-worked economies is not known.[96]

Rothschild in the Americas

Nathan Rothschild also began to support countries and colonies important to British trade. For example, the bank marketed bonds for

Portugal 'secured on Brazilian revenues' in London in 1823. Ten years later, independent Brazil obtained the same services from Rothschild. The Bank continued 'floating' Brazilian bonds in London in 1852, 1858, 1860, 1863, 1865, 1871 and 1875 – that is, during Brazil's slave-owning years.[97] 'They were European bankers to the Brazilian government and funded much of the railway development.'[98]

Rothschild entered the American market many years after Barings, but by the 1840s 'they were reported … to be large operators in Louisiana securities in London and New Orleans'.[99] The bank was also involved with the Spanish colony of Cuba in the 1830s. It advanced loans to the Spanish government on the basis of profits from copper and tobacco exports, and quicksilver mined in Spain. Together with Barings, Rothschild served as bankers to the main exporter of sugar.[100] In the late 1830s Rothschild decided 'to expand their involvement with the Cuban and Philippine trade', but to 'eschew bond issues'.[101] In 1843 Rothschild in Vienna had secured an agreement with the Austrian government to supply it with 12 million Havana cigars annually. But we do not know whether this involvement in the Cuban slave-worked tobacco manufacturing industry was as an owner, agent or financier.

Rothschild in South Africa and Egypt

Rothschild moved into South Africa by investing – somewhat reluctantly – in the De Beer diamond mines and held £27,000 worth of shares in the Rand (gold) Mines.[102] Lord Rothschild was close to Cecil Rhodes, the architect of apartheid South Africa. For example, it was in his own house that in 1889 Lord Rothschild introduced Cecil Rhodes to Joseph Chamberlain, the Colonial Secretary; and was called upon to ensure that Chamberlain saw Rhodes immediately on his arrival on his 1896 visit to London. At the close of the Boer War, with its high cost in British soldiers' lives, Lord Rothschild warned Rhodes that 'feeling in the country was running high', and there was 'considerable inclination on both sides of the House to lay the blame for what has happened on the shoulder … of those interested in South African mining'.

By the twentieth century the Rothschilds were such 'prominent financiers' that the British government used their influence to further their policies in South Africa. And the influence was wide-ranging and profound. For example, Lord Selborne, the High Commissioner for South Africa, noted in 1907, when discussing the importation of Chinese labour, that he had received

> a message from Rothschild that not one penny of money would the Transvaal get in London or Paris or Berlin until they had put the Rand mines labour supply on sure and permanent footing, but if they did that, they would have as much as they wanted at once and on easy terms.[103]

Rothschild financed Prime Minister Benjamin Disraeli's bid to buy the 40 per cent shares in the Suez Canal held by Egypt's Khedive Ismail, who had been bankrupted by the somewhat questionable dealings of some European banks. Five years later, in 1882, Britain occupied Egypt – and Sir Evelyn Baring, of the rival banking house, was appointed as 'Consul General' to rule in the name of the Queen.[104]

The effects of anti-Semitism

Though in 1819 Nathan had been asked to give evidence to the government's secret committee on the Bank of England, and though the company became the official gold broker to the Bank of England, it was not until 1868 that Alfred, son of Lionel Rothschild, was permitted to become a director of the Bank of England. The Jewish 'disabilities' also affected their direct participation in government: though from 1847 Nathan's eldest son Lionel was elected many times to Parliament by the City of London, it was not until 1858 that he was able to take his seat. (There had been many petitions to Parliament against the admission of Jews into Parliament.[105]) He served until 1874; his son Nathan was MP for Aylesbury from 1865 until 1885, when he became the first Jew elevated to the House of Lords – despite the opposition of Queen Victoria. Mayer Rothschild, another of Nathan's sons, was MP for Hythe from 1859 until 1874 – and there were other family Members of Parliament over the years.

If these companies, then how many others? Only new and extensive research will reveal the full extent of British commercial and banking support and involvement in slavery, without which the slave trade would not have flourished. Such research would also reveal the extent of the dependence of British wealth on the labour of enslaved Africans after 1807.

CHAPTER 4

Cuba and Brazil

By the 1840s Parliament had passed Acts forbidding British participation in the trade in slaves in any form, and in the ownership of slaves. British slaves in the Caribbean had been finally emancipated in 1838. They were given no compensation for having been robbed of their homeland, of their families, their culture, language, religion; no compensation for having been used – misused, abused – as non-human beasts of burden. Their 'owners' were given £20 million – almost £1000 million in 2005 – to compensate them for their loss of property (i.e. the slaves) and profit from unpaid labour.

Britain presented itself to the world as the epitome of Christian righteousness for this achievement and campaigned with great vigour to pressure other slaving countries to cease their activities. Was this perhaps to ensure no 'unfair' competition from slave-grown produce?

While there were no laws actually forbidding the support of foreign slave-worked economies, this would clearly have been against the *declared* intentions of Britain: after all, if you support them, you are in fact supporting and even encouraging slavery and the trade in the enslaved. But was there a hidden agenda? Were there no inhibitory laws because Britain was making too much money out of supporting such economies?

Though Cuba and Brazil were both slave-dependent economies, neither exists in British historical imagination or interest. I certainly

knew nothing of British involvement with either country until I
stumbled across the prosecution of Pedro de Zulueta in London for
slave-trading, as recounted in a previous chapter. So, when I was
planning this book, I thought I ought to just 'check out' Cuba and
Brazil. What I found horrified me. These two countries' growing
economies depended on slave labour until the 1880s. And they were
also at least partly, if not mainly, dependent on British investment.

After the mainland North American colonies won their independence from the 'Mother Country', British imperial interest in the
Americas shifted to the islands and the South American mainland.
Once the native peoples had been conquered, and in some instances
eliminated, Europeans fought each other, with guns, money, trade
and diplomacy, for possession. When Britain stopped attempting to
take over the Portuguese and Spanish colonies, her attention shifted
to commercial and financial conquest.

Could one argue that it had become more lucrative to support
these slave-dependent economies than to have attempted to take them
over and develop them with free labour – which might have meant
more expensive coffee? Curiously, while the campaign in Britain for
emancipation had included a large women's movement against the
use of West Indian slave-grown sugar, there was no similar campaign
against the use of, for example, some 2 million tons of slave-grown
coffee imported from Cuba in 1842. Was it only British-owned slaves
these undoubtedly brave women could 'see'? How could they be so
blind? Or blinded?[1]

This chapter will examine British involvement in these countries.
As with other areas I have discussed, there is no previous research
focusing on the many aspects of British involvement in Cuba and
Brazil until slavery was ended in 1880 and 1888 respectively.

CUBA

A little history

The largest of the Caribbean islands, Cuba was occupied by Spain
in the first decade of the sixteenth century. The Spaniards eliminated the native population by warfare, forced labour and disease,
and then added the island to the Spanish Empire. At first the main

crop grown was tobacco, using very little slave labour. However, in 1762, when for a brief year Britain conquered and ruled the island, experienced planters rushed in from neighbouring English-occupied islands, and 10,000 slaves were brought in to establish sugar plantations on virgin, very productive lands. When the island was returned to Spain, naturally the Spaniards continued to expand the plantations that had been opened.[2] By 1870 the white population numbered just over 600,000 and there were 141,677 free 'coloured people', who lived mainly in the towns and cities, and worked as domestic servants and in semi-skilled jobs. There were also, according to the official census, 300,989 enslaved women, children and men. However, this was probably a gross undercount as owners of slaves tried to avoid registering them.[3]

The slaves on the neighbouring sugar-rich island of Haiti overthrew and expelled their French masters and in 1804 asserted their independence. This resulted in the collapse of the plantation system, which grossly reduced the amount of sugar available for the world market. The price of sugar increased. Naturally the colonial masters elsewhere tried to increase sugar production, which required more labour. The Spanish government tried to regulate the slave trade and tax the owners of enslaved Africans, so some slaves were imported legally, while others were brought in via the smaller ports, avoiding surveillance and registration.

Britain had forced (or persuaded, depending on your perspective) Spain to sign a treaty to stop trading in slaves, and in 1820 gave Spain £400,000 in compensation for agreeing to stop. But enslaved Africans continued to arrive in Cuba in ever-increasing numbers. Cuban ships flying foreign flags brought them from the West African coast and usually landed them, as they had done previously, in the smaller ports, in order to avoid officials attempting to enforce the treaty. The enforcers were few: though some of the Spanish governors/rulers (called Captain-General) made vague attempts to stop the trade, most actually participated in it and received a 'commission' per landed slave.

After the Napoleonic Wars, Spain was heavily indebted. By the 1850s Spain's debt to Britain had grown to $250 million. Spain's largest creditor was Britain, and Cuba was her 'treasure trove'. This meant that Spain desperately needed her income from sugar to appease her creditor.[4] So the importation of enslaved Africans went on ... and on, despite further treaties being signed. Spain, after all, had to pay her debts to Britain. As Spain had lost all her colonies in the Americas except Puerto Rico and Cuba by 1824, it was Cuban sugar that had to fulfil the Spanish government's and merchants' needs. And also Britain's, if the debt was ever to be repaid.

Sugar production, which had been a mere 18,000 tons in 1787, rose from 205,608 tons in 1846 to 462,000 tons in 1855. The population of slaves also grew, from 38,979 in 1774 to 436,495 in 1841.[5] Some authors believe the numbers were much higher by then, as plantation owners were reluctant to add newly and illegally purchased slaves to the official census.[6] It has been estimated that 'roughly half the slaves brought to Cuba ... were brought during the period of the illegal slave trade from 1821 to 1867'.[7] In the early 1840s the price of an African on the coast was about $50–60, paid in goods, cowries or, later, silver dollars. He or she was sold in Cuba for about $340–360.[8] The price rose to $1000 in 1860 and even higher in the early 1870s.[9]

Cuban slavery was not outlawed until 1880. Slavery was not discontinued from any philanthropic feelings, but probably because the price of sugar on the world market had fallen so low that it no longer covered the cost of importing slaves.[10]

How Britain fits into this history

Britain had won the right to supply enslaved Africans to Spanish colonies in 1713. This did not include the right to trade with the Spanish colonies, but Britain avoided this by trading with Cadiz, the city which supplied Spain's colonies with both goods and human beings. When this *asiento* was suspended in 1739, Britain found a new way to avoid obeying the law: the Spanish colonies were now supplied with British goods from the British colonies. Among the goods sent to Cuba for local consumption were cotton goods, machinery and foodstuffs. But, of course, the 'locals' included the slaves who had to be clothed. The *asiento* was restored in 1786, but British slavers had to compete with illegal Dutch and French slave traders.[11]

The new treaty Britain persuaded Spain to sign in 1835 confirmed the illegality of slave trading and agreed to the mutual search of suspected slaving vessels. Spain also promised to make participation in and connivance with the trade illegal, but waited ten years to pass the required legislation! When passed, it was easily circumvented; importation continued from Africa and also from nearby slave-states such as Brazil and Puerto Rico, a Spanish colony.

Given that the trade was illegal and thus covert, the estimates of the numbers reaching Cuba vary widely. For example, the British Foreign Office's estimate of the numbers arriving between 1840 and 1854 is 222,834, while the Havana Slave Trade Commissioners reported 187,639; another estimate gives an *annual* importation figure in the 1850s of 40,000 men, women and children.[12] The British and Foreign Anti-Slavery Society (BFASS) estimated in 1855 that the total number of slaves on the island was about 800,000–900,000.[13] The majority of the slaves were probably shipped in vessels built in the USA.[14]

It is believed that about half of the cost of slave purchase and transportation was covered by credit obtained from British bankers and merchants. The profits could be large, as a British judge of the Mixed Commission Court advised the British government: after deducting the interest payable on the loan which financed the voyage, the cost of the vessel, wages and necessary bribes, the clear profit on the sale of 450 slaves he calculated would be about $389,850, or about £80,000.[15]

The Mixed Commission Court in Havana had been established by Britain and Spain in 1820, in order to judge the cases of detained/arrested slaving vessels and to reduce and hopefully prevent the 'nefarious' trade. The numbers of illegally imported enslaved Africans demonstrate the ineffectiveness of the Court. Between 1840 and 1850 the Court only tried seven vessels: it freed three, condemned three and couldn't reach a decision on the seventh.[16]

British settlers in Cuba

Given the money that could be made in Cuba, it is not surprising to find that some Britons, despite the language 'problem', settled there. How many Britons emigrated there is not known. Some migrated from the British West Indian islands when the slaves there were freed. (Machinery also 'migrated': Sir Stephen Cave, reporting on his visit to the Americas, reported that 'since 1846 there has been more than one instance of Spaniards purchasing the machinery of abandoned Jamaica Estates and re-erecting them in Cuba.'[17]) From various travellers' descriptions, we know that there were English shopkeepers, even 'dealers in ready-made clothes'.[18] In 1819 there were 201 settlers from England and Ireland; a few years later John Howison noted that 'Spaniards of the better class do not in general associate with those British and Americans who reside in Havanah'. He also observed 'a knot of English shipmasters' in a Havana square when a lottery was being drawn. What trade their ships were engaged in Howison does not mention – or query.[19] 'Of the English', Alexander von Humboldt wrote, 'a large number are connected with the mining interests'. He also noted 'machinists and mechanics', during his visit, probably in the 1820s.[20] In 1844 Dr J. Wurdemann believed there were only 327 English among Havana's foreign population of 18,977; elsewhere on the island he met 'an intelligent English physician' and a Hamburg-born Englishman, John Baker, who was in charge of a coffee plantation. Was the Dr Finlay he met British or American?[21]

By the 1840s about 20 per cent of the British market in sugar was supplied by Cuba and Puerto Rico. (The English women, who had campaigned against the trade in slaves and then against British slave-grown sugar, were almost silent about this outrage.) Though the actual settler numbers may have been low, Cuba had become sufficiently important to Britain for a regular mail service to be established. This cost £250,000 per annum. The first Royal Mail steamer was the *Dee*. Was this interest based on what one historian described as 'English manufacturers and capitalists [being] deeply … involved in furnishing the equipment and goods with which the [slave] trade was carried on'?[22]

One of the largest businesses in Cuba was the merchant house of Drake & Co. James Drake had emigrated in the 1790s, married a woman from one of the 'ten most distinguished families' in Cuba and become a plantation owner and merchant. The company had a number of offices around the island, marketing British and slave-grown products, and undoubtedly buying or importing slaves to work their plantations. How much wealth the family had accumulated is demonstrated by their being owed approximately half a million pounds by two planters in 1853. Philip Drake of Stockford, Lancashire, was a 'factor' in his uncle's firm trading under the name of Villeno & Co., and also owned several plantations. The Drakes' bankers – and partners – were the British firm of Kleinwort & Cohen; they also banked with Baring and Rothschild.[23]

Other British companies were Campbell & Potts and Duarte & Warren of Bahia (Brazil); British plantation owners included Fowler and J.G. Taylor. George & Burnell and R. Bell were sugar refiners. I have not been able to find more information about these companies. Tracing their partners and contacts in Britain would, of course, reveal more about British involvements with the slave-worked economy of Cuba.

Not all the British residents in Cuba were merchants, mine owners or planters. For example, George Backhouse, appointed judge of the Mixed Commission Court in 1853, hired 'a very reliable Irish Catholic man, Thomas Callaghan', to replace his previous clerk James Dalrymple, who was facing trial for robbery. He was acquitted, on the grounds of insufficient evidence. Dalrymple, who had stolen the valuables entrusted to the British Consul by resident Britons, was an alcoholic, a declared bankrupt, had previous convictions and had been 'associated with the slave trader Marty'. He was the son of a previous Mixed Commission Court judge, who was known to use *emancipados* and slaves on his estates.[24] Other Commission staff also owned slaves. The wife of Joseph Crawford, British Consul from 1842, used slaves on her plantation. She was the daughter of another previous consul, Charles Tolmé, a merchant, who was known to be 'notoriously accommodating to slave interests'. Judge Backhouse himself was from a Liverpool family involved in the slave trade.[25]

David Turnbull, while a very contentious British Consul in Havana, mentions that he was accompanied by another Englishman named Goff when he set out to investigate the charges against an Englishman named Forbes, a coffee planter who had allegedly imported 120 Bahamian 'Negroes' and used them as slaves. He was subsequently refused permission to search the plantation. When Turnbull left for the Bahamas, having been relieved of his duties, probably because he had been so outspoken about British capital funding the Cuban slave trade, he continued his investigations. What he found was that 'several hundred ex-Bahamian slaves had been shipped to Cuba to labour as slaves on plantations owned by British subjects in the area between Gibara and Holguín, commonly referred to as "English Cuba"'.[26]

A few years later Consul Clarke at Santiago de Cuba, when he was recommending that Forbes should replace him while he went on leave, assured the Foreign Office that Forbes was not a slave owner, 'Only three other British subjects here whose standing in society would warrant the Consulate being entrusted to them ... All the partners in Wright Brooks & Co are ineligible as they are large holders of slaves, added to which Mr Wright was a notorious Slave Trader in former years ... Dr Forbes assures me he does not possess any slaves.'[27] Are we to believe him?

British merchants and bankers in Cuba

Britain shipped goods to Cuba both for local use and for trans-shipment to Africa to be exchanged for enslaved men, women and children.[28] These transactions were not hidden, though they were illegal. Antonio Gallenga, a visitor to Cuba, observed that 'in this infamous trade not only Spaniards, but men of other countries, England ... have always been and are deeply implicated.'[29]

Historian Hugh Thomas elaborates on that contemporary journalist's observations:

> many leading merchants in Havana, including slave merchants, had close connections with London firms, several of which, as in Brazil, saw no reason why they should not supply goods for the slave trade, even if they seem to have hesitated before concerning themselves directly.

The sums of money advanced or deposited was in the millions of reales (Spanish dollars). Imports from Britain rose from £288,000 in 1839 to £354,000 in 1840. Exports to Britain soared from £617,000 to over £1 million in the same period, according to Consul Turnbull. This represented about a quarter of Cuba's total exports.[30]

In 1842, for example, 32,270 tons of copper, 2 million lb of coffee, 23.25 million lb of sugar and 35,580 gallons of rum were shipped by Britain from Cuba. All produced by slaves. Much re-exported. Four years later, though the amount of coffee shipped was down to just under half a million lb, when Britain lowered the import duty on slave-grown sugar, the amount of imported Cuban sugar more than doubled![31] (On this issue, see Chapter 6.)

Because of the disgraceful lack of research, we do not know which British merchants directly assisted the trade in the enslaved, either by supplying money or goods, or which traded in slave-grown produce. Londoner Thomas Brooks had agents in Havana from the 1840s and extended credit to slave merchants. Another Londoner, Samuel Dickley, also provided finance to slave traders, including the father-in-law of Julian de Zulueta, whose activities will be described later. Zulueta and other slavers also received finance from the London firms of Hudson Beattie, Aubert Powell and Simeon Himely, as well as Lizardi of Liverpool.

Another banker was the firm of Drake, Kleinwort, & Cohen. Alexander Kleinwort, who had been trading mainly in cigars from Cuba, set up a banking business with Edward Cohen in about 1850. Approximately half their capital was provided by a 'sleeping partner', James Drake. The firm of Drake & Co., as mentioned previously, had been trading in Cuba since the eighteenth century.[32] Frdk Huth & Co., merchants and bankers, was for a time 'the leading firm in the Latin-American trade'. The firm's founder, Hamburg-born Frederick Huth, had settled to Britain in 1809 after some years in Spain. Huth & Co. had a branch in Liverpool. Frederick himself became a director of the Bank of England and had seats on the boards of five insurance companies; he left £500,000 in his will of 1864 (c. £24 million in 2005).[33]

Baring Bros is another name mentioned by Hugh Thomas as being involved in Cuba. The company acquired Brazilian slave-worked diamonds and tobacco as security for its loans to Portugal.[34] According to Barings' competitor banker Baron Alphonse de Rothschild, who visited Cuba in 1859, 'Barings [are] the chief among a handful of houses making all the profit from commissions, credits and consignations.'[35]

Obviously, given the number of British financial firms involved with Cuba, this slave-dependent economy was an 'attractive proposition' – and a lucrative one. Equally obviously, it mattered not to any of these bankers that they were supporting the trade in slaves by investing in slavery.

Investments and profits

Of course, there was also money to be made out of importing Cuban produce: sugar, coffee, copper and rum. In 1845, for example, the value of Cuban imports was just under half a million pounds (worth about £26 million in 2005); in the same year the value of exports was £1.4 million (£74 million).[36]

Though it is difficult to gather data, economic historian Irving Stone has calculated that British investment in Cuba was only £1 million in 1840 (just under £45 million in 2005) but rose to £3 million in 1854 (£139 million). In 1865 even the British government loaned Cuba £600,000 (£2.8 million)![37]

We have to note that money flowed both ways. Half the Cuban capital invested abroad was placed in England. For example, having made their fortunes as slave traders, Gabriel Lombillo and José Antonio Suárez Argudín invested in textiles in Manchester and coal mining in Wales.[38]

Britain builds Cuba's railways ...

It was with British money that Cuba began to build railways as early as 1834. The first line was so successful that 'small, unconnected railroads [were soon built] throughout the sugar cane growing areas of the island'. It was a British loan of $2.5 million that financed the first railway, according to Alexander von Humbolt, and it was built by slaves, *emancipados* and convicts. David Turnbull believed that a loan of £450,450 had been negotiated by one Alexander Robinson.[39]

Given that the steam engine had been developed in Britain, the first batches of engineers and engines must have been imported from Britain, even if later in the century they came from other European countries as well as from the USA. The capital for the railways 'came principally from England, raised under the auspices of the Cuban Junta de Fomento', according to historian Franklin Knight, who has also shown that in 1851 out of a total of 802 foreign workers on four major railways lines, 663 were Irish and 37 English.[40] Britain invested £360,000 in railways in Cuba in 1865 (almost £17 million in 2005) and a total of £175,000 in the setting up of a telegraph system in the period 1870–75.[41] The skilled labourers on the lines were mainly Irish; the unskilled were slaves. So British money, inventions, skills and labour – and slaves – were used to build railways to aid the export of slave-grown sugar and tobacco, while officially – publicly – Britain was opposed to slavery and the slave trade.

... and supplies plantation machinery

Cubans, led by Julian de Zulueta, were eager to adopt modern equipment on their plantations. Zulueta was one of the planters first to install railways on his plantations for transporting sugar cane to his factories. By 1846, 20 per cent of sugar milling was done by steam-powered machinery; by 1861, it was 71 per cent. There is at present almost no information on how many of these mills were supplied with machinery from the UK, but in the late 1830s David Turnbull reported that they were either English or American. All I have been able to find is that the Liverpool firm of Fawcett & Littledale exported a total of 74 'engines' to Cuba between 1813 and 1845. Another Liverpool firm, Fawcett & Preston exported 'horizontal sugar mills' to Cuba. (I don't know how these differed from other mills.) The patents of the Scottish manufacturer Stewart & Macdonald 'were used in the machinery in many plantations to 'extract sugar from the cane', according to economist L.H. Jenks.[42]

Other imports from Britain

David Turnbull, visiting the island, noted that coal was shipped from Liverpool to Cuba. Mr Trist the American Consul told him that he 'see[s] passing through the customs house here, without attracting ... notice ... casks of shackles of British manufacture'. Some 10 per cent of the vessels registered as entering Cuban harbours in 1837, he reported, were English. Over the past five years, on average 7.5 per cent of legal, registered imports had come from Britain, Trist claimed. (This seems to me to be a gross underestimate. Or were a large proportion of British goods imported illegally without registration?[43])

Probably the main imports from the UK were what were called 'coast goods', cotton materials, guns, gunpowder and iron bars. According to the BFASS,

> there are manufactured in this country, in enormous quantities, articles known by the name of 'coast goods' ... [T]he consignees of the British merchants and manufacturers or branch houses of their establishments in Brazil and Cuba dispose of such goods to persons well known as traffickers in human beings ... [F]etters and manacles employed in the slave trade and in the punishment and torture form part of the export trade to Brazil and Cuba.[44]

(Sometimes these contraband goods were shipped to Cadiz or some other intermediate/neutral port. The British merchants' agents or partners in these ports were instructed to ship the goods to the coast of Africa or to Cuba.[45])

British abolitionist Joseph Gurney, visiting Cuba in 1839, found that 'certain it is, that the articles used in the slave trade, and often transmitted to Africa on American bottoms, are manufactured in England and employ a large amount of British capital.... [T]he filthy lucre is often found too strong for moral principle.'[46]

Britain and Cuban mines

Again, there is very little information. The El Cobre copper mine, which was the world's largest supplier of copper in the early to mid-nineteenth century, was owned by the Royal Santiago Co. of London. Michael Williams was the company's agent in Swansea; most of the experienced miners were imported from Cornwall. They were augmented by 400 enslaved Africans. Whether the 'Consolidated Cobre Mines' was the same company by another name, or just another British company working copper in the area, is not clear from the consular despatches.[47]

David Turnbull, who was later appointed British Consul in Havana, travelled around Cuba in the late 1830s. He reported that the then Consul, Hardy, was one of the principal proprietors of the mines, as well as its manager! On his retirement from Cuba, Consul Hardy was replaced at the mines by another British official, Consul Clarke of St Jago de Cuba.[48] Britain, as far as I could discover, made no moves to 'relieve' Clarke of his consulship when his new managerial role was made public. Clearly the British government was not deeply concerned about its senior employees owning slaves. Neither did Britain see any reasons to disbelieve Clarke's recommendations, as noted above, for another possible slave owner to take over his role while he was on leave.

Other Britons involved in mining were Messrs Brooks and Wright, and Wright, Shelton & Co. Nothing is known of them. About half the miners were slaves, Turnbull found, some owned outright by the mining company, others hired. Some of the copper, he reported, was shipped to Swansea. He believed that the profits of the company, 'regularly quoted on the London market', were about £12,000 in 1837. The British government had been told that about £400,000 worth of partly slave-mined ore was sent to Britain annually; in 1846 the

British government collected £42,245 (*c.* £2.7 million in 2005) in duty on this.[49] I wonder what proportion of Swansea's population was employed in the shipping and processing of slave-produced copper.

The *Anti-Slavery Reporter* for 10 February 1841 (p. 37) lists the directors of the Brazilian Mining Association. One is Timothy A. Curtis, the Deputy Governor of the Bank of England.

British-built slaving vessels

As building vessels for the trade in slaves was illegal, much subterfuge had to be employed. For example, both British- and North American-built slaving vessels were either actually or nominally sold in Cuba. The US Consul in Havana was noted as being 'slack' regarding ship registrations. The vessels then left Cuba with an American crew, which often seemed to include some British seamen. Some Spaniards were usually embarked as 'passengers'. Trade goods, and the equipment required to transport human beings, were picked up on a small island, such as St Thomas. For the return voyage the Spanish crew took over, and the flag and, sometimes, the ship's name were changed. This was because some parts of the African coast were open to non-British/American slavers and thus the vessel was less likely to be seized by the Anti-Slave Trade Squadrons.

As indicated in a previous chapter, that slaving ships were being built in Britain was relatively well known. The BFASS, for example, was constantly publicising it, and noted in its 1842 *Annual Report* that 'vessels have been built in this country specially for the slave trade and overtly prepared for the traffic in British harbours'. Even Hugh Thomas, not a historian who easily questions British morality, says in his book *Cuba* (p. 158) that 'ships could still be built in Liverpool for Havana merchant houses.... The ships sailed under several flags.'

There is no research to indicate why the government took no action, or what falsehoods appear on documentation. As indicated in previous chapters, the fact is that most of the ruses were known and thus the building of slavers for the slave trade could have been stopped. But, of course, the builders might have objected to being deprived of lucrative business.

One Cuban slaver we know about is the steamer *Wilhelmina*, built in Hartlepool. Crewed by Spaniards and Portuguese, it sailed to Cadiz, and from there to Africa, where it filled its holds with slaves and disembarked them in Cuba. Renamed the *Noc Daqui*, it made a number of such trips.[50] It is not known how many of the estimated 151,000 enslaved Africans imported into Cuba in the years 1821 to 1843 were transported on British-built vessels.[51]

Julian de Zulueta

One of the few Captains-General who made some attempt to stop the illegal trade was Domingo Dulce, who was brave enough in 1865 to send into exile in Spain one of the foremost slave traders, Julian de Zulueta. This grandee of Cuba, one of the wealthiest plantation owners, used more than 1,500 slaves on his plantations. Historian Franklin Knight calls Zulueta 'the acknowledged political boss of Cuba' and reports that he was charged with illegal slave trading, but was exonerated on technical grounds. Such involvements were clearly not thought to be reprehensible, as Zulueta was made a Marquis, a member of the Spanish Parliament, and became a mayor of Havana.[52]

Julian de Zulueta was the cousin of Pedro de Zulueta, the naturalised British citizen whose indictment for slave-trading is described in Chapter 3. He owned a number of plantations, one of which – Alava, at almost 5000 acres in 1845 – was the third largest in the island. He had 'three ox-drawn railroads running from the extreme ends of the plantation right up to the mills'. About 20 years later, according to Antonio Gallenga, Zulueta was the owner of three plantations, just one of which was valued at £300,000. By 'ransacking all the industrial marts of Europe and America to make iron, coal, charcoal and steam do the work formerly done by slaves', he reduced his expenditures. Zulueta 'is daily purchasing and enlarging new ones [plantations]; he has a large mercantile establishment in town; and he has a hand in almost every industrial and commercial speculation in his own country or out of it', Gallenga reported. Though 'by his own account' he had come to Cuba from Alava in the Basque provinces as an impoverished youth, Zulueta 'is the heart and soul of every public institution, political or social, in Havannah ... and in great emergencies the Captain-General would little venture upon any measure without consulting him.' Naturally, he had great influence 'in Madrid and throughout the Peninsula ... [He] was "a born king of men".'[53]

However, it is unlikely that Julian had arrived in Cuba quite as impoverished as he claimed. In any case, as he was the nephew of a wealthy coffee planter he would immediately have moved into a life of luxury. Eventually he inherited his uncle's estates and became even wealthier when he married the daughter of a leading slave trader. It is also quite possible that the Zuluetas were involved in slave trading from Spain. They were Basques, and in the eighteenth century there were many Basques residing in Cadiz, Spain's chief slaving port. The Cadiz Slave Company was directed by a Basque, Maguel de Uriarte.[54]

Julian was the Cuban agent of his uncle, Pedro Juan Zulueta, a London-based merchant from Cadiz. Don Pedro Juan was forced to live in exile in England for some years. He had been the President of the Courts, and Representative of Cadiz, until internal Spanish turmoil forced him to flee. The firm of Zulueta & Co. had been 'established as merchants for upwards of 70 years in Spain and twenty in England', Pedro Jr. stated at the court hearing when he was charged with slaving. Julian had an office in New Orleans for purchasing slaves, and was, according to Hugh Thomas, responsible for importing 'most of the 100,000 or so slaves imported in the years 1858 and 1862'. In 1863 the British Commissary Judge in Havana reported to Earl Russell that four steamers had been fitted out in Cadiz for the slave trade; he believed that Julian de Zulueta held a 50 per cent share in these.[55]

Far from being dishonoured as a slaver, Julian de Zulueta was made a Senator for life in Madrid, given the title of Marquis, and was worth 200 million reales when he died in 1878.[56] Perhaps his influence on the continuation of the trade in the enslaved can be gauged by the fact that slavery in Cuba was abolished two years after his death.

But, of course, Zulueta wasn't the only slave trader in Cuba. Pedro Martinez of Cadiz had established a vast slaving empire, with a branch in Havana. It is believed that of the 140 known unloadings of slaves in Cuba in the period 1831–43, he and his partners were responsible for 60. One of his ship's captains later became an independent slaver: this was Pedro Blanco, who received goods from Zulueta & Co. in London, as previously described. Blanco and Pedro Forcade were the prominent traders until about 1851, when they were overtaken by a company named Expedición por Africa, whose main shareholder was – Julian de Zulueta![57]

When the price demanded by traders for enslaved Africans rose rapidly, Julian looked for labour from elsewhere. In 1847, with the help of his London cousin, he imported enslaved 'Indios' from Yucatan in Mexico and from Venezuela. But the numbers obtainable proved insufficient, so Pedro Jr in London suggested their substitution with labourers from the newly opened Chinese ports. The Spanish government consented to Zulueta & Co. importing 600 labourers annually, on eight-year contracts. An intermittent trade in contract labour lasted from 1847 until 1871, when concern by the Chinese government regarding conditions of labour and the growing international condemnation ended this exploitation of not-quite-enslaved labour.[58]

By 1853 about 30,000 Chinese labourers had been imported; it is estimated that the final total was 60,000. This trade was helped by Judge Backhouse (see above), whose brother John was – very conveniently – British Vice-Consul in Amoy, China. In Liverpool Zulueta & Co. worked with Tait & Co. on the importation business. The Chinese were not technically slaves, as they were paid 4 pesos per month. But the planters ensured that most became heavily indebted so that their eight-year contracts could be extended – again and again. According to Richard Dane, a US traveller in Cuba, the 'coolies' were in fact sold for about $340 each; and the 'dealer did not deny their tendency to suicide'. Historian Martínez-Fernández believes that most died.[59]

Labour-hungry Cuba also obtained workers, supposedly free, from Sierra Leone. J.G.F. Wurdemann, visiting Cuba in the early 1840s, was obviously outraged at one particular sight:

> even now are the manacles of the captured Africans wrought by English workmen.... [E]nlistment of emigrants from Sierra Leone to labor for the lowest wages for a fixed period of years, under an ex-Jamaican planter, who is not bound to feed and clothe, and administer to them when sick and helpless ... What can the stupid African know of written contracts and articles of indenture ... England emancipate[d] her West Indian slaves, while she refuses to remove the shackles from her other oppressed colonies.

Wurdemann is clearly referring to Liberated Africans, that is, Africans freed from slave ships and deposited in the British colony

Slaves on a sugar cane plantation, *c.* 1860

of Sierra Leone. There they were compelled to accept either local 'apprenticeships' or similar 'employment' wherever they were needed, usually in Britain's West Indian colonies. But from this evidence, they were also shipped to Cuba, perhaps via the British West Indian colonies. It was reported to the US Congress that in 1856 Cuba wanted to import 40,000 'African apprentices'. The Spanish government had approved the proposal – and the 'British government [had] given their sanction to the scheme'. They were, according to the British and Foreign Anti-Slavery Society, re-enslaved.[60]

Cuba was dependent on slave labour. Spain was dependent on Cuba for much of her income. Some British merchants, manufacturers, bankers and shipbuilders were dependent, either partly or wholly, on supporting the Cuban slave trade and slave-grown produce. How did this fit in with Britain's professed anti-slavery? It didn't. But if no-one (except occasionally the anti-slavery societies) spoke about it, if the government ignored it, then the myth of British purity could be maintained. And is maintained to this day.

BRAZIL

The area of the South American mainland that we know as Brazil had been conquered and settled by the Portuguese in the fifteenth century. It was officially declared a 'possession' in 1500 and Portuguese settlers began to arrive – and to grow sugar. The first enslaved Africans were landed in 1538. Attempts were also made to enslave the native peoples, but they were not exterminated as they had been in Cuba. All Native Americans were declared free in 1755.

When Napoleon conquered Portugal, with the aid of the British Navy, the King fled to Rio de Janeiro in Brazil. The city then became the capital of the Portuguese Empire, leading to its rapid development. In 1821 the Brazilians forced the King to return to Lisbon. His son Pedro remained, declared Brazil's quasi-independence and proclaimed himself as its emperor. In 1827, in return for various trade concessions, Britain consented to recognise Brazilian independence. But soon much civil strife ensued, and it was not until 1844 that Brazil achieved more concrete measures of independence from Portugal. However, the country was still ruled by the Portuguese royal house, though there was a partially elected General Assembly. In 1891, after an army revolt, Brazil declared itself a republic.

In 1830 Brazil formally abolished the slave trade, but, as in Britain, the Act was circumvented. British abolitionists, according to some writers, encouraged the abolition movement in Brazil, which succeeded by 1850 in getting stricter laws passed to suppress the trade. Relations with Britain, which some argue had become problematic, now improved. This was despite the non-abolition of slavery. According to a report of 1865, Britain now gave loans for public works, and 'large amounts of English capital poured into the Brazilian Empire'.[61]

The estimates of the slave population vary widely. The British and Foreign Anti-Slavery Society believed that there were about 2.5 million in the early 1840s. A few years later Surgeon T. Nelson of the Royal Navy estimated that there were about 3 million slaves. Historian Roger Conrad believes that a total of about 5 million

Africans had been imported into Brazil.[62] Slavery was not abolished until 1888.

The slave trade to Brazil

As in Cuba, most of the labouring work in Brazil's mines and plantations was done by enslaved Africans. As Brazilian records have been destroyed, there is huge disagreement between those trying to estimate the numbers of slaves imported, even during the nineteenth century. One estimate for the numbers of enslaved imported from 1710 to 1810 is 1.9 million, with perhaps as many as another million people landed by 1840. For the period from the 1840s to 1851, the lowest estimate of the numbers of Africans imported is 289,892 and the highest 371,615.[63] The well-enforced 1850 Act stopped importation; the last known landing of enslaved Africans was in 1855. However, the internal trade in human beings continued, mainly to the lucrative coffee plantations in the south.

The situation regarding the collusion of government officials with the slavers was very similar to that described for Cuba. 'Brazilian authorities of every rank co-operated with the slave traders', wrote historian Roger Conrad. 'Customs officials accept false names [for slave vessels]. At a higher rank, they marry into Senatorial families and serve as imperial councillors ... [there was] much, and constant bribery.' One judge in the 1830s who tried to uphold the law against slave trading was persecuted into resignation![64]

The British government also colluded. A Brazilian official, G.A. d'Aguilar Pantoja, informed British Consul H. Hamilton that 'several English merchants, moved by the desire for gaining great profit, have imported from Great Britain merchandises calculated only for the slave trade.' He asked the Consul to 'enlighten the English government ... [so that it] may take the necessary steps to prevent the exportation of the said merchandise to Brazil'. The British government ignored this plea.

The landing of slaves was also similar to that practised in Cuba. The enslaved were landed at small ports along the coast. The vessel was cleaned up there and sailed on to a supervised major port in ballast. It was then loaded up with goods to take to the coast of Africa to purchase more women, men and children.[65]

British involvement has not been studied. However, it is clear that apart from the often mentioned provision of goods for the slave trade and the insuring of slave vessels, some of the British residents in Brazil were often directly involved in the trade. Two Quaker visitors to Brazil in the early 1850s found an Englishman who 'employed his steam-boat to convey contraband slaves from the ships of the manstealer to the shore'. They also noted that 'not a few English-men hold slaves ... some Englishmen have bought slaves since Lord Brougham's Act of 1843 [which] made it unlawful for an Englishman to buy or sell a slave in any land'.[66]

While in 1829 Consul Ponsonby at Rio de Janeiro could not find evidence of direct British involvement in the slave trade, he did report to the Foreign Office that

> vast amounts of British manufactures are employed in the slave trade. There are few merchants here who do not annually receive large shipments of goods.... It is calculated that one third of all British manu-factures imported into this harbour consists of Articles destined for the commerce with the coast of Africa.

In 1835 the British Mixed Court Commissioner at Rio repeated Ponsonby's exoneration of direct involvement in the slave trade, but advised that 'any considerable number of the slaves imported into Brazil are in fact employed in Establishments conducted and supported by British agents and capital ... and many individuals claiming British protection ... are openly seen ... buying and selling slaves'. The Commissioner repeated his charges in 1838 and also sent the information he had gathered to the Attorney and Solicitor Gener-als in the UK. This included references to a British man named Platt, who was importing slaves 'in his own small vessel'.[67] The reports were ignored by the government in London.

Retired Ambassador W.D. Christie reported in his reminiscences that

> three British houses in Brazil have lost £12,000 [about half a million pounds in 2005] by [slave] vessels' condemnation ... British capital suffered severely in Rio from recent captures ... A Brazilian paper has recently reported a Brazilian Minister talking of British insurance for slave trade vessels and British goods used on the Coast ... there is no hope of seeing a notorious slave trader getting punished as he has friends among English merchants and owes them money.

So naturally the slave traders tried their hardest to influence the Brazilian government against prosecution: they had to avoid bankruptcy by paying off their debts by whatever profits they could reap from slave trading.[68] And, of course, the British merchants and financiers wanted the debts repaid, so they would have supported the Brazilians. That is, they had good reasons – from their perspective – for supporting the slave trade.

Britain had begun its involvement in the slave trade to Brazil soon after the 1807 Abolition Act, by investing in 'foreign commercial houses'. By 1821 'at least 80 per cent of the cargoes bartered in Africa for slaves carried to Rio' were British. Robert Conrad in his study on the African slave trade to Brazil, has written that

> in the 1830s and 1840s, British merchants, now based in Havana, Rio de Janeiro, Bahia and Recife, sold these *panos da costa* (coast goods) to slavetraders, who bartered them in Africa for men and women. In those years, as far as Brazil was concerned, Atlantic commerce resembled spokes of a wheel. At the hub in Rio and other Brazilian ports were dozens of British merchant houses that arranged shipments of coast goods from Britain; sold those goods to slavetraders, often on credit; acted as agents for the purchase of American vessels that carried those products to Africa and returned with slaves; shipped slave-grown coffee to Europe and the United States; and sometimes even insured slave ships against seizure by the Royal Navy.

Conrad goes on to argue that the

> British government ... was generally tolerant of the unlawful activities of its own subjects. British involvement in the slave trade to Cuba and Brazil was nearly ignored in London if such activities were not too blatant.... [T]he power and influence of commercial interests in Britain perhaps account for the comparative scarcity of references to British involvement in slavetrading transactions [reported] in the British [official] slave-trading correspondence.[69]

As if this were not bad enough, according to information sent to the Anti-Slavery Society, among the auctioneers of slaves in Brazil were two English companies, Cannell, Southam & Co., and A. Lawrie & Co.[70]

Mr Henry Wise, the pro-abolition US Consul in Rio de Janeiro, assiduously informed both his own government and Hamilton Hamilton, his British equivalent, of the details of American and

British involvements in the slave trade. He also gave Mr Hamilton the names of some of the British crew on American slavers. He named the local agent for the British firm of Hobkirk & Weetman as negotiating the charters for slaving voyages with the notorious trader in slaves Manuel Pinto Fonseca. The US government took Consul Wise's charges so seriously that in February 1845 the President sent a message to Congress about the situation. The President described the methods used to avoid detection, and the purchase and shipping of 'coast goods from Britain'.[71] This was then sent to the British government.

Foreign Secretary Lord Aberdeen's reply is eight printed pages long. But, to my mind, it does not negate Mr Wise's assertion that the 'disposition of the British authorities [in Rio] is to be at least blind to, if not wink at the infamous slave trade'.[72]

I have to add here that the British government was given plenty of evidence of British complicity in the slave trade by the Royal Navy, the BFASS, its own Consuls, and visitors to Brazil. US Consul Wise reported to his own government that he had ensured 'that there is no question but that both the minister and the consul of Great Britain at Rio now know of the participation of British subjects in the slave trade ... and are fully informed of the direct and indirect mode and means of carrying it on by British capital, goods and credit, from both English and foreign ports'.[73] But nothing was done.

British support for slave-worked Brazil

Investment and banking

British private investments in this flourishing, slave-worked colony/ country were huge – 'bottomless', according to Naval Surgeon Nelson. For example, John Bright stated in Parliament that between 'four and five millions of capital and 3 millions of export went to Brazil in 1849'.[74]

It seems that obtaining accurate data for investment is difficult and interpretation hazardous. One author claims that investment in 1865 was almost £2.5 million (c. £116 million in 2005) while another calculates £7.3 million (£330 million in 2005). Some of this investment was in local manufacturing, such as textiles, shoes and food processing.

These authors also differ on the amount of government loans, one giving £1.4 million and the other £13 million. Perhaps what matters is that the sums were large and increasing. In 1876, for example, the British government underwrote a loan of £43 million (£18,748 million in 2005) to Brazil.[75]

According to L.H. Jenks the British government loaned a total of £24.6 million (well over £1 billion in 2005) to Brazil in the years from 1860 to 1876 – that is, while slavery was still legal; 84 per cent of these loans were negotiated, for a hefty fee of course, by the London-based Rothschild banking house, who are also described as the 'financial agents of the Brazilian government'.[76]

Britain was also heavily involved in the Brazilian banking system. In 1863 the London and Brazilian Bank was established and opened branches throughout Brazil. One of its directors was a coffee trader from Liverpool, Edward Johnston. Two years later the newly formed Brazilian and Portuguese Bank had its headquarters in London. Soon 'almost all the international trade of South America was financed by bills of exchange drawn on London and Liverpool'.[77]

There was nothing hidden about British involvement. In 1840 the *Jornal do Commercio* carried an article appreciating 'the contribution of British merchants in Rio to the "ransoming" of blacks in Africa, the supplying of trade goods and loans to the merchants and their willingness to insure slave ships'.[78]

Trade

In the 1820s, three-quarters of Britain's trade with South America was with Brazil. The annual value of exports then was about £3 million. By the 1870s it was about £8.3 million (c. £349 million in 2005).[79]

What goods were imported? Everything from machinery to woven cotton goods, hardware, earthenware, and 'fancy' goods for the middle classes such as glass, silver and table linen, hats, musical instruments and umbrellas. In the early 1820s, Maria Graham, the wife of an English naval captain, visiting a family which owned 180 field slaves, observed that 'everything was served up on English blue and white ware'.[80]

Brazil's growing economy required machinery. The earliest exports I could find were the engines shipped from Liverpool in the years 1816–20 to A.M. Pedra & Co. in Rio and Thomas & William

March in Bahia. Another Liverpool company involved with Brazil was Deane, Youle & Co., which had branches in Bahia and Pernambuco. Historian Alan Manchester believed that 'the export of machinery intended largely for sugar mills more than doubled between 1845 and 1847', after Britain equalised the duty payable on free and slave-grown sugar.[81]

Britain also built and then installed the gasworks to light the cities of Pará and Pernambuco. British companies built bridges, telegraph systems, sewerage works, tramway, drainage works and exported and installed sugar presses. 'Sugar plant engines' were shipped to Jukes Coulson & Co. in Bahia from as early as 1813.[82] All of this must have been mainly financed by the profits and taxes on slave-produced exports.

British merchants were also much involved with Brazil's exports. In 1843, for example, almost 40 per cent of the sugar exports, 50 per cent of coffee exports and 63 per cent of cotton exports were shipped by British merchants, 'although, except for cotton, very little of these products actually landed in England'. 'Exporting firms, shipping, insurance, banks and the railways' were in 'British and other alien hands', wrote economic historian P.L. Cottrell, and 'the majority of Brazil's imports came from the UK.' By 1860 British imports from Brazil reached £4.5 million – about £99 million in 2005.[83]

Mining

The gold mines of the Minas Gerais district were owned by Britons. When the gold ran out, the slaves were sold to the Imperial Mine at St Juan del Rey, another British company. Naval Surgeon Nelson estimated that there had been a total of over 160,000 enslaved Africans working on the mines in the Minas Gerais district in the 1820s – far outnumbering the white population. John Candler and Wilson Burgess, visiting Quakers, reported that the del Ray gold mines were owned by an English company and used British capital. The work was carried out by slaves bought prior to 1843 and others hired from their owners for a maximum of seven years, at the rate of £15 a year – paid to the owners, of course. The company, they believed, owned about 800 slaves and hired another 1000. In a June 1843 letter to the government the company stated that it employed about '2000 ... the only labour is the negro population'.[84]

The Imperial Brazilian Mining Association, founded in 1825, had their offices in London's Broad Street. They owned gold mines at Gongo Soco, which employed about 250 English miners. It was alleged by an ex-employee, though the owners disputed this, that the mines used between 600 and 700 slaves. The General Mining Association, whose largest shareowner was the London firm Rundell & Bridge, also owned slave-worked mines. The Candonga Mining Co., owned by British subjects, also used slaves, according to the Rio Mixed Court Commissioner.[85]

Cornish miners and expertise were exported from the 1820s. Though miners were also recruited from other parts of the UK, Cornishmen outnumbered them. Cornish money was also invested and about a third of South American mining companies had Cornish directors. Machinery and equipment, from steam engines to shovels and boots, were also manufactured in many counties, including Cornwall. Though some of this equipment was shipped from Liverpool, Portsmouth, Plymouth and Swansea, it has been argued that shipments to South America were a major contributor to the growth of Falmouth as a port. What proportion of this traffic was with Brazil is not known.[86]

Does anyone in Falmouth care, I wonder, or even know about the town's growth having partly depended on slavery? I presume that the Cornish miners were well paid – so how much money did they send home to their families? How many Falmouth seamen crewed ships to Brazil? Or manufactured the boots and so on shipped there?

Railways, shipping, postage

The first plan for a railway was presented to the Emperor in 1827 by a resident Englishman, Charles Grace. But the Emperor was not interested. About ten years later, Fred Forum, an English merchant at Santos, in consultation with Robert Stephenson, proposed another scheme. Again, the proposal was turned down. It is possible that this was due to intense US competition. Finally, Thomas Cochrane was granted the concession for a track between Santos and São Paulo – but he could not raise the money. In 1856 a new company was formed, combining Brazilian and British investors; this was so successful that two more companies were formed to build other lines. The British government provided guarantees. Ex-Ambassador W.D. Christie wrote that two of the three railway companies in the period up to the 1860s had been organised in London by Rothschild and that their 'directors were London merchants, bankers and MPs'. According to railway historian Anthony Burton, 'lines throughout South America had a strong English accent'. By 1880 – that is, still during the era of slavery – there were 11 railway companies operating in Brazil. The designers of these lines were all British, as were the administrators, the machinery and the engines. The skilled labour was provided by immigrant Europeans, including British, while the unskilled were – of course – slaves. Most of the enslaved were rented from their owners, at 16 pence per day – paid, as always, to the owners, not the enslaved workers.[87]

Once postage rates were agreed by the two governments in 1851, the British Steam Packet Line was awarded the contract for carrying mail to Brazil. The British government anticipated this service, which included carrying other cargo, to become so lucrative that it agreed to cover two-thirds of the postage costs.

According to the Quaker travellers, in the 1850s Brazilian coastal steamers were provided by Britain, or were 'captained by Englishmen'.[88] At about this time 167 – that is, about 25 per cent – of the foreign vessels entering Rio de Janeiro harbour were British. In 1844 it had been noted that of the 200 ships arriving in Britain from Brazil, all were British. They employed 2333 crew. Of the 302 leaving for Brazil, 255 were British, employing 3143 seamen.[89] As it is possible that the ships leaving and arriving were the same vessels, it is likely that no more than about 3000 sailors earned their living from this slave-worked economy. How many had been involved in building all these vessels?

British residents

I have not been able to obtain any information on how many Britons had decided to emigrate and settle in Brazil. Did some of the Cornishmen settle there? Those not in favour of abolition, and enticed by the possibilities of making large profits from slave-grown produce, would of course have been much attracted to this relatively independent country. In the 1820s it was reported that 'English pot-houses lined the streets of Rio near the beach', and that there were 'about sixty British houses in business in Rio and nearly twenty houses in

Bahia, sixteen in Pernambuco ... and smaller numbers up and down the coast'. Thirty years later the Quaker travellers noted that 'some of the best houses and gardens in and near Bahia and Pernambuco belong to British merchants'.

Undoubtedly many of those involved in the activities outlined above must have settled in Brazil. For example, according to the US Consul in Rio, nearly the whole of the slave trade in American bottoms is transacted by the house of Jenkins, from New York, and an Englishman named Russell and a Portuguese named Guimaraés.[90] Who was Russell and how did he become a slave trader in Rio?

Conclusion

Even from this very limited research it is obvious, I trust, that Britain was much involved in the slave trade to Cuba and Brazil and that Britons owned slave-worked enterprises there. Both were illegal. It seems equally evident that the British government knew this. As US Consul Henry Wise suggested, 'one of the duties of Great Britain [is that] the facts as they are should be exposed there. Let her powerful press and her mighty debates not continue to cry shame upon Brazil and Spain even whilst not a finger is pointed at her own manufacturers, merchants and brokers in the slave trade and whilst they are smug and secure in their secret gains.'[91]

That nothing was done, that this wealth-creation from slavery was not and *still has not been acknowledged*, is why this book had to be written.

Trading with and investing in countries dependent on slave labour did not break any British laws but was certainly not in accordance with the supposedly abolitionist spirit of Britain. It was also, of course, in total contradiction to the much publicised abolitionist politics and propaganda of the British government.

That the shameful treatment of 'Liberated Africans' also involved their shipment to these slave societies surprised me, though it should not have. I fully agree with Consul Henry Wise's suggestion to his British counterpart in Rio that 'Great Britain should change her policy of making apprentices of the Africans captured from slavers.... Is not the apprenticeship system a part of the foreign slave trade? ... Far better would it be to restore the captives to their native land.'[92]

Just how large these profits were is unknown at present. But that the profits made were large enough to encourage the government to turn a blind eye, is also, I trust, obvious. Equally absent from any research is any information on how many Britons in the UK made a living out of Cuba and Brazil, as workers in British factories and shipyards, as ships' crews, as clerks in merchants' offices, as carters, as bankers, as insurers...

CHAPTER 5

Africa

How was the modern map of Africa created? Did African countries develop 'naturally', through the rise and fall of empires, kingdoms, chieftaincies, as European countries, or as China evolved? Certainly not.

As previously outlined, by the nineteenth century, some Europeans had been trading with Africans for four centuries, as had the Ottoman Empire, the Arabian kingdoms, and the Indian and Chinese traders for even longer. All these traders influenced the development of the countries of Africa, but probably none as much as the European trade in enslaved Africans and the subsequent devastations wrought by colonialism.

It was the development of German interest in acquiring colonies in Africa that led to an international conference in Berlin in 1884–85. A conference which, of course, did not include a single African representative. The European powers, as well as representatives from the Ottoman Empire and the USA, sat around a table drawing lines on the map of Africa, dividing the continent among themselves and agreeing that if at all possible they should not fight wars with each other for possession. Some areas were declared 'spheres of influence' while others were 'possessions'. Historic, natural and linguistic boundaries were ignored, thus creating 'artificial creations, [which] have created very serious problems, many of which have still not

Slave market in Zanzibar
(from Rev. Jabez Marrat, *David Livingstone*, 1877)

been solved', according to Professor Adu Boahen of the University of Ghana.[1]

The trade in enslaved Africans

There had been slavery in various forms in Africa, as there had been elsewhere in the world, probably since time immemorial. The 'English' were enslaved by the Roman conquerors; my Magyar forefathers were enslaved by the Turkish conquerors of Hungary in the sixteenth century. There had been a trade in slaves in Africa, marching the enslaved women and men north, across the Sahara for about a thousand years.[2] European slave traders arrived on the West African coast in the fifteenth century. There was a trade in slaves from the east coast also, going north and east and eventually across the Atlantic.[3]

Africans, of course, resisted. Though there has been some research on revolts on slaving vessels, research on resistance in Africa has been relatively recent. This is not surprising as British (and other

'Western') historians have only admitted within the past few decades that *Africa had a history*.[4]

Britain, as stated previously, had begun trading in enslaved Africans in the sixteenth century. The Abolition Act of 1807 and all the subsequent Acts, listed in Appendix 1, and the many treaties signed with slave trading and/or slave-holding countries, had very little effect.[5] Historian David Eltis has estimated that about 16 million African were embarked from the shores of Africa after 1808; about 80 per cent of them arrived at their destination.[6] How many survived there is not known. Nor do we know how many were killed in the process of enslavement or how many died while awaiting shipment.

So, after the much-lauded Abolition Act of 1807, the export of the enslaved continued, and the use of domestic slaves in Africa increased. The last British Acts abolishing the legal status of slavery were passed almost one hundred years after the 1833 Act of Emancipation: it was in 1927 that slavery was abolished in the British colony of Sierra Leone. On the Gold Coast, where 'slave dealing' had been abolished (at least on paper) in 1874, the legal status of slavery was not abolished until 1928.

The British government and governors, even after they turned the trading forts into official 'Protectorates' and colonies did little to stop slavery. As explained by historian Patrick Manning, 'the desire to run inexpensive colonial governments and to utilize African labour cheaply ... encouraged [British colonial officials] to wink at slavery'. The government used 'forced labour' for road building and other construction projects.[7] While such labour was usually used only for a relatively brief period, it was still slave labour as it was unpaid. The system was in use during both world wars, when such labour (called 'political labour' in Nigeria) had to be furnished by the chiefs for both private companies and for pubic works.[8]

Although in this chapter I shall concentrate on the slave trade and slavery in the areas known today as the countries of Nigeria and Ghana, let me give just one example of the British involvement on the East African coast.[9] I have chosen this as it not only illustrates British attitudes and policies but in some aspects has a remarkable similarity to what had been 'accomplished' in the West Indies.

Britain established a consulate in Zanzibar in 1841 in order to protect her trade routes to India and the Persian Gulf. A large island off the coast of what was then called Tanganyika, Zanzibar had a population comprising about 80 per cent enslaved Africans, obtained from the mainland.[10]

They produced cloves, most of which was bought by British traders. In 1873 Britain signed a treaty with the Sultan of Zanzibar to abolish the slave trade. The treaty was renewed in 1876, 1885 and 1890, when Britain proclaimed the island to be a British Protectorate. An emancipation decree was passed in 1897 and the *owners* of the enslaved received compensation money. But the newly freed men and women lost their subsistence plots and could be declared vagrants if they refused to sign a labour contract with the landowner! These contracts stipulated three days' labour a week all year in exchange for a subsistence plot of land. In fact, the trade in slaves and in slave-grown produce continued well into the twentieth century.[11]

The Anti-Slave Trade Squadron and the Mixed Commission and Vice-Admiralty Courts

If the 1807 and 1833 Acts are the jewels in the British crown, then so is the work of the naval Anti-Slave Trade Squadron, established to give some force to the 1807 Act. But was the West African Squadron more successful than the 1807 Act? And could we argue that in some ways the British – at least some Britons – profited even from the Squadron? And thus from slavery?

To implement the Act of 1807, the British government sent two ships to the coast of West Africa in 1808 to seize slaving vessels. It was a hopeless task for the two small, old vessels, but the Royal Navy was busy fighting Napoleon. After the war the numbers of vessels was slowly increased, but they were usually still old and much slower than the many modern slavers. Captured slaving ships had be taken to the newly set up Vice-Admiralty Court in Sierra Leone, which was declared a Crown Colony in order to be used as a centre for suppression work.[12] By 1816, the Court had heard indictments for 130 ships, of which *22 were owned or had been outfitted in British ports.* How many of those not captured were British? Clearly, British slave traders were still in business.

Mixed Commission Courts were set up in 1819 in Freetown and subsequently in the Americas, where an even smaller Anti-Slave

Trade Squadron was deployed. These Courts consisted of judges from the nations that had signed the Treaties agreeing to stop shipping slaves. So a Spanish ship, for example, would be tried by a Spanish and a British judge. After 1819, only vessels whose nationality could not be determined, or whose home countries were not represented by the Mixed Commissions, were tried at the Vice-Admiralty Court. (In 1847, for example, the Court tried ten vessels 'without colours or papers'.[13])

The effectiveness of the Courts is questioned by Capt. F.W. Butt-Thompson in his book *Sierra Leone*.[14] According to the Captain, the British government forgot to appoint a judge to the Vice-Admiralty Court until 1811, when the colony's Chief Justice reminded London of this omission. The Court remained understaffed for some years and its work was 'always difficult, and made more so by the questioning and the upsetting of its decisions by the Lords Commissioners at Home ... Doubts as to legality of the Court seemed always in the minds of the Commissioners' (p. 151).

Some of those appointed to serve on the Mixed Commission Courts were, Butt-Thompson argues, in sympathy with their captured compatriots. He quotes Capt. Denman of the Squadron explaining that such Commissioners had their captured mariners released from prison 'at the earliest available opportunity'. Slaving vessels were sold at auction – very frequently to slavers. Their contents, Denman reported, after it was decided to break up captured slavers, were sold – again frequently to slave dealers. The contents included not only 'trade goods', but guns, cannon and gunpowder (p. 158).

The numbers of vessels captured was a very small proportion of those involved in the trade, as evidenced by the many thousands of enslaved women, men and children landed in the Americas. It was not until 1844, when the Squadron was much increased that the numbers captured rose rapidly. Between 1819 and 1845 a total of 528 ships were taken before the Freetown Mixed Commission Court. If the vessel was condemned by the Court, the 'Liberated Africans' were set ashore in Freetown. A total of 65,000 were emancipated by the Freetown Court. The Africans had to stay on board before and during the court hearing. If the vessel was not condemned they were shipped to their lives of enslavement.[15]

This low number of vessels caught is due to many reasons, including:

- the poor quality of the British ships;
- the 'aimless methods adopted by the officers';
- the impossibility of patrolling thousands of miles of coastline;
- the lack of international treaties permitting the Royal Navy to stop *all* slavers.[16]

The success of the avoidance tactics used by the slave traders also resulted in low numbers of captures. These tactics included carrying multiple 'papers of convenience', not only to evade capture, but to avoid paying import duties. Historian George Brooks explained how the Americans did it: 'they carried double papers, so they could appear British in British ports, American in American ports, thus evading duties in both.... Usually this was achieved by partnerships between British and American merchants.'[17] Many ships of other nations used this tactic. Others pretended to be what they were not by sailing 'ostensibly as licit traders to St. Thomas and Prince's Island', according to one Squadron captain. These islands in the Bight of Biafra had little to offer in terms of 'legitimate' trade. They served as entrepôts for the 'trade goods' used to purchase slaves on the mainland. Or to Madeira, as another captain explained: the British Consul there for some time was quite amenable to certifying that British vessels had offloaded their slaving cargo and turned a blind eye to the vessel reshipping the same goods to West Africa.[18]

Eventually further treaties were signed with other countries, permitting the 'arrest' of vessels only equipped (known as the 'equipment clause') for trading in slaves, but with no slaves actually on board. (Some of these treaties are listed in Appendix 1.) This resulted in more ships being condemned and put an end to the murderous practice of slaver captains hurling slaves overboard in order not to be caught with them on board!

While one may accept that Britain was short of ships during the war with Napoleon, why it took so many years for Britain to send a larger, but still inadequate squadron to enforce its much-publicised anti-slavery stance has to be questioned. Even Lord Palmerston remarked on their hopelessness in 1862: 'if there was a particularly old, slow going tub in the navy, she was sure to be sent to the coast of

Africa to try to catch the fast sailing American clippers'.[19] And why were the ships often ill-equipped to deal with the slaving coast's difficult-to-enter river estuaries which made ideal slave-trade posts? The Gallinas, for example, was described by slave-trader Conneau as 'the notorious slave mart ... a river whose entrance and interior is not navigable but to boats and small crafts.'[20]

Some of the African Squadron commanders were exceptional men, wholly dedicated to their task and resentful of the government's lack of support. Captains Denman and Matson were two such men.[21] Captain Joseph Denman was the son of Chief Justice Lord Denman, an outspoken abolitionist. His son was an assiduous chaser of slaving vessels, and sometimes a very frustrated one. He could only chase after vessels loaded with slaves or blockade the mouths of rivers in order to capture loaded slavers when they tried to sneak out. But when he ran out of provisions and had to return to Freetown, or the winds drove him off, or on exceptionally dark nights, the slavers quickly escaped. In 1840 his patience ran out. Having been instructed to rescue a woman and her child who had been abducted from Sierra Leone and taken to the Gallinas, he went ashore and persuaded 'Chief Siacca' (or Siaka) to sign a treaty to abolish the trade in slaves throughout his kingdom. Denman removed 841 slaves and burnt the barracoons (holding prisons) to the ground. Captains Nurse, Matson and Foote followed in their colleague's 'footsteps' and burnt down barracoons along the coast, liberating about 2000 slaves who had been held in them. The owners of the barracoons sued the captains for a total of about £630,000 for compensation for loss of property. The cases dragged on for eight years as different British governments took opposing views as to the legality of the captains' actions. Eventually it was found that Denman (and the others) could not be the 'subject of a suit for damages'.[22]

Questions and issues relating to the Squadron

- The 1807 Act offered bounties or 'head money' for each African liberated.[23] The officers received the largest share, but even the 'ordinary seamen' received one share of the net proceeds. Senior officers could get rich: for example, the Commander of HMS *Waterwitch* received £2629 between 1839 and 1843 – that's over £120,000 in 2005.[24] *Why did this inducement have to be offered?* Was the

Royal Navy opposed to the 1807 Act? Are we to believe the captain
of the US brig *Dolphin*, who reported that when he suggested to
an African Squadron captain that he should blockade the entrance
to the River Gallinas, the response was:

> this is an unhealthy climate; we come out to take prize money; if a
> slaver is captured without her cargo, she is sent to Sierra Leone where
> the expense of condemnation amounts to nearly the whole value of the
> vessel, which is the perquisite of those in the employ of the Govern-
> ment.... We get nothing. If we capture a vessel with slaves on board,
> we receive £5 sterling a head for each of them.[25]

If this was a commonly held view, then did the Squadron attempt to capture all the slaving ships it caught sight of? There
have been allegations that they were not keen to chase after
empty slaving vessels as they only received prize money for
liberating slaves.[26]

- Where did the prize money come from? Some came from the
  profit from auctioning the condemned vessels and their contents.
  In 1835 a public outcry against this in England provoked the
  colonial government into agreeing to scuttle the vessels. This
  was not always carried out. Most of the slavers had been sold,
  and continued to be sold, to slave traders. Leading slave trader
  Pedro Blanco's English agent in Freetown was as happy to buy
  condemned vessels as he was to buy the 'trade goods' in them. The
  agent shipped the goods to Blanco at the 'Gallinas on an English
  cutter'. The Governor stated that this was not illegal.[27] Another
  dealer in the enslaved, Theophilus Conneau (or Canot), recorded
  not only how easy it was, but how the crews of the condemned
  vessels were re-employed:

> at Sierra Leone in 1829, prize vessels were publicly sold and fitted out
> (for the trade in the enslaved) with very little trouble for the coast of
> Africa. Availing myself of the nonchalance of the Government officers,
> I fitted my schooner in perfect order to take a cargo of slaves immedi-
> ately on leaving port. My crew consisted of prisoners from the prizes
> and men of all nations; however, I took good care that my officers
> should be Spaniards.[28]

- Not all naval captains were averse to making a little extra money
  to add to their bounties: in 1827 a condemned vessel was bought by

'the commander of a British Squadron in West Africa'; he sailed it
to Cape Verde, where he sold it to a Portuguese slave trader for
$5000 (c. £50,000 in 2005).[29] *Did other captains behave like this?*
- As the Royal Navy could not 'sit around' awaiting the decisions of
  the Vice-Admiralty or the Mixed Commission Court, the crews
  needed an agent to collect their prize money once the condemned
  vessel had been sold. Zachary Macaulay, ex-governor of Freetown,
  became this agent – for a large fee, of course.[30] Perhaps because
  he foresaw the enormous increase in trade given Freetown's new
  position as a Royal Naval port, he had set up a company together
  with his nephew Thomas Babington to trade with Freetown. The
  company rapidly became the largest in the colony, partly from
  provisioning the army and the navy now stationed there – and
  as prize agents. Some of the prize vessels, probably the best, the
  most modern, were bought by Macaulay and sailed to the UK,
  where they were 'registered and sold at a large profit'.[31] *Profit that
  went into professed abolitionist Macaulay's pockets.*

    Among Macaulay & Babington's exports was timber, probably
felled by slaves. Is it unfair to presume that the 'gold and other
produce' exported by the firm was also slave-produced? By 1823,
when he estimated that his private fortune had reached £100,000
(over £5 million in 2005), Macaulay retired to 'devote himself
entirely to anti-slavery work'.[32] Clearly, obtaining vast profits from
the labour of slaves and from the sale of slaving vessels was seen
by Macaulay and his anti-slavery colleagues in a different light
from participating in the actual trade in the enslaved. *But it was
still profit from slavery.* And how are we to see the profits from the
fees collected on the crews' prize moneys? Isn't that also amassing
wealth from the trade in slaves?
- And what happened to the Liberated Africans on board the slavers?
  Some died in the monstrous conditions aboard the vessels while
  they were being sailed back to Sierra Leone.[33] Others died on
  board while in port, awaiting the Court's decision. For example,
  a medical officer visiting the London-based slaver *Elizabeth*, found
  that of 602 slaves shipped, 155 had already died and the rest were
  suffering from opthalmia, a disease causing blindness common in
  the filthy ships' holds. On another vessel 127 died. One estimate
  is that 25 per cent of slaves died before they were allowed off

the vessels.[34] Couldn't another system have been devised which preserved rather than destroyed lives?

• What was done with those who survived? They were supported by the British government for a year, after which they were 'apprenticed', at first to local farmers and traders, in the military (the 'West India Regiment' and the 'West Africa Corps'), and a few were recruited by the Royal Navy.[35] As the numbers grew, 35,850 were 'recruited' as 'apprentices' for the West Indies. What this actually meant and how they were used remains a subject of debate.[36] Naturally this led to criticism by other Europeans powers, who claimed that the main reason for liberating the enslaved was to provide labour for British West Indian colonies where slavery had been abolished in 1838.

A few did not escape re-enslavement. Some of the Liberated managed to return to their homelands.[37] Of those who remained in the colony – sadly – a few became slave traders. But most became traders and farmers – thus the colony needed more and more land to sustain itself. But how was this to be acquired? In most of Africa the notion of *selling* land was unknown: usually land was held by the village chiefs who allocated it to families as it was needed. Conflicts therefore soon arose over land usage: the Africans believed they had permitted temporary usage, whereas the British in charge of Freetown thought they could do whatever they pleased with the land. This, and the many settlers in the colony created problems, which, one could argue, remain there to this day.[38]

The ongoing export of slaves

The trade in slaves escalated, both externally and internally. As indicated above and in previous chapters, traders found a multitude of ways to circumvent the laws and the treaties and the African Squadron. The external trade was stimulated by the need for labour on the slave-worked plantations in the Americas, both North and South, and on the islands, as their exports to Europe grew. As historian David Northrup noted, 'so long as an external demand for slaves existed, it was possible and profitable to sell them'.[39] The *West India Reporter* for January 1830 noted that 'wars on the coast of Africa have been purposely excited to supply the demand for captives' (p. 205). 'To catch slaves is the first thought of every chief in the interior; hence fights and slavery impoverish the land', wrote explorer John Speke in 1863, while David Livingstone, also in East Africa, believed that the slavery 'pressed people into accepting demeaning forms of protection'.[40]

The internal trade in slaves was stimulated by the expansion in the export of African produce. Though gold production also grew, the main increase was in palm oil, a natural and locally used product, normally grown by small farmers. As external demand for the oil increased, the chiefs and merchants who had grown rich on the trade in human beings invested in setting up plantations. Well-practised in obtaining slaves, they now captured them for their own use. Land had to be cleared, the palms planted, the nuts gathered and the oil produced. Much of the actual production work was done by enslaved women.[41]

These facts were brought to the notice of the British public and Parliament in many publications, some by African Squadron captains. For example, Captain Colomb, who had been in charge of HMS *Dryad* of the Africa Squadron, wrote that

> The disease from which Africa suffers ... is the slave trade; that part of it believed to be most agonising, is the interior slave trade.... What is the painful yet undoubted fact about the West Coast, now that the export trade is suppressed? It is that the articles exported are slave-produced, that a raging slave trade sweeps over the interior, and that furious wars everywhere surround the British settlements [which are] one of the instruments employed in that suppression [of the slave trade].... Take Gambia in 1865 ... cultivation of ground nuts by slaves for export ... Wars constantly taking place between the natives, the prisoners are made slaves, and are either retained to work for their masters, or are sold to other parts of the country for the same purpose.... [It is the] same on the Gold Coast and in Lagos. Where there is most commerce there is the most slavery.[42]

The British purchasers of palm oil and palm kernels wanted to pay the lowest possible price, so naturally they did not question the status of the workers producing them.

It was not only the importers of slave-grown African produce who reaped handsome profits from this trade. Naturally those manufacturing exports both for the purchase of the enslaved and for sale to African merchants also profited. The exports were mainly cotton cloth, tobacco, rum and the guns necessary for procuring the slaves. The numbers of guns exported reached 35,017 in 1825. From 1827 until 1850 the combined value of guns and gunpowder exported never dropped below about £74,000 a year and reached £136,383 in 1849.[43] Another major export was 'rum and spirits': the amount exported rose from 109,205 gallons in 1827 to 310,047 gallons in 1841. In 1844 the Emir of Nupe wrote to Bishop Samuel Crowther that 'rum has ruined my country; it has ruined my people. It has made them become mad.' So large was this export trade that special distilleries were established in Liverpool for supplying ships bound for Africa with 'trade gin'. How many Liverpudlians, and other distillery workers, I wonder, earned their living by manufacturing gin?[44]

Slave exports from Nigeria

Nigeria had been the home of many peoples, speaking many languages and living in vastly different social structures. Some of these were empires, others were kingdoms; some peoples lived in clan or village groups, electing their leaders. Some societies were patrilineal, meaning inheritance passed through the males, whereas others were matrilineal. In some kingdoms the status of king or ruler passed from clan to clan in regular rotation, while in others it could be passed down from father to son.

Britain had been regularly trading for slaves, gold and tropical products along the coast since the seventeenth century. After 1807 there was a slow growth in 'legitimate' trade in some areas. Internal warfare, usually fought for the purpose of acquiring slaves, impeded this trade in 'legitimate' goods. British traders sought government support to remove the impediment. So, to 'bring peace', Britain in 1861 seized Lagos, deposed its king and annexed some of the Yoruba lands. British fear of French and German expansionism led to 'acquisition' of more lands, and then to the creation of the Niger Coast Protectorate in 1885.[45]

Encouraged by this, the following year most of the British traders amalgamated to form the Royal Niger Company, to expand and defend their interests on the River Niger. This resulted in further British conquest: Yorubaland was taken over, King Jaja of Opobo (who had almost succeeded in outwitting the British traders) was removed in 1887; the ruler of Itsekiri and the capital of the Bida Kingdom were destroyed in 1894; and Benin was conquered in 1897.[46] The Protectorate of the Oil Rivers was proclaimed in 1891 and that of Southern Nigeria in 1900. Slowly Igboland in the East was also conquered. The Royal Niger Company's rule was taken over and the Protectorate of Northern Nigeria was established in 1900. The caliphate of Sokoto was conquered in 1906.[47] Northern and Southern Nigeria were merged into 'Nigeria' in 1914.

It has been estimated that the average number of enslaved women, men and children exported after 1807 from this area was between 12,650 and 16,200 annually. The Bight of Biafra was a major export area until the 1830s, when the presence of the African Squadron began to have some effect. Treaties were signed with local exporters by the Squadron captains. These can be seen as bribery, no different from the compensation offered to British slave holders in the West Indian colonies. For example, Captain E. Rodney of the African Squadron offered $2000 yearly for five years to King Pepprell (or Pepple) of Bonny in 1848 to stop the export of slaves. The King accepted the treaty. Three years later a similar treaty was concluded with King Amacree (or Amachree) of New Calabar, but he was only promised $1000 for three years. Somewhat peeved, King Amacree continued selling slaves until 1853, when on capturing yet another slaver at New Calabar the British refused to hand over this compensation and threatened him with destruction. The King conceded.[48]

Slave exports from the Gold Coast

To understand British complicity in slavery in the Gold Coast, we have to look at some aspects of the history of what became the independent country of Ghana in 1957.

As in Nigeria, what became the British colony of the Gold Coast was the home of many peoples, languages and social and political structures. For example, in what is now known as the Northern Region, there were – and are – at least 21 different peoples. Kingdoms expanded, disintegrated; peoples merged, migrated. But 'in the traditions of all these ethnic groups, slave trading and raiding for slaves are not mentioned', according to historian Benedict G. Der.[49] But the North became an entrepôt for slave dealing and was eventually seen as nothing but a source of labour – men and women enslaved, 'contracted', 'pawned' (supposedly given as security for loans or debts), 'recruited', embezzled, exported.[50]

Initially slaves were brought to the Kingdom of Asante in central Gold Coast from the North and the East in exchange for gold and kola nuts. (Kola is a mild drug; many years later it became the base ingredient in 'Coca-Cola'.[51]) When it became sufficiently lucrative, the Asante supplemented their gold trade with the South by exporting slaves. Wealthier than many other kingdoms because of their tripartite trade, the Asante could buy more guns than their neighbours. This enabled them to conquer many 'polities' (peoples, nations) to the north, from whom they extracted slaves as tribute. In the South, where they wanted to control the trade in slaves with the coastal European forts they attempted to conquer the coastal peoples. As the trade grew, so did wars, kidnappings and pawning.

The coast of the 'Gold Coast' was literally strewn with the trading forts of the Portuguese, the Dutch, the Danes and the British. Erected partly because of the rivalry and hostility between these European nations, the forts also served as holding prisons for the enslaved awaiting transport to their new worlds. The cannon at these forts, as I saw, face outwards, towards approaching shipping. Clearly rival, competitive Europeans had much to protect from each other: it has been estimated that about 32,000 ounces of gold were exported to Europe every year from 1651 to 1850. From 1690 until 1807, about 20 per cent – or about half a million – of the total number of enslaved Africans bought and transported by British traders were obtained from the Gold Coast. As much of this Coast did not offer the camouflage in river estuaries necessitated by the patrolling African Squadron, after 1807 the trade in slaves from the Gold Coast was reduced considerably – to an estimated 2000 in 1815.[52]

From 1750 British trade was in the hands of and governed by the African Company of Merchants. After the official abolition of the trade in the enslaved, the Company fell into debt, which demonstrates both how important the trade in slaves had been to them and that abolition along this stretch of the coast was effective. In 1822 the British government took over ruling the British 'possessions' of Cape Coast and Accra, but abandoned Whydah (or Ouidah), a major slaving port to the east, incorporated into the kingdom of Dahomey.

After the death of Governor M'Carthy in the 1824 war against the
expanding central kingdom of Asante, the British government decided to abandon the Gold Coast. Protests from the African Company
of Merchants, of whom Matthew Forster was the most vociferous,
resulted in the trading forts being returned to the Merchants in 1828,
with a subsidy of £4000 per annum. The Merchants created a council
to rule over themselves and the Africans and 'Euro-Africans' settled
in and near the British trading forts. In 1840 Dr Robert Madden, appointed by the British government to ascertain the state of the settlements, toured the West Coast. His accusation of British merchants'
ongoing complicity in the illegal trade in slaves was questioned by a
Parliamentary Select Committee (see Chapter 6). Nevertheless the
government resumed control in 1843 by appointing a governor. This
official was to preside over a council, elected by the resident British
merchants. These resident merchants were usually the agents of the
merchants in Britain, who had been so strident in their questioning
of Dr Madden at the Select Committee.

The British government – that is, the Council of the Merchants
– attempted to bring local chiefs along the coast under its influence,
and restrict commerce to themselves through bribery. For example,
in 1843 Foreign Secretary Lord Aberdeen advised that 'it will be
expedient to conclude with the Native Chiefs of Bimbia a Treaty
… the prevention of the slave trade, and a *clause for preventing the
Cession to other natives of exclusive Commercial advantages prejudicial to
Great Britain....* [I]t is proposed to give a present to the Chiefs in
token of friendship and in consideration of the conclusion of the
Treaty.... The value of this present might properly be two hundred
and fifty pounds sterling'[53] (*c.* £14,000 in 2005). After obtaining a
number of such treaties, a 'Bond' was signed with the rulers of the
coastal peoples in 1844 by which they accepted British jurisdiction
and the prohibition on exporting slaves. (Domestic slavery remained
untouched. See below.)

After considerable pressure by Matthew Forster in London (see
Chapter 3), Britain purchased the Danish forts in 1850. This extended
British power to the east of the Volta estuary, where trading in slaves
was common. There was no ensuing reduction in the trade in slaves
from the Volta region.[54] The Dutch forts were acquired in 1872 – in
exchange for Sumatra and Java. (*It is difficult for me to find the words to*

describe these 'purchases'. How could Europeans look upon millions of people and their lands as their 'possessions' which could be bought, sold, exchanged?) Britain formally established the Gold Coast Colony and Protectorate in 1874 and prohibited the buying, selling and 'pawning' of people. The Ordinance (i.e., local law) was ignored. As late as 1928 – the year slavery was nominally abolished – it was reported to the Colonial Office in London that slave dealing was ongoing.[55]

Some Africans were bewildered by the change in British policy towards slave trading. For example, the Asantehene (Asante king) asked: 'But if they think it is bad now, why did they think it was good before?' and continued to encourage slave trading in his kingdom.[56] After six wars, the British managed to conquer the Asante and enter Kumasi, the capital, in February 1874. The Asantehene was forced to sign a treaty, giving up any claims to the coastal forts and territories, and to his vassal states. The British thought this would be the end of Asante empire-building, but on his accession King Prempeh I slowly began to resuscitate his country and mobilise his troops. The British asked him to accept 'Protectorate' status. The King refused. The British invaded the kingdom, burnt down the capital city of Kumasi and looted it of all its treasures. The Asantehene and many chiefs were sent into exile in the Seychelles. But the Asante still owed the 'fine' imposed on them by Britain – a mere 50,000 ounces of gold. Britain demanded payment and the acceptance of Protectorate status. Led by Queen Mother Yaa Asantewa the Asante attacked the visiting British governor and an approaching Gold Coast troop of 250 soldiers, armed with some Maxim (machine) guns and a cannon. The troops were soon augmented by over 4000 equally well equipped men from the West African Frontier Force from Southern Nigeria, the West African Regiment from Sierra Leone, Central African Rifles and eventually even a Sikh troop. In October 1900 the Asante, probably armed with nothing more than the 'inferior smooth-bored guns' usually sold to Africans, surrendered. Yaa Asantewa and her most senior chiefs were sent to join Prempeh I on the Seychelles. The kingdom was declared a British colony in 1901. The territories north of the kingdom were added to the colony of the Gold Coast in the same year.[57]

Yet neither the conquest of the Asante, nor the extension of colonial status up to the border of what is now Burkina Faso, resulted in a reduction of slavery. All the historians of the Gold Coast note the undiminished domestic slavery and the ongoing export of slaves. As late as the early twentieth century, there was slave raiding in the north-east and north-west and well-documented markets for slaves inland at Salaga, Kintempo and Kete Krachi (among others).[58] Travellers estimated the numbers of slaves sold at Salaga as between 15,000 and 20,000 annually. From Salaga slaves destined for export were taken down the Volta river, to be sold at Keta or Ada at the Volta estuary. Historian Trevor Getz believes that as late as the 1890s slaves were sold in Accra. Reports were sent to the government in London, but there was never much effort put into suppressing this trade. Slaves were also exported to other coastal markets not under British control. Local governors were not very concerned: for example Governor Winniett was told in 1863 that slaves were being exported to Dahomey, but he ignored the report. As did London.[59]

Who were the traders in the enslaved? Quite possibly some were sold by the agents of the three major British companies in the Gold Coast: Forster & Smith, Hutton & Co. and F. & L. Swanzy, as well as British African (often of mixed descent) traders such as Robert Bannerman and W. Lutterodt, both of whom had been noted slave traders on the Coast.[60] Whether Forster and the other major companies were actually involved in selling slaves, or simply in furnishing the dealers with 'trade goods' used to pay for slaves, is not known. How, for example, are we to classify the British firm of Hutton, which set up a 'factory' in 1837 at Whydah, the notorious slave trading port in Dahomey? In his evidence to Parliament in 1842 W.M. Hutton said that 'slavers paid with bills drawn on London houses … [c]ould be used to purchase produce elsewhere on the Coast.' How could he have known this unless he was involved? Hutton was replaced by that other large British firm, F. & L. Swanzy, in 1868.[61]

Domestic slavery

Slaves for domestic use were captured similarly to those who were exported. Some were 'pawned' by debtors. As usually the interest on the debt was increased annually, not many 'pawns' were ever redeemed. As late as 1927 the District Commissioner for Ghana's Northern Territory described the slave raiding taking place there: the district was a 'permanent reservoir for slave hunting', he reported.[62]

The exact meaning of the status of a 'slave' varied according to time and place. In some societies there was a distinction made between newly captured slaves and those born in the society. In some areas slaves were permitted to marry into the family (or clan) that captured them and became absorbed in the main group. In other areas slaves were housed in separate villages under a headman who ensured that they fulfilled their duties. In most African societies the enslaved could improve their economic and even their social status, while remaining 'slaves'. The work done by slaves depended on their masters and their status: there were miners, agricultural labourers, traders, craftsmen, porters, domestic servants and recruits into the ruler's police and military. It was enslaved women who did much of the work of actually producing the palm oil. According to historian David Northrup, it was only among the Igbo people in eastern Nigeria that there was a 'close approximation of New World plantation slavery' in terms of harshness of conditions and the attitude of the masters, who 'held the power of life and death over their slaves, who were regarded as mere chattels'.[63]

All contemporary observers reported that the number of domestic slaves being used by African producers and traders increased with the escalation of the export of primary products. The export of palm oil increased from 1179 tons in 1811 to 10,890 tons by 1832 and 39,030 tons in 1855.[64] Though some was grown by farming families, *what increase in domestic slave labour did this necessitate? How many people in Britain (and elsewhere) grew rich on the trade in palm oil and the oil itself, as well as on other slave-produced African products? How many were employed in Britain whose jobs depended on this trade?*

Slavery flourished and Britain profited from it. According to that most unusually honest and outspoken British civil servant, Sir Alan Pim, 'in 1871 the British government admitted that "To slave labour we owe the flourishing commerce of all our West African colonies. Of the £1.05 million worth of produce shipped not more than £1,000 is the product of free labour and European merchandise is all carried into the interior by slaves."'[65]

Domestic slavery in Nigeria

It was slaves who worked on the farms and in the mines and it was slaves who carried or paddled the goods to the coast to the waiting European vessels. As about 226,000 tons of palm oil were exported from this section of the Coast, a large number of slaves were required.[66] In the 1850s, Consul Campbell admitted that domestic slavery was practised on a 'large scale' and estimated that about 90 per cent of the 25,000 people living in Lagos were slaves.[67] The leaders of the 1857 Niger Expedition reported that British subjects in Lagos, including three consular employees, owned and dealt in slaves.[68] Urban populations grew in other towns: for example, Old Calabar's population grew from about 3800 in 1805 to over 10,000 in the mid-1840s. All these urbanites, free and enslaved, required food. So the urban hinterlands became food-producing areas – naturally, mainly worked by slaves.

There were major political consequences to this increase in producing for export. For example, as the trade in palm oil increased, so did the disputes among the indigenous and foreign traders. Britain sent a consul to calm things down – and, as noted earlier, he ended up seizing Lagos, deposing its king and annexing some of the Yoruba lands in the hinterland, thus creating an official British colony.

In 1901 laws ending the legal status of slavery and prohibiting enslavement were promulgated in both Northern and Southern Nigeria. Their interpretation is somewhat questionable.[69] Lord Lugard, governor of Northern Nigeria, made the ex-slaves work for their own manumission, which could, of course, lead to prolonged demands for unpaid labour. Lugard's House Rule Proclamation also prolonged slavery by another name, as did his Master and Servant Proclamation. (These 'Houses' were local trading associations using slaves.) In the South the 'freed' men were forbidden to leave the 'canoe houses' where they were kept in perpetuity. Many slaves fled their masters, but Lugard's vagrancy laws discouraged running away. The House Rule Proclamation was not repealed until 1915, after much campaigning by the Lagos Auxiliary of the Anti-Slavery Society.[70]

Slavery did not stop. In 1933 the government amended the regulations regarding the use of 'political labour' to conform with the Geneva Convention on Forced Labour. The use of forced labour was made illegal except for transport and 'personal services to chiefs'. I presume the forced labour used to build the Baro-Kano and Eastern railways was classified as legal 'transport' usage. As late as the 1930s, Igbo children were being 'pawned' to raise money to pay the poll tax.

And though 'pawning' was made illegal in 1938, court prosecutions were noted as late as 1949. The use of 'political' (i.e. forced) labour was common up to and including World War II, and prosecutions for pawning continued into the late 1940s.[71]

On the Gold Coast

Producing gold and kola required a large number of slaves, for production and for transport. When the British demand for palm oil (and subsequently other export crops such as cocoa and rubber) increased, so did the use of domestic slave labour. Much of the food for the new merchant class, and their workers, was also grown by slaves. Work on the land was so closely associated with slavery that Rev. Schrenk, teaching at the Basel Mission in the North-East, remarked in 1875 that his pupils 'objected to any form of agricultural work because it was associated with slavery'.[72]

Domestic slaves were also used as carriers of goods to the markets. For example, a member of the Niger Expedition noted that the 'English cloth, guns, rum, planks, beams' were carried from a village to the Cape Coast market, eight miles away, 'on the heads of slaves'. But that was a short journey compared with that of the Accani traders, who 'loaded their purchases into bundles which the slaves carried on their heads.... From the sea they went to Assingrad ... five days journey from Cape Coast, but since the slaves were heavily loaded they could not travel more than ... about 23 miles in a day.'[73]

To avoid strictures by the government, these slaves were officially called 'pawns' – that is, men supposedly paying off debts by working for a supposedly fixed term.[74] Though 'pawning' had been made a felony in 1892, it continued into the 1930s.[75]

When in 1843 the British government made it illegal to 'carry away [people] to be dealt with as slaves', and for Britons to hold slaves, the Governor gained exclusion for the Gold Coast and even returned runaway slaves to their owners! He argued that liberation of slaves 'would endanger the government's own economic projects and threatened to alienate the powerful economic and political elites within the Gold Coast'.[76]

In 1851, British merchants pleaded with the Governor to help them, as 'these Euro-African and African traders held an unfair advantage over their European competitors through their access to slave labour',

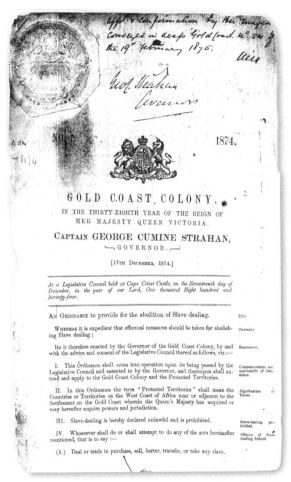

1874 Act for the Abolition of Slavery on the Gold Coast

which had been forbidden to them in 1843. African merchants, historian Susan Kaplow has argued, bought slaves with their profits as the slaves could not be seized by Europeans to pay off their debts. The merchants were often bankrupted by the commissions charged by the European traders for both exports and imports. Other historians point out that to avoid censure some of the British merchants had given their slaves to their African wives: for example, Mr Swanzy, one of the protestors, had given his slaves to his wife Kate, as had John Marmon, another British merchant in Accra.[77]

The Governor responded by declaring illegal the holding of slaves by 'educated natives'. This led to further protests, for example by the paramount chief at Cape Coast, who threatened to withdraw the (slave) labour he had promised for one of the Governor's construction projects. The Euro-African traders also protested, resulting in the Governor abandoning the enforcement of his own decision.

It was not only the government's construction projects that used slave labour. The governors 'borrowed' slaves for the Militia, paying their wages to their owners. From 1858 chiefs were required to produce 'free' recruits for the military – but how free were these men? A letter sent to Dr Madden in 1840 by the 'Militia of Cape Coast Castle' had described the conditions of service (I have not changed the spelling of the original):

> We were supposed to serve for one year ... and paid us very little to matain ourselves and now ... we serves niene years and three months ... They make ùs carry lymn and stones ... we refused, and they placed us in gaol for three months and a half, and chain some of us, and flog some of us and charge our wages to...

The men charged that they were 'still carrying stones' and cleaning the streets 'while we are a militia to protect the town'. These charges and others eventually resulted in the recruitment of slaves and pawns being nominally stopped in 1863. Yet there are reports that purchases of men for the 'Hausa Constabulary at Cape Coast' continued into the late 1880s. Later various forms of 'recruitment' were practised for manpower for the West African Frontier Force.[78]

When slavery was nominally abolished in British 'possessions' along the coast in 1874, though some Gold Coasters had argued for abolition, quite naturally slave holders asked for compensation. After all, Gold Coasters claimed, 'slavery was introduced on this Coast and for the gain of the West India planters – they were compensated for their property'. Why shouldn't they be treated just as well? Colonial Secretary Lord Carnarvon agreed, and even proposed including compensation for 'pawns' in the plans he suggested to Governor Strahan. But the Governor advised that the defeat of the Asante was sufficient 'compensation' as it freed the 'inhabitants of the Protectorate from defeat and disaster'. The Secretary of State did not argue with Strahan. Gold Coasters continued to press for compensation, and the government continued to refuse to pay, for the next twenty years or so.[79]

Domestic slavery continued in the twentieth century, though usually under other names. In the Salaga district instances have been found of the British Commissioner preventing slaves from leaving their masters in 1904.[80] 'Recruitment' of labour was introduced, for example for the much-hated underground work in the gold mines. Chiefs in the Northern Region were simply told how many men they had to produce; they were given 'head-money' for each 'recruit', and fined if they did not produce the number demanded. Similar techniques were used to 'recruit' labour for railway construction in 1908. The men could be flogged and taken to court if they deserted before their 12-month contract had been worked. (Of course, most could not have read the contracts, even if they existed!) This recruitment of labour by the payment of 'head money' was reintroduced in the 1920s by the mine owners: in some government reports these men were called 'indentured labourers'.[81]

There is ample evidence of the sale of enslaved adults and children, and of domestic slavery in the fast-deteriorating files at the National Archives in Tamale. For example, in his 'Informal Diary' for 1919–20 the District Officer in Navrongo-Zouaragu notes the recruitment of labour by private individuals, and his own despatch of labourers obtained from local chiefs. He appears to exclude himself from his observation that 'chiefs regard a request for labour as an order to be obeyed at once.... Through the chiefs one will have extortion, enforcement as with the recruits for the Regiment.'[82]

In the same period Governor Guggisberg introduced what he termed 'communal labour' for railway building: each district was assigned a quota of men it had to produce. One Provincial Commissioner explained that 'Commissioners persuade the Chiefs to endeavour to find labour, the Chiefs look upon it as an order and tell their people to come forward and volunteer for work.... The boys ... do not appear to realize they are required unless ordered.' By 1925 the 'head money' paid by the mines' recruiters reached £50. These forms of labour 'recruitment' were practised until 1950.[83]

The Gold Coast government of course knew about the sale and use of slaves. So did the British government, as the Colonial Office received reports about it.[84] Why did the British administrators on the Gold Coast and in London ignore the use of slaves in the colony and not enforce the many laws prohibiting their sale and use? It is worth reproducing the government document of 1873 which explained that

> it must be admitted that to slave labour we owe our flourishing com-
> merce with Africa … [O]f 17,882 ounces of gold dust sent to England,
> probably not one ounce was obtained by free labour. The European
> produce is carried from the coast by slaves. It is not unlikely that
> for some time to come the growth of our commerce with Africa will
> strengthen domestic slavery instead of diminishing it.[85]

Besides the desire for the cheapest possible export product, other reasons suggested by available documents for this appalling non-interference are:[86]

- Fear that trade could be affected if carriers of goods from the north, once they arrived on the Coast, claimed their freedom.
- Fear of 'disturbances' if there was any meaningful attempt to put down domestic slavery, on whose labour the wealthier Africans now depended.
- The supply of labour from the Northern Territory overrode all other considerations: the 'main aim of British officials in the north was to develop and maintain the free flow of general trade whether by land or down the River Volta. Administrators would not, therefore, have jeopardised that trade by intervening in every small case involving slave-trading or use of slaves as porters by major African merchants.'[87]
- The British merchants wanted their imports (whether gold or agricultural produce) at the lowest possible price, so they exerted pressure to prevent 'any kind of radical interference with Gold Coast slavery'. But, when it *was* in their perceived interest, they even pressed for war: for example, Colonial Secretary Earl Grey admitted in an internal minute of July 1848, referring to the expenses of a military expedition against a western Gold Coast state: 'Mr Forster, like all other merchants, has no objection to urging the Government to undertake warlike operations whenever it is fancied their own interests can be promoted by doing so.'[88]

The slave castle on the island of Goree on the west coast of Africa

- The British government was also profiting from slave labour: for example, by 1838 it was receiving £17,102 in import duties on palm oil (*c.* £835,000 in 2005).
- Especially after the Berlin Conference of 1896, which delineated 'spheres of influence', the British were 'careful not to take any actions which might drive the Asante into the hands of a rival colonial power'. (This meant, for example, returning runaway slaves if they could not prove they had been cruelly treated.[89])

In 1926 the League of Nations discussed the use of 'forced labour' and 'reached an understanding that whether used for private gain or public purpose, [it] created "conditions analogous to slavery"'. The League asked the International Labour Organisation to investigate. The ILO did so and proposed the eradication of such labour at a conference in 1930. Most interestingly, 63 nations, including France, Belgium and Portugal, abstained from voting. *Britain voted in favour, but did not abolish forced labour, as outlined above.*[90]

A.R. Slater, the Colonial Secretary, was concerned about the situation in the North of Ghana and the requirement to report to the League of Nations. In 1927 he discussed the enslavement of prisoners of war taken in local wars and then asked: 'Please refer to the S[ecretary for] N[ative] A[ffairs] for report as to whether we are in a position to assure the League of Nations if any question is raised that no vestiges of slavery remains in the Gold Coast. Legally, I imagine that Chapter VI of our Laws enables us to give this assurance, but in practice what is the position?'[91] In 1936, probably reacting to information reaching him, the Colonial Secretary warned all colonial governors that the 'continuance of any form of servitude ... cannot be acquiesced to indefinitely ... I request that Colonial Governments ... undertake a careful examination of the position'.[92] It was all to no avail, as there are reports in the National Archives in Ghana of 'pledging' for debts and of slave dealing the following year.[93]

There is considerable evidence in the files preserved at the National Archives in Tamale of ongoing domestic slavery. For example, in 1948 the sale of boys to work in Kumasi concerned the Acting Chief Commissioner sufficiently to put it on the agenda of the 'next session of the Northern Territories Council'.

Slave trade and/or legitimate trade

As some historians have argued that 'legitimate' trade supplanted the trade in slaves, it is important to examine this assertion.

'Badagry was struggling to develop a successful Atlantic palm oil trade while restructuring its commerce in slaves', according to a historian of this south-western Nigerian town. 'These merchants [in the palm oil trade] in certain cases were not averse to making some money on the side by dealing in slaves where the opportunity offered itself', according to economic historian A.G. Hopkins.[94] The trade in slaves and legitimate goods 'co-existed in harmony', according to another historian, and 'sustained each other'. They certainly did.

There are innumerable mentions in the contemporary accounts of 'legitimate' traders supplying goods to slave traders. As some of these have already been noted, let me give just two more examples, and then ask some questions.

Peter Leonard of the Royal Navy reported slave vessels

> in the rivers adjacent to [British] Sierra Leone, receiv[ing] considerable assistance in the pursuit of their illicit traffic from some of the merchants of this colony, in the shape of articles of trade and provisions.[95]

An American naval captain castigated not only Britain but his own country:

Some of the large English houses give orders ... not to traffic with
men reputed to be slave dealers; but if a purchaser comes with money
in hand, and he offers liberal prices, it requires a tenderer conscience
and sterner integrity than are usually met with on the coast of Africa,
to resist temptation. The merchant at home, possibly, is supposed to
know nothing of all this. It is quite an interesting moral question,
however, how far either Old or New England can be pronounced free
of guilt and the odium of the Slave Trade, while, with so little indi-
rectness, they both share the profits and contribute essential aid to its
prosecutors.[96]

Did the legitimate traders never trade in slaves? Imagine a slave
trader and a vessel awaiting legitimate cargo side by side in a 'port'
dealing in both forms of 'cargo'. The slave trader is loaded first, 'oblig-
ing the [other vessel] to remain in expensive and sickly indolence,
until the slavers and pirates are supplied with their unhappy victims'.
Would the 'legitimate' captains never succumb to (lucrative) temptation?[97] Especially those captains who were working for companies
owned by Liverpool (ex?)-slave traders such as John Tobin, Jonas
Bold and the Aspinalls, all well versed in the nefarious trade. For
example, Thomas Tobin, the younger son of John, had been a slave
trader in Bonny, and then combined supplying slavers with shipping
palm oil.[98] Awaiting cargo cannot be enjoyable when there is not
much entertainment to be found ashore, and perhaps even less so
when you know you could make much more money by 'going illegitimate'. And there is some evidence that this was so.[99]

According to historian Martin Lynn, oil and slave exports continued together until the 1850s from Lagos, Whydah and Badagry.
At least two of the Brazilian slave traders, Francisco Da Souza and
Domingo Martinez, sold both human beings and oil. Lynn believes
there was a 'symbiotic relationship between the exportation of slavery
and oil' with both using the same ports, the same West African areas
and the same traders.[100]

European goods were bought by Africans on the shore and carried
into the interior. How the goods were used there was of no interest
to anyone in Britain or in the British ports in West Africa.[101]

What is crucial for us to understand is that in Britain's colonies
in East and West Africa both the slave trade and slavery continued
well into the twentieth century and that Britain grew rich on the
profits derived from slave labour.

Effect on Africa[102]

The most immediate effects were the ongoing wars. To quote just a few contemporary descriptions:[103]

1825 The Commissioners at Sierra Leone, speaking of the great increase in the Slave Trade which had lately taken place on the coast between ... Sierra Leone and the Gallinas state that the increased demand for slaves consequent thereon was 'the cause of the destructive war which had raged in the Sherbro for the last eighteen months'.

1832 Slavery has produced the most baleful effects, causing anarchy, injustice and oppression to reign ... and exciting nation to rise against nation. All these evils, and many others, has slavery accomplished.

1833 The Sherbros ... had fallen on the unguarded [town of] Rokel ... The inhabitants who could not escape across the river to Magbelly perished, or were made slaves, and the town was reduced to ashes.

1837 The wars continue to rage with increasing fury. The whole line of the coast from the Gallinas to Grand Sesters is in a state of fearful commotion. Wars increase with the demand in slaves...

1839 There are ... five slavers in the Rio Pongas; the whole are under American colours, and it is likely ... the natives of that river will be at war again, as they were but a few months ago, all on account of these slavers, who are the instigators of all the disturbances and war on the coast.

1842 The land was desolate; only a few groups of huts remained amid the ruins of villages devastated by the cruel hand of inter-tribal war. The Egba guides were ever alert for the way was exposed to the attacks of a hostile tribe who were in league with the slavers of Lagos. These evil men lost no opportunity of waylaying small parties of Egbas and others who came within their reach ... they kidnapped and sold them as slaves to their Lagos allies. [Rev. Freeman is travelling from Freetown to Badagry][104]

1843 Even though Badagry had regained its independence, the people hardly dared venture unarmed across the lagoon before their town, lest they should be kidnapped by wandering bands of Dahomians.[105]

1848 At Badagry the difficulties were increasing. It was a veritable cockpit of rivalries – trading, tribal, and international. The townspeople were divided among themselves, and lived in constant fear of invasion by the people of Whyda or Porto Novo.[106]

1850s [I]t is utterly impossible to justify the wars by which the slave trade is supported. The annihilation of the Egbá [*sic*] nation is a case in point ... I have counted the sites of eighteen desolated towns within a distance of sixty miles between Badagry and Abbeokuta [*sic*] – the legitimate result of the slave trade. The whole Yóruba [*sic*] country is full of depopulated towns ... The Dahomy army killed and captured about 20,000 people ... The whole number of people destroyed in this section of the country, within the last fifty years, can not be less than five hundred thousand.[107]

1876 The Ashantees often sold into slavery a whole village full of his people, and no one's life or property was safe ... I myself saw the ruins of several large villages, and on inquiring the cause of the desolation the reply in every case was, 'the Ashantees sold all the inhabitants' [report of British government official visiting the King of Salaga].[108]

1886 It is heart-rending to think of the effects of this unfortunate war [the Yoruba wars which broke out in 1877].... Slaves who redeemed themselves sold by their former masters ... The distress in the country in general; not to talk of a few years ago, when salt and all articles of trade were scarce.[109]

The teasing out of the long-lasting effects of these ongoing and incessant wars and raids has not apparently intrigued many historians. Yet, as Benedict Der describes, the 'main effects of the slave trade on Northern Ghana (from where about half a million slaves were exported) were depopulation, devastation, insecurity and loss of life and property. Agriculture and the local arts were disrupted while people lived in constant fear for their lives or of the raiders. The long term effect of the slave trade ... was that it retarded development.' In 1899 Sir F.M. Hodgson, the Governor of the Gold Coast, was quite clear about the uses of the North: 'I would not at present spend upon the Northern Territories, – upon in fact the hinterland of the colony – a single penny more than is absolutely necessary for their suitable administration and the encouragement of the transit trade.' This led, in the opinion of economic historian Jacob Songsore, to 'the widespread use of unpaid labour for the construction of roads, rest houses and official buildings' and to the migration of labour to the South.[110]

But there were, of course, other consequences, with which a few historians are beginning to grapple. Was the power of kings affected by the increasing use of Western arms for attacking the less powerful in order to enslave them? Were more men enslaved in order to join kings' armies to fight such 'wars'? Trevor Getz believes that 'slavery was transformed.... [There were] diversifications of acquisition methods ... [and an] expansion of brutality and [of the] magnitude of the slave trade networks.... [The] legitimate trade stimulated the slave mode of production.' To this David Northrup adds that 'a greater market for foreign goods, an expansion of the economic infrastructure of markets, roads and currencies, and marked growth in the major trading communities of the hinterland and of the coast' were other effects.[111]

A new social class was formed of the merchants who dealt in both slaves and goods imported from Europe as well as produce exported to Europe. This resulted in the radical alteration of the traditional kinship obligations and networks.[112]

Whereas previous to the European trade indigenous slaves were used as local farm labour, now they were used more intensively, and often hundreds of miles from their homes. Perhaps the new African view of slaves, at least towards those sold to Europeans, is exemplified by a 'story' told in 1985 'along the lagoons of the republic of Bénin ... A slave was thrown into the sea and allowed to drown. Then cowries [the currency used to purchase goods and slaves] would grow on the body of the slave, and after a time the body would be dredged up and the cowries collected from it.'[113] So exporting slaves was acknowledged as the fastest route to wealth – and power.

Having been moved so far from their homelands, many of the enslaved could not return when freed. And many, after long periods of enslavement, would have become completely estranged from their homes. It was also quite possible that their lands in their native villages had been taken over. Or that the new, colonial system of government, often dependent on client chiefs and merchants, would not recognise their claims. Thus many searched for work in the urban areas or sought unoccupied lands on which to settle.

From the early nineteenth century the amount of imported British goods rose rapidly as the price of manufactures tumbled due to the increasingly efficient mechanisation of production. The value of British exports rose from an annual average of £193,571 in the period 1814–18, to £801,931 for 1844–48.[114] In the words of a retired government official, 'the general trend of the import trade [was] to convert luxuries into necessities ... and to make the Bight of Biafra and its hinterland depend on a large range of these and other necessities *which they had formerly either produced themselves* or gone without'.[115] This could be said of the whole of the West African coast.

This vast increase in imported goods resulted in the extinction of much African manufacture. For example, the smelting of tin had disappeared by 1923, as had the smelting of iron.[116] The weaving of cotton cloth was grossly reduced by the importation of cheap (partly because the raw cotton was slave-grown) cotton cloth from England, where 'special varieties [were manufactured] for the different areas'.[117]

Other European – British – introductions were:

- the use of threats and bribes to control Africans;
- avoidance of import duties by landing goods at unofficial ports;
- other forms of 'impropriety', such as the dilution of imported spirits from the stated 'proof strength';[118]
- non-taxation of British companies by the colonial authorities;[119]
- the non-payment of royalties for the products of mining;
- the formation of trade and shipping 'combines' which excluded Africans – for example, soon after the introduction of a steamship service to the Coast, it was reported to the Foreign Office that 'the Liverpool Houses had more than once offered to regularly charter [both] Packets on their homeward voyages with the view to prevent Native Traders shipping their Oil'.[120]

Conclusion

Of course, all societies undergo change over time. But there is a vast difference between what one could call 'natural evolution', and changes induced by overwhelming outside influences, and then by subjecting people to colonial rule. How would African societies, cultures, industries have developed had the Europeans not intervened? What was the effect of depriving East and West Africa of at least 20 million of its ablest, strongest peoples? Of inducing hundreds of years of warfare? And what was the effect of colonialism, which was about making the produce of Africa available to the West as cheaply as possible and creating a market for Western manufactures?

All these questions have to be taken into consideration when looking at Africa today. And another issue, that of social and psychological effects of enslavement, has to be recognised.

Although the official status of 'slave' has been eradicated, memories are not so easily obliterated. As Claude Meillassoux wrote in 1991, 'Once a slave always a slave. Even today, whatever their social rank, public opinion still attributes to them all sorts of stereotypical defects: greed, dishonesty, lack of moral values, obscenity, and so on. As soon as one of them gives in to the temptation of corruption – like most of his colleagues of high birth – he immediately becomes the living proof of the indelible nature of the servile strain.'[121] Is this so in Ghana and Nigeria and throughout Africa a decade and a half later? I have met people in Northern Ghana aged 50 or so, who recall being belittled as 'slaves' in their childhood. *If there, presumably elsewhere.*

CHAPTER 6

British people, government and Parliament

[T]here is too much reason to fear that British capital and British merchants are employed in the traffic [in slaves] ... At a public meeting in Reading ... information from Africa that British subjects openly and avowedly are engaged in landing cargoes for the purchase of slaves.... The opinion of the law officers was unfavourable to the success of prosecution, and it was abandoned.... My other informer is a large ship-owner in the city; he tells me that some parties standing well in the city applied to him last week to enter into a slave-trade speculation with them, and fit out a fast sailing clipper.... Consigning slave trade cargoes is a daily occurrence in this country.

The quotation is from an 1840 publication by Sir George Stephen, *A Second Letter to the Rt. Hon. Lord John Russell.* Sir George, a barrister, was a member of an abolitionist family: his father, a judge of the Prize Appeal Court, worked with Wilberforce, and his brother Sir James was a much-committed abolitionist Colonial Under-Secretary of State. So Sir George would have been well informed. It is not only his allegations that are important, but that he voiced them at a public meeting. So what was going on in Britain regarding slavery and the slave trade? Was the Anti-Slavery Society accusation that the main use of the African Squadron was 'a quietening of the conscience of the nation whilst permitting the continuance of this greatest outrage on humanity' a true description?[1]

Government and Parliament have been in and out of all the previous chapters, and even here there is no space for a thorough exploration. I shall not scrutinise the attitudes of the different political parties. Nor shall I comment further on the ongoing debates among historians on the numbers of Africans enslaved and transported. Or on the reasons behind the passing of the 1807 Act, or the 1833 Emancipation Act, or any of the other Acts, though these certainly should be researched. Nor can I investigate the twists and turns in the parliamentary debates whenever issues relating to slavery were on the agenda. But these questions are all relevant to any full discussion of Britain and slavery.

What I want to investigate here, however superficially, is the attitudes of 'ordinary' British people to slavery and especially how these were manifested in two very pertinent issues, the importation of sugar and cotton. I then want to at least glimpse at the information available to parliamentarians and the government and whether this impinged on decision-making, and to ask, how were those who challenged government treated?

British people

We cannot, regrettably, interview nineteenth-century British people to ask them how they viewed the parliamentary debates on slavery – or if they even knew about them. The 'working class' would not have had much leisure time to read (even if they *could* read) newspapers. Parliament did *not* represent 'the people', even after the Reform Act of 1832, but only those wealthy enough to qualify for the franchise. It is quite possible that most Britons would not have concerned themselves with issues about slavery and would not have known, or perhaps cared, if their wages were dependent either on slave-grown imports or on constructing ships and manufacturing exports for the trade in slaves. Are such attitudes current today? Do those, working in the armaments industry, for example, care where their products are exported? Do you care who made your shoes? Or the football you kick?

Very sadly, racism among British people was well-engendered by the nineteenth century. Historians who have investigated this note that though there were probably not yet many Africans resident in Britain, 'in the late sixteenth century, blackness was commonly equated with ugliness, lechery and wickedness in general'. By the mid-nineteenth century, supported by the new 'sciences', such attitudes had solidified into the 'belief of the superiority of one race over another'. In this racial hierarchy the British – no, the English – were at the top; Africans were at the bottom. 'Others' were homogenised into 'rigidly defined groups' and 'biological inheritance governed the individual's physical, intellectual and psychological attributes ... Negroes were classed in a common category of the brutish and perpetually inferior lower orders ... only Anglo-Saxons could be gentlemen.'[2]

Nevertheless, during the long crusade that succeeded in persuading Parliament to pass the Abolition Act of 1807, it had proved relatively easy for campaigners to procure support from the British people.[3] Millions signed petitions. But there were also petitions opposing abolition, from Liverpool, Manchester, Glasgow, Bristol and Lancaster.[4] Were the abolitionists free from racist attitudes, or could philanthropy overcome racism? Did people not want to see themselves as condoning the cruelties of the trade in enslaved Africans? Was this relatively easy to do because people – the 'ordinary' people – did not understand how they themselves might be profiting from the trade? Who signed the petitions? Only those who could read and write? Or were the non-literate people's names written on to the petitions by the collectors? Had they fully explained what the petitions were about? Did they hope that a by-product would be an improvement in their own conditions? Was it an issue of being a 'good Christian'? We have no answers to these questions.

After their partial victory – for some had hoped for the inclusion of the abolition of slavery and not just the abolition of trading in human beings – the campaigners entered a short period of quiescence. But not for long. After the defeat of Napoleon a campaign was inaugurated to persuade the European powers to sign up to the abolition of the trade in enslaved Africans. The Netherlands and Sweden agreed, but the 1814 Treaty of Paris gave the French five years' grace, despite her colonies being restored to France. Petitions of protest poured into Parliament – a total of 772, bearing nearly 1 million signatures. After considerable pressure from the British government, France agreed to abolish participation in the trade in 1815. Again, we do not know who signed, and why.

The campaigns for the abolition of the trade in enslaved Africans had been organised by 'Evangelicals' and the Abolition Society. Black Britons were apparently not welcome in this Society, but were well received when they (or was it only Olaudah Equiano?) toured Britain and Ireland soliciting support.[5] With success in 1807, the Society disintegrated, but was soon replaced by the African Institution and then the Anti-Slavery Society. Disagreements over various issues led to splits, new societies, and amalgamations among the abolitionists. (There is no space to discuss these here.) But they almost all campaigned, and attracted thousands to their meetings.

Campaigning women, 1820–1850s

As women are so often ignored by historians, let us look briefly at their involvements in anti-slavery work. Women had been part of the anti-slavery movement since the last years of the eighteenth century, but were relegated to the background by their male colleagues. The Anti-Slavery Society did not permit women to speak at its annual meetings, or to sit on the committees. William Wilberforce led the reluctance to accept them as equals.

Perhaps outraged by the revelations of the conditions and treatment of slaves on Sir John Gladstone's plantations in Demerara (see Chapter 2), and perhaps dismayed by the seeming lack of interest in the abolition of slavery among their male counterparts, women formed their own anti-slavery societies. The first society to work for slave emancipation was formed in Birmingham in 1825. A further 72 were established by 1833.

The women's tactic was to approach consumers of slave-grown products. Upper- and middle-class women, and some from the 'artisan' class, located in cities, towns and villages throughout Britain and Ireland, campaigned against the use of slave-grown sugar. Their approach was personal: they knocked on doors, asking women not to use it; they talked with other women, distributed their own printed materials, and withdrew their custom from shops selling, and producers using, such sugar.[6]

The campaign for emancipation and against apprenticeship heated up in the early 1830s. Was this a response to the slave rebellion in

Jamaica (known as Sam Sharpe's Rebellion), which ended with hundreds of rebels being hanged?[7] Were women particularly influenced by the publication of *The History of Mary Prince, A West Indian Slave, Related by Herself*? Again, we do not know, but certainly women began to canvass vigorously: about a quarter of the 1.3 million signatures on anti-slavery petitions sent to Parliament in 1833 were from the women's organisations. In 1838 they sent petitions to the Queen with over 700,000 signatures against apprenticeship. Women, in the words of anti-slavery campaigner George Thompson, 'formed the cement of the whole Antislavery building'.[8]

The 'free labour' movement was started by an American Elihu Buritt who had come to live in Britain in the late 1840s. Though their numbers had diminished, women took up this rephrased issue. Cloth manufactured from slave-grown cotton was not to be tolerated. There was a major problem in locating supplies of free-grown cotton, but the women persevered, supporting manufactures from free-grown cotton, and also the sale of free-grown produce (not dissimilar to the fair trade campaigns of today). Anna and Henry Richardson produced their own journal, *The Slave*, from 1851, devoted to publicising 'free labour' issues. They worked quite independently of the Anti-Slavery Society, which appears to have paid very little attention to the issue of the importation of slave-grown produce.[9]

The Birmingham Ladies' Negro's Friend Society issued a two-page 'flyer' in 1849. In this the women emphasised that 'the exclusive Consumption of the Produce of Free Labour is the most effective means of annihilating the existence of Slavery'. Most ingeniously, the women calculated that this level of consumption meant that 'every seven British families employ at least one slave!'[10]

Two years later, under the aegis of these Birmingham Ladies, almost 60,000 signatures were collected from women around the country on a petition, again to the Queen. This urged Her Majesty to set an example by using only free-grown produce, and to encourage cotton growing in India. The Queen did not bother to reply. But the women got a lot of publicity, thereby putting the issue back on the public agenda.[11]

During the 'cotton famine' created by the lack of imports from the USA during the Civil War, the well-to-do women abolitionists gave practical aid to the unemployed women workers, abandoning their staunch anti-slavery for the sake of hungry women and children. These women workers' attitudes towards the ongoing struggle against slavery in the USA has not been adequately researched.

The emancipation issue

All the 1807 Act and its amendments set out to do was stop Britons trading in slaves. The issue of slavery itself lay dormant until the 1820s. Wilberforce felt 'negroes' had to become 'fit to receive freedom' – some time in the future.[12] At first Parliament only wanted to consider emancipation as resulting from a long period of a gradual 'amelioration' in the conditions of slavery.

Apart from some abolitionists, there were now some merchants interested in emancipation. These were the traders who wanted to import sugar from India at the same low rate of import duty as was charged on West Indian sugar. (They were known as the 'East India interest'.) They were opposed by the 'West India interest' – the plantation owners and merchants and shippers bringing in slave-grown sugar from the West Indian colonies. The government did not want to alienate either party, and moreover needed the co-operation of those who governed the colonies. Both groups campaigned tirelessly. In the 1820s Parliament passed many resolutions for the amelioration of the conditions under which slaves laboured. These were communicated to the colonial governments. They generally ignored them. The government in London did nothing to enforce them.

For some in both the government and Parliament the issues of preferential duty on West Indian sugar and slavery became amalgamated, but for others it was simple: the abolition of slavery had to be paramount. Some were perhaps a little confused. For example, the President of the Board of Trade argued that it was irrelevant that the West Indian plantation owners used slave labour. 'It was not the fault of the owners, it was their misfortune!' The 'East Indian interest' and pro-abolitionists were often grossly outvoted in Parliament. However, in 1825 import duty on (slave-grown) sugar from Mauritius was lowered to the West Indian rate.

The government 'sat on the fence', not moving from a policy of 'gradual emancipation'. The colonial governments continued to ignore 'advice' from London regarding the conditions under which the enslaved lived and worked. The Anti-Slavery Society, set up in 1823, went along with this until about 1830, when the free-trade argument was brought into play: protective duties kept slavery alive, it was argued. Abolish protection, paid for by the English worker in high prices, and slavery would fade away. This argument held some sway: support for the 'West Indian interest' began to fade. Liverpool's West India Committee organised: it sent a deputation, including Sir John Gladstone, to the Prime Minister.[13]

Though the new Parliament elected in 1830 was busy with the proposals for electoral reform, staunch abolitionist and reform campaigner Lord Brougham was appointed Lord Chancellor. There was now hope for some progress in the struggle for the abolition of slavery. Fowell Buxton, the leading abolitionist Member of the House of Commons, promptly announced that he would move a resolution for immediate emancipation. Among those against the motion was Sir Robert Peel MP, son of a cotton manufacturer millionaire.

Peel and the 'West India' and slavery supporters won a partial victory: a new Slave Code was issued by the King in December 1831, but only to ameliorate conditions. The West Indians protested. Yet another committee was appointed. At a huge public meeting the Anti-Slavery Society passed a resolution demanding 'speedy termination'. This was, of course, opposed by the West Indians, who presented a petition to Parliament 'praying for relief from the distress' they were suffering. Yet another committee was set up, this time by the House of Commons.

In the meanwhile, pressure for the reform of Parliament grew apace. The proposals included extending the franchise to all who owned a house valued at £10 and to tenant farmers paying more than £50 a year in rent; the electoral boroughs were to be reformed. When the Lords voted against the measures, there was rioting. So the Act was passed: 'rotten boroughs' – that is, constituencies often with two seats in Parliament but with hardly any electors, and often just about 'owned' by the local landlord – were abolished and the seats were transferred to the new industrial areas.[14]

Hopeful of the new reformed Parliament, in 1832 the advocates of both sides toured the country giving lectures. They plastered London with placards. An anti-slavery petition carrying 187,000 signatures, collected mainly by two women, was presented to Parliament; 104 of the newly elected Members of Parliament pledged themselves to support a motion for immediate emancipation.[15] It was known that the King was not in favour of emancipation and the British government was not in favour of reducing the duties it garnered from sugar. What would happen to sugar production if the slaves were freed? And what would happen to all those who held the mortgages on so many of the plantations in the West Indies, if sugar production dropped drastically? Parliament gave the new Colonial Secretary, Lord Stanley, eight weeks to come up with a plan.

Campaigning continued. The Anti-Slavery Society, divided on the issue of compensation to the planters, eventually agreed to go along with it. The clergy preached on the sinfulness of slavery. A million and a half people signed petitions supporting emancipation. The West Indians sent a deputation to the Prime Minister. And another. The second one asked for immediate compensation and to be able to keep slaves 'under contract' for a period of 41 years. They organised a public meeting, attended by 1500 planters and about 3500 supporters, including *'almost every banking and commercial house in London'* (my emphasis).[16]

Lord Stanley presented his proposals to Parliament on 14 May 1833. After warning of the possibility of a 'servile war' if emancipation was refused, he suggested a loan of £15 million to the planters and a 12-year period of apprenticeship for the slaves. During the many days of debate, representatives of 'Proprietors, Shipowners, Manufacturers, Traders' and others interested in the 'welfare' of the West Indian colonies met and sent a demand to the government for an outright compensation of £30 million. When refused, the demand was reduced to £20 million. In the vote, 304 of the members of the reformed and enlarged Parliament approved; 56 were against.

Now it was the Anti-Slavery Society which sent a deputation to Lord Stanley, demanding a reduction in the period of apprenticeship. Stanley refused. But after listening to the debates, he relented and reduced it to seven years. The bill was now passed. Slavery was to be abolished from 1841 – no, not throughout Britain's colonies, as many believe, but in the West Indies, Mauritius, Canada and the Cape of Good Hope. India, Ceylon and the African settlements were not mentioned.

Who won? The planters were relieved of their huge debts while the few efficient ones became even richer. The freed women, children and men were given *nothing*, except apprenticeship and ultimately the freedom to work for paltry wages. When rumours reached Parliament of the apprentices' ill-treatment, a Select Committee was set up to investigate. Among the Committee's members was William, the son of Sir John Gladstone. The Committee could see no problems, but abolitionist Joseph Sturge did not believe their findings. He toured the West Indies and returned to Britain with James Williams, whose manumission he had paid for. They toured Britain, describing the often appalling conditions of the apprentices. Petitions poured in and in 1838 apprenticeship was abolished.[17]

The sugar duties question

In the 1840s the now free-grown West Indian sugar was imported at a lower rate of duty than other, including Indian, sugar. (This was for raw sugar; the duty on refined sugar was prohibitive, in order to support the British refineries.) The 'East India interest' was naturally avid to have the duties at least equalised. They were supported by the Manchester Chamber of Commerce, and Liverpool and London merchants, who petitioned Parliament regularly from 1821 onwards for reduction or equalisation. What was the interest of these cotton pro-ducers/shippers/merchants in Indian sugar (and coffee and cotton)? The improvements in technology had been providing a surplus of goods: they needed new markets. The millions in India could earn enough to buy British goods if they could export more agricultural produce to Britain. It was simple really.[18]

The 'West Indians', already feeling threatened by the talk of emancipation, protested and petitioned.[19] Competition they certainly did not want. The issue to some Parliamentarians was the reduction in price for the home consumer. The alarm of the 'West Indians' grew. Parliament, not wanting to alienate either side, resorted to its favourite tactic when faced with a problematic issue: it set up a Select Committee to investigate sugar duties.

Naturally the 'West India interest' resisted: they were already facing a drop in income due to the reduction in sugar production on their plantations since the passing of the Emancipation Act. The pro-equalisation lobby mobilised: the Manchester Chamber of Commerce was now supported by commercial organisations in London, Liverpool, Glasgow and Bengal. They succeeded, partially:

duties for free-grown Indian and West Indian sugars were equalised in 1836.

Concern grew, but not regarding slave labour. It must have been foreseen by many that equalisation was just a matter of time. It was the fate of the West Indian planters that concerned many, even the Commissioners of the 1841 Census. They entered the debate, arguing that there were 'grave doubts whether, after the sugar duties are equalised, our planters can sustain the competition of the planters of Cuba and Brazil, who command the services of slaves'.[20]

Manchester was not satisfied. Neither was the Liverpool Brazilian Association. They clamoured for a reduction in the duty on *foreign* (i.e. slave-grown) sugar. Then they wanted total abolition of duties. Why was Manchester involved in this? They were interested in developing their trade with Brazil. Why should Britain charge exorbitant import duties on Brazilian produce when Brazil admitted British goods on favourable terms? After all, Brazil was a larger market for British cotton than the West Indian colonies! The matter was urgent: the commercial treaty with Brazil was coming up for revision in 1842. Sir Robert Peel, protecting colonial merchants' interests, lowered the duty on coffee, much of which was re-exported.[21] But not on sugar.

The struggle over sugar duties now became one between pro- and anti-slavery factions. The Anti-Slavery Society argued it was justifiable to charge a higher duty on slave-grown sugar. Many branches of the Society had sent petitions to Parliament, pleading for the equalising of duty on all *free-grown* sugar. Petitions from the West Indies and the West Indian 'merchants and proprietors', protesting against equalisation, were also presented. The planters, others argued, should not be burdened: they needed time for giving 'the experiment of slave emancipation a full and fair trial'.[22] Some merchants argued that the West Indian planters had had ample compensation; and in any case, why was it more reprehensible to import slave-grown sugar than slave-grown cotton? The Manchester merchants repeated their previous arguments: 'Hostile tariffs' had driven Brazil, 'one of the largest customers for our goods, into a state approaching hostility'.[23] In 1846, Parliament listened – and voted to reduce the duty on slave-grown sugar! Among those who voted for this was Matthew Forster MP.

The effect of the Act was disastrous. To quote just one assessment, from Lt Henry Yule of the African Squadron, who could see the results: 'disastrous Sugar Act ... which might well have been entitled "a Bill for the Better Promotion of Slavery and the Slave Trade".'[24]

The new government under Lord John Russell was more amenable to Manchester pleas. Or was it perhaps interested in actually helping the British people obtain cheaper sugar? After all, sugar cost seven and a half pence per pound in Britain, while you could buy it for four and a half pence on the continent![25] The Select Committee to investigate the issue recommended that the duty on foreign free-grown and slave-grown sugar should be equalised, but for the duty on West Indian sugar to be ten shillings lower for six years. Equal duty was finally achieved in 1854, despite West Indian protests.[26]

Cotton barely questioned

you know these FACTS [on the trade in slaves] will surely be repeated, as long as nations continue to pay man-stealers ... and slave workers, by buying their Sugars, Coffees, Rice or Cotton.[27]

This argument in a pamphlet published in 1850 is one of the very few that I have been able to find which mentions cotton. This seems to me to be very curious. Have I just missed them? If they were not written, then the attention paid to cotton by both free-trade and protectionist campaigners, and pro- and anti-slavery campaigners, is truly abjectly minimal. Only four references came up when I searched the British Library catalogue under various 'cotton' headings. Searching the British archival database produced nothing. I can find very few references in the many books I looked at, and there is very little in the *Anti-Slavery Reporter*. Is this because cotton was just too important to the economy? For abolitionists in and out of Parliament, was it easier to concentrate on the endless debates on the efficacy of the Anti-Slave Trade Squadrons? And for 'the people', was it easier – less personal – to support visiting African-American abolitionists and the campaigns of the American anti-slavery movement? (Much as today we teach African American but not Black British, or Caribbean or African history in our schools?)

Perhaps the issue was just too 'delicate', as teaching about slavery in schools is deemed to be today. After all, *The Times*, during the period of its support for a reduction in the import duties on slave-grown sugar, pointed out that 'Nay, we are guilty of the gross absurdity of making that a virtue in sugar which we show to be a matter of indifference in every other article. The whole world is crying out at our hypocrisy.' The newspaper was echoing the argument of the Manchester Chamber of Commerce:

> we consume slave-grown coffee ... employ our people in the manu-
> facture of slave grown cotton, and even wear it ourselves ... all our acts
> forbid the belief that a sense of moral obligation was the true ground
> for making that distinction [between free and slave-grown sugar].[28]

But this blatant hypocrisy was ignored by the Anti-Slavery Society. And *The Times*, naturally, did not take it up after the sugar duties issue was won.

It seems to have been the indomitable abolitionist Joseph Sturge who embarked on a campaign, with support from the Quakers. He had been one of those who supported free trade, but still opposed the reduction in sugar duties. Now he decided to promote the Free Labour Movement – that is, for restricting, hopefully eliminating, the importation of slave-grown cotton. He toured England in 1845–6, visiting manufacturers and holding public meetings, as a 'sort of daily practical protest against all encouragement of slavery'. He was very disappointed, feeling that

> the voice was of one crying in the wilderness ... [T]he spirit of the
> trade was then, as it ever is, deaf to the pleadings of justice and human-
> ity.... All the good people of England, with tears in their eyes from
> reading 'Uncle Tom's Cabin', found it pleasanter to express their love
> for freedom, their sympathy for the slave and their hatred of oppression
> by denunciations and remonstrances addressed to sinners in America,
> than by making any serious efforts to sacrifice to clear themselves of
> complicity in the sin at home.[29]

Is it possible that it was in response to Sturge's campaigning that Liverpool felt obliged to defend its support for equalising sugar duties and thus supporting slavery? At a meeting held in June 1848, the *Mercury* reported that one of the speakers at a public meeting had said that

> [S]ome say we are encouraging slavery by admitting slave-grown
> sugar.... [This] comes with a bad grace from those who close their
> eyes and lips on the enormous importation into this country of slave-
> grown cotton and tobacco.[30]

But such views appear to have been rare. Sturge was up against the Manchester and Liverpool merchants, manufacturers and shippers:

men who naturally campaigned for a reduction on the duty on raw (slave-grown) cotton imports. West Indian cotton could be imported free of duty from 1821 onwards – yet another helping hand for those improvident plantation owners, some argued. (Yet this was pretty meaningless, as by then West Indian cotton only formed about 2 per cent of imports – a massive drop from 35 per cent at the turn of the century.[31]) The duty on all cotton was reduced in 1828 to 4 per cent from other parts of the British empire and 6 per cent from elsewhere. In 1831, when the government proposed increasing the duty, Manchester merchants organised a protest, which included pleading for support for cotton from India. The government reduced the proposed increase.

Manchester merchants were dissatisfied. Though the East India Company had improved the production and quality of cotton, it could not compete with American cotton. So the Mancunians wanted their slave-grown produce. And they wanted it cheap. With their fellow merchants in Glasgow, Nottingham and Belfast they organised meetings, petitions, memorials, deputations. In 1845 the government acquiesced: duty on cotton was abolished.

By the late 1840s, 90 per cent of cotton imports came from the USA and Brazil, slave-worked in both countries. The manufacturers wanted to ensure that their raw material was delivered, irrespective of political upheavals in the countries of supply. Would British-controlled countries be a safer source of supply? They also wanted to reduce prices by the introduction of competition among raw cotton suppliers. So the Manchester Chamber of Commerce undertook new cotton campaigns. It attempted to influence both the East India Company and the government by suggesting not only India as a source of supply but possibly the Cape of Good Hope and Natal, and then West Africa and Egypt. In 1857 the city set up the Cotton Supply Association to investigate cotton sources, deal with the government and protect its trade. The trade was huge: £32 million worth of cotton manufactures were exported in 1853.[32]

Cotton from India

There is another side to the cotton question which we must look at briefly. At the end of the eighteenth century, Britain imposed a duty of 78 per cent on Indian cotton goods coming into the UK. This was

to protect the nascent home manufacturing industry, as Indian cloth could be sold 'at a price 50% to 60% lower than those fabricated in England' – and still make a profit. By 1835 British cloth imports into India had risen to 51 million yards, from less than 1 million in 1814. Cloth exports to Britain dropped from a quarter of a million 'pieces' in that year to 63,000 in 1844. The effect was 'wholesale destruction of the Indian manufacturing industries'. The Governor General reported in 1835 that 'the misery hardly finds a parallel in the history of commerce. The bones of the cotton-weavers are bleaching the plains of India'.[33] (This could well have been an exaggeration. Not all the Indian cotton workers were forced into unemployment by the loss of the British market: the East India Company used Indian cotton and opium to pay for the tea imported into Britain from China, and cotton 'piece goods' also continued to be exported to Southeast Asia, East Africa and the Middle East.[34])

The British government ignored the warning of colonial administrator R. Montgomery Martin to the 1840 Select Committee:

> I do not agree that India is an agricultural country; India is as much
> a manufacturing country as an agricultural; and he who would seek
> to reduce her to the position of an agricultural country seeks to lower
> her in the scale of civilisation.... To reduce her now to an agricultural
> country would be an injustice to India.[35]

The British 'need' for raw cotton provided work for the now unemployed cotton workers. The plantation system was introduced, with the aid of 'experts' from the British West Indies. Such experts had also been imported to set up the plantation production of indigo, for dyeing the cotton. They have been described as a 'rather rough set of planters, some of whom had been slave drivers in America and carried unfortunate ideas and practices with them'. An 1860 inquiry into their practices 'revealed frightful abuses by the European planters'.[36]

I have not been able to discover what safeguards were put in place for the workers on these new cotton plantations to ensure that they were paid. Not only was slavery still legal in India, but the Act 'for the more effectual suppression of the importation of slaves into India by sea' did not receive the royal assent until 1842.[37] In 1844, 88 million lb of raw cotton was exported from India – a massive increase from the 9 million lb in 1813 – was it grown by slaves perhaps working under the indigenous forms of unpaid labour?

The issue of American cotton being slave-grown was raised in a very British-centred fashion by John Bright in Parliament: should the slaves there be emancipated, cotton production might be reduced, he warned Parliament in 1850. More cotton should be obtained from India. He suggested the appointment of a Commission to investigate any obstacles that prevented a greater growth in exports, and 'any circumstances that may injuriously affect the condition of the native cultivators'. The government spokesperson assured Mr Bright that 'the ryots [peasants] were not serfs, as he seemed to suppose'. After much defence of the East India Company, Bright's request was turned down.[38] Did John Bright, usually regarded as a radical, have evidence of the mistreatment or misuse of Indian labourers on cotton planta-tions? Or was he just interested in ensuring the supply of cotton for British manufacturers?[39] This was not many years after the 'laying on the table' of the House of Lords the *Despatch from the Governor General of India ... dated 8 February 1841 ... on the Subject of Slavery in the East Indies*. The owning of slaves was only made illegal in 1862.

Yet what all those in power seemingly cared about was their own wealth, though it was sometimes disguised as caring for others' welfare. Mr Cope, a Macclesfield manufacturer, told the 1840 Com-mittee that

> I certainly pity the East Indian labourer, but at the same time I have a greater feeling for my own family than for the East Indian labourer's family: I think it is wrong to sacrifice the comforts of my family for the sake of the East Indian labourer because his condition happens to be worse than mine.[40]

The influence of merchants and bankers

Both merchants and bankers, of course, had enormous interests in influencing government policies – as they do today. After all, a nation survives partly on its trade, and trade needs bankers. So perhaps the issue is whether the 'interest' of the merchants and bankers is solely about enriching themselves. If Parliament itself is the domain of merchants, bankers and landowners, then one could argue that the interests of the 'people' are at the bottom of the league table.

Especially when 'pleasing' your electorate in order to be re-elected means only having to please your fellow merchants or that social class. Was Sir George Stephen correct when he wrote that 'two thirds of the [West Indian] plantations were held in fee or in security by English houses.... These men banded together like forty thieves, they sold their votes in a lump.'[41]

It was natural for British merchants to club together to form associations to protect and promote their interests. How important were the merchants? Very. According to historian Andrew Porter,

> the economic and political weight of Lancashire and the North-West often compelled governments in boom and slump alike to heed local industrialists' and associated merchants' needs for markets and raw materials ... Lancashire's interests were frequently consulted in connection with overseas commercial and colonial development policies at least until the late 1940s.[42]

Influence was also exercised over the colonies close to Manchester's interests. The Chamber of Commerce, in the words of its president,

> had no hesitation in proffering advice to the Government of India, whether under Company or Crown ... a responsibility rested on the mercantile body of Manchester as far as possible either to guide and influence the Indian government, or to overhaul, if possible whatever errors might be found in that Government.[43]

Again, just a few examples.

Regarding the Anti-Slave Trade Squadron

In 1845 the government passed an Act to enable the Anti-Slave Trade Squadron to seize any vessel equipped for the trade in enslaved Africans. As one would expect, the merchants involved one way or another with this trade were appalled. In 1849 the Manchester Chamber of Commerce petitioned Parliament to revoke the bill as it hampered trade. Two years later the plea was repeated by the Manchester Commercial Association together with the Liverpool Brazilian Association and the Glasgow Chamber of Commerce. For once, they were unsuccessful, though they tried repeatedly until the Act was revoked in 1869.[44]

So a way round had to be found. And it was. The materials for manufacturing the 'equipment' – that is, wooden planks for additional sleeping decks, staves for making barrels for food and water, and iron to be made into manacles – were shipped out separately. Trade goods could also be sent out in an innocent vessel and either delivered to a shore-based trader or put on board a moored vessel beyond the 'waters' 'belonging' to an anti-slaving port. A slaver would then be sent out, sometimes in ballast, to be fitted for the trade on the Coast.

The Liverpool merchants were not hesitant in blaming the activities of the Squadron for creating problems for them. Legitimate traders were being forced to abandon the Coast, Thomas Horsfall, ex(?)-slave trader and then Mayor of Liverpool, told the Slave Trade Committee in 1848. Mr Tobin naturally echoed his slaver colleague, and, when asked, expressed his views about slavery clearly:

> 'Did the slaves generally regard their exportation with great apparent horror?'
> 'Not at all', he replied.
> 'They did not lose their natural cheerfulness?'
> 'No'.
> 'You regarded the transportation of slaves from Africa to our colonies as an exchange from an inferior to a superior society?'
> 'I did.'[45]

Regarding South America

How else was this influence used? Did these organisations intervene in British foreign policy? They certainly did. For example, as their trade with Spain's colonies (Mexico, Colombia, Peru, Chile and Buenos Aires) reached £4 million in 1821, the Manchester Chamber of Commerce (with support from other Chambers, including that of Birmingham) persuaded the government to open consulates in the major towns there. Three years later, when these colonies began fighting for their independence, the Chamber urged the government to aid them, despite Britain's declared neutrality. In 1825, when they won their independence, though Spain still claimed sovereignty, the Chamber urged – and won – their recognition as independent states. As profits always appear to dictate policy, when fighting between the newly independent peoples began to impede trade, the Chamber now urged the government to 'interpose its good offices with the Court of Spain ... putting an end to all pretext for those petty hostilities'.[46]

But that was not the end of commercially sponsored British interference in South America. It went on... and on.

For example, Matthew Forster

The redoubtable Matthew Forster can be viewed as an example of an individual merchant doing all he could, in and out of Parliament, to influence government policies and actions. Though he has already been dealt with in Chapter 3, and appears again below in the section on Dr Madden, it is worthwhile listing some of his other interventions:

- In June 1844 Forster presented a petition to the House of Commons from 'the principal manufacturers and merchants' in the UK who were 'connected with British trade to Cuba and Brazil and Africa'. The petitioners claimed that the charges that they supported the trade in slaves were 'caluminous and unfounded'. He wanted an inquiry. Then he wanted the government to present to Parliament any documents it held confirming 'the participation, directly or indirectly, by any British subjects in the slave trade'.[47]
- In 1845, during the debates on the sugar duty, Forster pushed for a reduction in import duty on a number of other items.[48] In whose interest? I wonder. His own, or those of his fellow merchants? Shall we ever discover the full range of Forster's trade?
- In 1846 Forster asked in Parliament whether the government was buying maize from the USA. It was not the question of whether this was slave-produced that bothered him, but that such purchases would 'paralyse private enterprise'. Was Forster just interested in maintaining free trade, or did he have some other interest? As the following year he alleged that the importation of flax seed into Ireland would 'materially affect private enterprise', perhaps we can presume that his interest lay in unencumbered trade.[49]

It would be very interesting to go through Forster's enormously lengthy correspondence with various government departments to ascertain what his interests and influences were. And how many other merchants exercised, or attempted to exercise, such influence?

...and bankers

Here all I can do is ask questions:

- Why did Rothschilds arrange the loan to pay the £20 million compensation to the West Indian planters when they lost their

unfree, unpaid labour? Did they have an interest in sugar production? Did they have outstanding loans to the planters? Were
they interested in freeing the enslaved? Why did they lend the
government £4 million at short notice and at the very low interest
rate of 3 per cent to buy the majority holding in the Suez Canal?
Was it in order to increase their already 'vast influence on the
British government [gained through] their wealth, financial and
political acumen and international connections', as suggested by
one historian of the bank?[50]

- What sort of influence did the Members of Parliament from the
  Rothschild and Baring families have on Parliament? We must
  recall that Thomas Baring opposed the bill introduced in Parliament to proscribe the investment of British capital in the trade in
  the enslaved.
- And what influence did they have on the Bank of England? For
  example, Thomas Baring was a director as was Humphrey St John
  Mildmay, a partner of Baring Bros.[51]
- One of the many new banks set up to cope with the demand for
  finance from the Americas and the colonies was the Colonial Bank.
  It was established in 1836, in response to the 'flow of money into
  the Colonies' derived from the slave compensation pay-outs: 'a
  group of merchants conceived a plan of establishing a Bank …
  with Branches in the West Indies and British Guiana'. Among the
  Bank's directors were four men who were 'all active members of
  the Committee of West India Merchants'. Not among these four
  names, yet also known as a West India merchant, was Aeneas
  Barkly, whose son, listed as the owner of Highbury plantation in
  British Guiana in 1820, later became governor there. The Bank was
  reported at the 1840 Anti-Slavery Convention (p. 516) as having
  had 'for some time a branch at Porto Rico and has been making
  strenuous efforts to establish another at Havana'. How many of
  the founders of this bank apart from David Barclay of the slave-
  owning Barclay family, were also, or had been, owners of slaves?
  Were they financing slave-worked plantations in Cuba and Puerto
  Rico in the 1840s?

  The bank was amalgamated into Barclays Bank in 1925.[52]

The government

One important question is: what did the government know about the ongoing British involvement in the trade in slaves and about British participation in slavery? That, of course, leads to another question: if the government and Parliament knew the 'facts', why was there no effective action taken?

That the government had been kept well informed has been demonstrated in all the previous chapters. Information flooded in from British consuls, the Vice-Admiralty and Mixed Commission Courts, the Treasury Solicitor's Department, the African Squadron and from the evidence presented to the endless numbers of committees of both Houses of Parliament. I have put some samples of this information in Appendix 3.

If researchers documented the information contained in the reports listed above, we would have much more information on who was involved when and in precisely what. That is, we would be able to assess far more clearly the reliance of Britain's 'development' on slavery and the trade in enslaved women, children and men.[53]

Parliament

It would be very interesting to see an analysis of the debates in both Houses of Parliament. Who said and who voted for what? Were those opposed to emancipation, abolition, and other issues related to slavery financially involved in the slave trade or profiting from slavery? What could we learn about British attitudes, for example to labour issues? Was there a difference between attitudes to workers in British possessions/colonies and workers in other countries and others' colonies?

These questions have, I believe, a bearing on Britain today, and not only regarding modern slavery. The National History Curriculum includes a section on African Americans, but not one on Black Britons: is this a reflection of nineteenth-century attitudes? Nothing is taught about the Caribbean, and the one topic on Africa (apart from Egypt, which is seldom depicted as being in Africa) is optional. Would it contradict the much-vaunted glories of 'Britishness' to teach the realities of the past?

To give just a few examples of issues debated and attitudes expressed in the two Houses of Parliament:

- On 20 September 1841 Lord Brougham presented a petition by the British and Foreign Anti-Slavery Society to the House of Lords. This asked for legislation to stop the use of British capital in the trade in slaves and in slave-worked mining companies in Cuba and Brazil; and the building of slave vessels in the UK. The petition was 'laid on the table' (*Hansard*, cols 608–10).
- On 2 August 1842 the House of Lords debated a resolution that 'measures' should be taken 'with all practicable Expedition to prevent the Employment of British Capital in promoting the Slave Trade carried on by Foreign States'. Lord Brougham was asked to 'frame an efficient measure' (*Hansard*, cols 936–52).
- Two days later, the Lords received from the Commons the proposal for an 'Act for extending the powers of the Governor and officers of the East India Company ... for the more effectual Suppression of the Importation of Slaves into India by Sea'. This was actually approved, and received the royal assent on 10 August 1842. Was it enforced? Perhaps I should ask whether it was ever forwarded to him. There is some evidence of British officials on the West African coast not being informed on what was and was not legal.[54]
- In 1843 Lord Brougham introduced a Bill, of which I have not been able to find any copies. After much debate, the Bill was printed: 'intituled An Act for the more Effectual Suppression of the Slave Trade'. Section (1) stated that all the previous prohibitive Acts were to apply to British subjects 'wherever residing'. Section (2) stipulated that 'pawns' should be treated as slaves and come under the provisions of the Abolition of Slavery Act. Sections (3) and (4) dealt with trials and the determination of offences. Section (5) dealt with the 'vessels fitted out for the Slave Trade, or suspected of being concerned in the Slave Trade ... procuring articles of merchandize along the Coast ... to prosecute such illegal traffic. ... [As] further provisions are required in order to prevent such lawful trade from directly or indirectly aiding and abetting the Slave Trade ... it is lawful for Her Majesty to establish such ordinances and regulations and

issue such prohibitions and restrictions ... [and] to take such reasonable security ... by bond or recognizance' as might be necessary to stop such actions. In Section (6) Brougham asked that 'Mining and other Operations in Foreign Countries' which used slaves 'shall within six weeks ... enter into a bond in the sum of £5,000.... Shall not hold, hire, retain or employ Slaves (except Slaves held prior to this Act).'[55]

The Imperial Brazilian Mining Association protested from the beginning of the debates on this Bill. In its letter to the Foreign Office the Association argued that 'injury and injustice will be done not only to the Company I represent, and those similarly circumstanced, but also to the Negroes themselves'. Joshua Walker enclosed a petition from the directors of the St John (*sic*) del Rey Mining Company. George D. Keogh, the company's secretary, argued that 'the amount of capital ... in Mining in Brazil is very large'. He admitted that the only labour is 'the Negro population' but the 'true remedy' lay in the prevention of the illegal traffic.[56]

(The Anti-Slavery Society had asked the British government in 1857 to investigate the illegal use of slave labour by British companies in Brazilian mines. Among the companies named was the St Juan Del Rey Mining Company (*sic*). Some questioning appears to have resulted in an agreement to free its slaves by 1859. This was not done. The Society took up the case again 20 years later. The slaves had to sue the company for their freedom in 1882.[57])

On 16 May 1843 the House of Lords voted to have the bill withdrawn. Lord Brougham presented another. It was 'read' on a number of days in June, until it was 'committed to a Committee of the Whole House' to meet on 11 July. At that meeting the petition from the Imperial Brazilian Mining Association was presented, with its pleas that parts of the Bill which 'relate to the Foreign Mining Companies may not pass into law'. The Earl of Shaftesbury reported that the Committee had made 'Amendments to be ingrossed'. After the third reading of the reformulated Bill, it was sent to the House of Commons. The MPs made more amendments. These were then agreed by the Lords and the new Act received the royal assent on 28 August 1843.

In the Act there is nothing referring to Brougham's Section (6) which tried to prevent the supplying of slave traders on the Coast. The actions of the 'joint stock companies' established prior to the passing of the Act regarding their slaves remained unhindered.

These modifications are hardly surprising, when one reads the words of a supposedly pro-abolition Member of Parliament. This was William Ewart, the very wealthy local merchant and MP for Liverpool, where he claimed his views had often 'incur[red] hostility'. At the 1843 Anti-Slavery Convention at which he was a visitor, he said:

> our great pervading and animating principle must be an extension of the commerce of the world. Commerce I believe to be the great emancipator. Although I would seize the vessel of the slave-trader, and make his trade piracy, yet I look beyond these coercive means, to the extension of commerce to its enlightening and enfranchising influence.[58]

- Mr Hutt MP advised the House in 1845 that the current campaign against the slave trade was useless. He didn't seem very concerned about those 'distant and barbarous people'. I suppose we should not be surprised at this attitude as he had been a trader on the West Coast for many years. But, he assured the House, he and his partners 'had never been parties to any transaction connected with slavery or the slave trade'. However, as they had 'discovered that seven tenths of the goods with which the Brazilian and other slavers fed their trade were British manufactured goods, they ship out same goods to exchange for palm oil. Attempts to suppress the trade in slaves', he avowed, 'simply resulted in an increase in cruelty'.[59]
- In 1847 Mr Hume MP suggested that the West Indian planters should go to 'West Africa and buy slaves there and free them in the West Indies'. He had been told by a friend from Havana that the profits of the plantations had risen, so they should be able to afford the $400 or so purchase price. The Foreign Secretary, Lord Palmerston, pointed out that 'wars, burnings, and the murdering of women and children' were entailed in the acquisition of slaves.[60]
- On 22 August 1848 the House of Lords refused to debate the proposition that the government should 'give Directions for the Enforcement of all Treaties with Foreign Powers for the Extinction

of the Slave Trade ... and for the Prosecution of British subjects at home or abroad, directly or indirectly violating the Laws against that Crime'. Had such an Act been passed, the merchants would no longer have been able to sell goods to slave traders. It is – very sadly – hardly surprising that their Lordships refused to entertain the Bill.[61]

- As far as I can discover, the suggestion that if a higher price was paid for palm oil the dealers would stop trading in slaves, made by Capt. Denman of the African Squadron earlier in the same year, was never taken up by the government or parliament.[62]

Dr Richard Robert Madden

The treatment and experiences of Dr Richard Madden can be used as an example of how a convinced abolitionist was treated by different governments and by Parliament. Even when very abbreviated, the history of Dr Madden's early service with the British government provides a glimpse of government strengths and attitudes, and the influence that one manipulative man (the much-mentioned Matthew Forster) can have on the conduct of Parliament as well as the government.

A Dublin-born physician trained in London, Paris and Naples, Dr Richard Madden was a staunch abolitionist. He gave up his medical practice when he was appointed a Special Magistrate in Jamaica in 1833 to oversee the 'apprenticeship' system. A firm believer in treating Blacks and Whites as equals, he aroused hostility in the entrenched planter interests. 'One of the cases he dealt with caused such emotion that he was assaulted in the streets of Kingston.' Probably feeling that he could accomplish little, he resigned in 1834.[63]

While in Jamaica, he was instrumental in securing the freedom of a number of slaves, including Timbuktu-born Abu Bakr al-Siddiq, whom he helped return to his birthplace. On his return to Britain Dr Madden reported his experiences and submitted recommendations to the government, and gave evidence to the Select Committee on Apprenticeship. He advocated immediate emancipation.

Wanting to gain a wider audience for the realities of Jamaica, Madden published a book, *A Twelve Months Residence in the West Indies*, in 1835. This included some of his correspondence with Abu Bakr and the following (remarkable, even for an abolitionist) comment:

the natives of some parts of Africa are not so utterly ignorant as they are represented to be, and the Negroes, generally, are as capable of mental improvement as their white brethren ... Slavery ... in our colonies is not killed. Its name is changed: its character remains to be changed.[64]

Clearly not disapproving of his work or his publication, in 1836 Foreign Secretary Lord Palmerston appointed Dr Madden to the position of Superintendent of Liberated Africans in Havana. As his abolitionist views had preceded him, he was received with great hostility. As soon as the Cubans discovered just who he was, they demanded his withdrawal: the island's Governor General complained to his Spanish overlords that 'Dr. Madden is a dangerous man ... will have too many opportunities to disseminate seditious ideas.'[65] But Palmerston refused to bow to such pressure.

Never one to give up easily, Dr Madden also challenged the United States and Spain. News reached him of the recapture by the US Navy of the *Amistad*, a slaver bound for Cuba, which had been taken over by the enslaved Africans on board. On his way back to London on leave, he attended their trial in Connecticut and gave evidence on behalf of the Africans. He described the slaves' conditions in Cuba and pointed out that Spain had signed a treaty many years previously to stop slave trading. Dr Madden's 'performance was impressive and convincing'.[66] The Africans were released.

On his return to London, Dr Madden addressed the 1840 Anti-Slavery Convention on what he had found in Cuba – this was sub-sequently published as *An Address on Slavery in Cuba*. Also in 1840 he published his translation of the autobiography and poems of Juan Francisco Manzano, a Cuban slave he had helped liberate.[67] Nine years later he collected his experiences in *The Island of Cuba*.

Though Dr Madden was in London only on leave, in 1840 Lord Palmerston offered him another appointment. He accepted it, although he must have suspected that it would prove to be as problematic as his previous two appointments. Presumably both he and Lord Palmerston felt that he was well suited to take on this new task. He was to investigate slavery and the slave trade on the West Coast of Africa. The need to investigate arose after the newly appointed governor of Sierra Leone admitted that slavery was ongoing by proclaiming (however useless this might have been) that both trading in enslaved

Africans and domestic slavery were forbidden. There were also allegations that George Maclean, Governor of the Gold Coast, had
permitted slavery within 'his' territories and that slaving vessels were
equipped there with guns and gunpowder.[68] Dr Madden was on the
Coast for about two months, admittedly not long enough, especially
as his investigations were hampered by illness.

By the time Dr Madden submitted his lengthy and detailed report,
the government had changed.[69] Neither the new Foreign Secretary,
Lord Aberdeen, nor the new Colonial Secretary, Lord Stanley, were
as rigorous abolitionists as their predecessors. And Matthew Forster
now had a seat in Parliament.

When asked in Parliament on 29 September 1841 when Members
would see Dr Madden's report, Lord Stanley replied that there were
four reports; he had 'no objection' to producing the medical one,

> but the other three treated matters of greatest importance and secrecy,
> of matters related to individuals, affecting our foreign policy and our
> relations with the trade legally and illegally carried on on the coast of
> Africa. In the present position of the Government [I] do not feel war-
> ranted in laying on the Table of the House, the whole of these matters
> [which] are under anxious considerations of the ... Government.[70]

The previous day Forster had written to Lord Stanley, the new Colonial Secretary, asking that 'no hasty measure may be resorted to on
the evidence or recommendation of parties imperfectly acquainted
with the subject, until the fullest inquiry has taken place'. Stanley
had obviously listened – or had come to the same conclusions without
Forster's solicitations.

The issue was raised again on 5 October in the House of Lords
(*Hansard*, cols 1114–28). Lord Ripon, the head of the Board of Trade,
advised that he had discussed the issue of the release with Lord
Stanley. However, 'as the report contained statements of very important and delicate nature, involving the names and conduct of private
persons ... their publication would tend to defeat rather than advance
the great object', they could not agree on its release. Why precisely
the 'object' would be 'defeated' the Lord did not bother to explain.

Dr Madden's report was certainly damning, both of government officials and British merchants. Having seen the results of enslavement,
he was, I presume, sufficiently angered by what he saw that (undip-
lomatically) he named names. While his revelations might have been

more acceptable to Lord Palmerston, for Lord Stanley and Matthew Forster, whose name figures in the report, Dr Madden's work was too threatening. Forster, accused by Madden of supplying slave traders, used his new position as a Member of Parliament to increase his correspondence with the Colonial Office as well as the Foreign Office both in length and in volume.[71] That he was someone to be reckoned with is indicated by the draft of a letter in the Colonial Office files, probably drafted for Lord Stanley. This warns that 'His Lordship … would suggest that if any comment be made to Messrs. Forster & Smith, it should be in the most cautious (guarded?) terms.'[72]

Except for the named names, Dr Madden's allegations were very little different from the reports which had been coming back from the Royal Navy and some of the Sierra Leone governors and judges. Lord Stanley resorted to the old ploy of appointing a Select Committee to investigate. Presumably to demonstrate where his interests lay, he appointed Viscount Sandon, the MP for Liverpool, as its chair, and Matthew Forster MP as a member – MPs not exactly indifferent to such an investigation! The Committee of 19, which included aristocratic and merchant MPs, met seven times from April to August 1842. Only Sandon and Forster attended all these meetings. Attendance by other members was spasmodic: two members attended no meetings, while three attended only two. In today's terminology, the Committee was certainly compromised.

Attendance at the actual hearings was better, but again Forster outshone them all. And he managed to ensure that his fellow West African merchants should be among those invited to give evidence – and some others who would support him.[73] Interestingly, Lord Stanley only attended on the days when Dr Madden and Pedro de Zulueta (named in Madden's report; see Chapter 3) were being questioned. Perhaps the government's concern regarding commercial interests is demonstrated by Dr Madden's report having been sent to Zulueta & Co. for their comment before the first meeting of the Committee. Or, more simply, could the government not afford to antagonise Pedro de Zulueta?

Given the paucity of Committee members at the meetings, it must have been easy for Forster to shift the focus of attention away from himself and to discredit Dr Madden.[74] Forster was outraged at some of the questions put to Pedro de Zulueta, 'one of the first (meaning 'best') Spanish houses in this country, and perhaps in Spain'. He put many motions to the Committee regarding the alterations required in the report prior to publication. Trade was not to be interdicted, even if the goods ended up being exchanged for enslaved Africans. If it was, business would be put into the hands of foreigners. Governor Maclean certainly did not own slaves or condone slavery. (Maclean was a friend of Forster's.) Pawning was perhaps not 'abstractly unjust or unreasonable'. Captain Denman had undermined trade by burning slave-holding barracoons.

Was it Forster who solicited the letter from Foreign Secretary Lord Aberdeen, which was enclosed in the Committee's report? Aberdeen doubted the legality of Denman's actions, which had been approved by the previous government. He went further, issuing instructions that naval officers should be forbidden to carry out such actions.

When it did appear, Dr Madden's report was consigned to the end as an Appendix to the Committee's report. Another victory for Forster, Sandon and Lord Stanley! According to the *Anti-Slavery Reporter* of 2 November 1842 (p. 61), 'some material had been omitted … and it was interspersed with commentaries by others, diminishing Dr. Madden.' My reading is that his recommendations were either ignored or so altered as to be almost meaningless; and all reform was to be gradual, very gradual.

Matthew Forster's vituperative attacks on Dr Madden before, during and after the sittings of the Committee were not only addressed in private letters to the government and to Dr Madden himself, but also appeared in the newspapers. As Dr Madden recalled in his *Memoirs*, 'on this Committee a seat was given to an affluent West African merchant largely implicated in the slave trade, and by him and his friends no stone was left unturned and no abuse spared in the futile attempt to controvert the report'.[75] Dr Madden responded by publishing many of his own letters to the *Morning Chronicle* (and other journals and newspapers) in 1843, as *The Slave Trade and Slavery: The Influence of British Settlements on the West Coast of Africa in Relation to Both.*

The Anti-Slavery Society was outraged at the treatment meted out to Dr Madden and his report. As early as April 1842 the *Anti-Slavery Reporter* analysed the exclusion of Dr Madden's report: 'it seems … clear that the reasons for withholding it are derived … from a wish to screen certain individuals from exposure' (p. 61). In

November 1842, the *Reporter* reminded readers that the Committee had questioned the involvement of Forster's vessel the *Robert Heddle* in the trade in slaves, and commented: 'now we know why the new Tory government suppressed and then manipulated Dr. Madden's report' (p. 172). Many on the Committee and the witnesses, the *Reporter* alleged, were Forster's 'friends and servants', including the captains of Forster & Smith's vessels, and merchants 'engaged in similar traffic and their employees'. The Society for the Extinction of the Slave Trade noted that 'the Committee were prevented from recommending any prohibitory enactment against this indirect participation in the slave traffic [i.e., by supplying trade goods to slavers] by the difficulty of prevention'.[76]

Moreover, the Anti-Slavery Society believed that Lord Palmerston had been considering prosecuting Matthew Forster prior to the Whigs losing the election.[77] This charge was also made in the *Leeds Mercury* in February 1843: it was 'no secret', the paper reported, 'that the late Government had resolved to institute a criminal prosecution against the house of Forster & Co. of London, which was most largely implicated in the practices brought to light by Dr. Madden … [T]he present Ministry is totally changed … [and has] placed Mr Forster MP for Berwick upon this committee [dealing with Dr Madden's report]'.[78]

To escape from it all, after the dismissal of his findings by the Tory government and Parliament, Dr Madden moved to Lisbon as a special correspondent for the *Morning Chronicle* and worked on what became a seven-volume work, *The United Irishmen*. In 1846, Lord Grey, the Colonial Secretary of the new Whig government, offered him the position of Colonial Secretary of Western Australia. Dr Madden accepted.

I wonder whether Lord Stanley was shown the letter below, forwarded to the Colonial Office? And if he was, how did he react? But perhaps his diplomatic officials decided to spare him any embarrassment. The letter had been written by John Jackson, a Coast merchant, who had been President of the Council on the Gold Coast in the late 1820s. Having seen the published report, he wrote in confidence to Mr Hutton, who had forwarded the letter (again) in confidence to G.W. Hope MP, who in turn forwarded it to the Colonial Office.

Mr Forster, I suppose, imagines himself the champion for us all whereas the truth is to screen himself and defend Maclean [the Governor];
he has assumed the Public garb he wears ... We are unfortunate in our
friends ... [This is] useless bravado of [a] vain attempt to defend an
untenable position against public opinion, against the very powers able
to crush us at a blow before whom I shall expect Mr Forster himself
will have to succumb before they have done with him.... Most unpleas-
ant is the domestic slavery question ... I would rather they would by
compensation emancipate all with a certain boundary. Take Madden's
advice and pass a new Act...[79]

Conclusion

As indicated in all the chapters, most often the government did
nothing, or nothing wholly effective, in response to the petitions,
pleas, evidence and arguments in and out of Parliament. In the words
of shipbuilder and African explorer Macgregor Laird,

We have not repaired the injuries we have inflicted on the African race,
that has given rise to the costly and useless attempts we have been for
the past thirty-six years and are now making, to put down the African
slave trade by treaties and preventive measures.[80]

It is very important, I think, to list at least some of these 'inactions'
if we are to understand what lies behind Britain's proclaimed anti-
slavery stance.

- The 1811 Act made trading in slaves a felony, punishable by transportation. This clause was retained in the Slave Trade Consolidation Acts of 1824 and 1842. As far as I have been able to discover,
not a single person was ever transported for this crime.[81]
- The Anti-Slave Trade Squadron was increased, at least until they
were withdrawn during the American Civil War, and the numbers
of slaving vessels captured increased. But Britain did not keep pace
with the new vessels employed by the slavers, as Captain Henry
Matson of the RN explained:

where steamers are found to be inefficient, the worst of the bad ones
are sent to the coast of Africa ... Again, with respect to the sailing
vessels; they are rigged for Channel or North Sea service, and have
not sail enough to compete with the slavers ... there is not a sloop on

the African station that can compete in sailing with a well-found slaver
… If we are to expend money on an African squadron, let it be an
effective one.[82]

Given the increase in the numbers of slaves imported into
Brazil and Cuba, the effect of the Squadron was minimal. Nevertheless, it must be acknowledged that some Africans were freed
from the slaving vessels. How they fared as freed men is briefly
examined in Chapter 5.

- The issue of supplying slaving vessels and slave traders with trade
goods and the use of British capital was never dealt with. Neither
were British companies and officials on the Coast and in the
Americas involved in slavery.

- Innumerable treaties were signed with other countries involved in
slavery and the trade in the enslaved (see Appendix 1 for some of
these). They were, until the latter half of the nineteenth century,
ineffective.

This particular example is worth quoting as it demonstrates
both the uselessness of treaties and the indifference of Britain to
the activities of British companies on the Coast. A vessel named
Juliana was 'condemned' at the Brazilian/British Mixed Commission Court in Sierra Leone. It was bought and resold by a
'British subject' and left the port under a Spanish flag. The case
was referred to the Queen's Advocate, who informed the Foreign
Office that the 'course taken was in accordance with Treaties for
Abolition … vessels sold must be permitted to clear out and leave
the Port, notwithstanding any suspicion … that … they may
again be equipped and employed in the Slave Trade'. The 'British
subject' was 'Messrs Kidds [who] have been reported for years….
The Governor gives them Certificates, and Customs clears them as
Spanish.' That Customs continued to clear such vessels appears to
demonstrate a lack of co-operation by the Customs officials, whom
Governor Jeremie had 'instructed not to clear condemned vessels
purchased by Foreigners'.[83] (There was, of course, no other trade a
Spanish-flagged vessel would be engaged in on the West Coast.)

- The countless Select Committees expended an enormous amount
of time and energy (and money) collecting a vast amount of
evidence about individuals, companies, techniques of involvement

and avoidance. But prosecutions were almost non-existent, were seldom successful when attempted, and new Acts passed on the basis of the evidence submitted were as ineffectual as the previous ones.

It is appropriate to conclude with the words of Sir George Stephen, commenting on the Committee enquiring into the ongoing importation of slaves into Mauritius in 1827:

> the committee ... examined such witnesses as were immediately at hand, in a superficial way, and made a report, that, like many others from Parliamentary Committees, amounted to little or nothing.[84]

He would, I feel sure, agree with me that what he said in 1827 would have been just as relevant ten years later, or twenty, or thirty, or forty.

Conclusion

This has been a difficult book to write – and I'm not referring to the research involved. It was difficult for two main reasons:

First. We are talking about what was done to women, children and men until not very long ago. We're not talking about numbers, but about human beings. For me there is no difference between my feelings when I search for my relatives' names on the tall obelisks bearing the names of Hungarian Jews murdered by the Nazis, and my feelings when sitting in Northern Ghana listening to memories of degradations experienced by people of slave ancestry; or when I visit Elmina or Cape Coast castle in Ghana and breathe in the fetid air of the prisons which had held the enslaved awaiting transportation. That there are not even names on those walls is heartbreaking.

Second. My anger and frustration with historians and nationalist propagandists grew and grew and I read more and more. Yes, Britain passed the 1807 Act. But, unless I am wrong, it made more money out of slavery and the slave trade after 1807 than before. Where are the analyses, the investigations, the books on this?

I think the abolitionists' sole success was getting the Abolition Act through Parliament in 1807. They failed, with the exception of the 'equipment clause' (see Chapter 5), to get any other Acts through Parliament that *effectively* closed the gaping loopholes that permitted the passage of all those traders, all those goods, all those investments in slavery and the slave trade. (Somewhat like the arms trade today.) What does that tell us about the workings of Parliament?

Unless I am mistaken, the abolitionists did not take up the issue of British manufacturers' dependence on slave-grown cotton, or of British exporters' dependence on it, and, for example, on slave-grown tobacco. This to me indicates that these imports (and trades) were just too important to the British economy to be tampered with. Cotton cloth and yarn, manufactured mainly from slave-grown cotton, accounted for 40 per cent of Britain's exports in 1850.

Slave owners in the British West Indies could be paid off with £20 million compensation for the loss of their 'property'. How much more money would have had to be raised by the government as compensation to the cotton manufacturers, shippers and exporters if the factories had to be closed because the government prohibited the entry of slave-grown cotton? And, while the newly freed African people in the West Indian colonies received no compensation, they were *out there*, while millions dependent on employment in the cotton industry would have been under the eyes of parliamentarians *in Britain*. Could they have watched them starve? How much would it have cost to feed them? And to house and clothe them? And where would they have found new employment, given that cotton manufacturing had been absorbing more and more workers since the 1820s? No – cheap, slave-grown cotton had to continue coming into Britain.

Yes, Britain did spend some money, mainly on the African Squadron. But, as I hope to have demonstrated, for most of its existence the Squadron was not particularly effective, and some of its officers appear to have had a pecuniary interest in their work. Why didn't Britain assign more efficient vessels to this work? I think this was because Britain needed the slave-worked economies to flourish. For Britain the produce of slave labour in the Americas was indispensable for her own 'development', especially after the demand for exports of cotton manufactures had increased hugely. Britain also benefited from the increased investment opportunities which emerged as the economies of slave-worked countries expanded. This expansion was partly, if not mainly, due to Britain lowering the import duty on slave-worked sugar and on the massive increase in imported raw cotton.

I think much of the activism by the government and Parliament, the meaningless Acts, the almost annual Select Committees looking at various aspects of these issues, were just good publicity.[1] The local and international value of that propaganda and the immense wealth gained from *not* dealing effectively with the trade in enslaved Africans and from slave-grown produce outweighed the expense of the Squadron and the Select Committees. We live with the heritage of that entrenched propaganda today. (It could be argued that it is akin to the 'tick-box' approach to 'race relations' today.)

It is important, I think, for us to recognise that it was not only the traders, bankers, shippers and insurers directly involved who grew rich, or made their living out of the trade in enslaved women, men and children. Apart from those working in the cotton and related industries, how many British workers, for example, manufactured the 'trade' or 'coast' goods crucial to this 'nefarious' trade? How many seamen were on the vessels shipping slave-grown produce or manufactured goods to and from Britain and also in the direct export trade in the Americas? Could Britain have become the foremost among industrialised nations without these profits from the trade in enslaved Africans and the profits derived from slavery? No, not just up to 1807, but until the 1880s, when slavery was ended in Cuba and Brazil. That is, was British 'development' dependent on slavery?

There is another reason for looking at all these issues. These days there is much discussion about the definition of 'Britishness'. This ought to – this must – include an acknowledgement of the misinformation we have all been fed about British philanthropy and the glories of the 1807 Abolition Act. We have to reassess ourselves in the light of realities, not propaganda.

APPENDIX I

British and European
Acts of Parliament and international
treaties regarding slavery

Why list these? To demonstrate just how meaningless signatures on official pieces of paper can be. European powers signed treaty after treaty, passed one Act of Parliamant after another, issued one royal decree after another. But how many were actually put into practice? The chapters in this book have begun to illustrate just how meaningless they were, to far too many Europeans. As Philip Curtin argues,

> Various European powers made the maritime slave trade illegal for their subjects at various dates scattered through the first half of the nineteenth century, but the date of illegality made less difference than the date of willingness or ability to enforce the prohibition.... [V]arious subterfuges were used to continue the trade in fact if not in theory.[1]

Some international Acts

1792–1803	Denmark abolishes trading in slaves.
1794	French revolutionary government prohibits slavery and the slave trade.
1802	Napoleon reinstitutes the French slave trade and slavery.
1803	The Netherlands abolishes trading in slaves.
1804	The USA: no more slaves to be imported.
1813	Sweden abolishes trading in slaves.

1814	Netherlands declares slave trade originating in Dutch ports illegal.
1814	Spain declares abolition of slave trading.
1815	Congress of Vienna declaration against the slave trade signed by Austria, Britain, France, Portugal, Prussia, Russia, Spain and Sweden.
1815	France abolishes slave trading.
1815	Portugal abolishes slave trading north of the Equator and exporting restricted to her own 'possessions'.
1817	Spain declares abolition of slave trading, again.
1818	Congress of Aix-la-Chapelle: the five powers who declared against the trade in slaves in Vienna repeat their declaration.
1818	France abolishes slave trading again and sends three warships to the West African coast.
1820	Spain abolishes slave trading south of the Equator on receipt of £400,000 from Britain.
1822	Congress of Verona: repeat of Congress of Aix-la-Chapelle and Congress of Vienna declarations.
1822	Spain declares abolition of slave trading, again.
1826	France declares that fitting out a vessel for the slave trade is the same as trading.
1826	Brazil abolishes slave trading north of the Equator in exchange for the recognition of her independence (from Portugal) by Britain.
1829	Mexico abolishes slavery.
1830	Portugal abolishes trading south of the Equator.
1835	New constitutional government of Spain signs treaty forbidding slave trading under the Spanish flag.
1836	Another Portuguese decree forbidding participation in the trade in slaves.
1839	Pope Gregory XVI condemns the 'odious traffic'.
1840	France abolishes slavery.
1841	Quintuple treaty between Britain, Austria, Prussia and Russia, agreeing to the seizure of vessels equipped for slaving.
1842	Portugal declares slave trade a piracy – not enforced.
1842	Uruguay abolishes slavery.
1845	Spain declares slaving a piracy – not enforced.
1847	Denmark emancipates slaves in its West Indian colonies.

1847	Ottoman Sultan closes the market for slaves in Constantinople and stops importation via the ports on the Persian Gulf.
1848	France and Denmark abolish slavery.
1850	Brazil declares the end of slave trading.
1863	US abolishes slavery.
1875	Portuguese Empire abolishes slavery.
1878	Spain abolishes slavery in her colony of Puerto Rico.
1870	Slaves who fought for Spain in Cuban war of independence declared free by Spain.
1878	Portugal abolishes slavery in all her 'possessions'.
1880	Cuba abolishes slavery.
1888	Brazil abolishes slavery.

British Acts and decrees

Listen to Lord Palmerston addressing the House of Lords on 26 July 1844, by when innumerable Acts had been passed and treaties had been signed by Britain with other European countries, all promising to cease trading in enslaved Africans.

> from 120,000 to 150,000 slaves are landed annually in America. It is calculated that of three Negroes seized in the interior of Africa, to be sent into slavery, but one reaches his destination, the two others die in the course of the operations of the slave trade. Whatever may be the number transported, therefore, we must triple it to obtain the true number of human beings whom this detestable traffic kidnaps every year from Africa.[2]

And to Joseph Pease of the Anti-Slavery Society, who stated in 1895 that

> Today there is probably more slavery, for which we are to a large extent responsible, in our Protectorates than we have at any time known in our colonies in the West Indies.[3]

To Lord Lugard much involved in East Africa and created High Commissioner of Northern Nigeria in 1901, who had advocated:

> The gradual abolition of the legal sanction of slavery, and not compulsory emancipation ... the development of East Africa must depend on Negro labour.[4]

And to Sir Harry Johnston, Vice-Consul in the Niger Delta 1885, Commissioner of South Central Africa 1891–96, and of Uganda 1899–1901, who believed that

> The African slave trade ... White peoples [are] punishing the Negro for his lazy backwardness.... The races that will not work persistently and doggedly are trampled.[5]

And

> On the continent of Africa we have little but backward peoples to deal with.[6]

This list does not include all the Acts of Parliament, royal decrees and ordinances passed by colonial governors. I have listed just enough to demonstrate that passing laws was relatively easy. Enforcing them, as demonstrated in this book, was (and is) a different matter altogether.

1807	British Act abolishing British participation in the trade in slaves; bounties offered to British ships capturing slave trading vessels.
1811	Slave trading by Britons declared a felony; penalty is transportation for 14 years.
1813	Ships condemned in the Vice-Admiralty Court may be registered as British ships.
1814	Act to Prohibit British Subjects from Lending Capital to Assist the Carrying on of the Slave Trade to the Colonies of Foreign States (Amended).
1822, 1823	Acts to amend and consolidate Slave Trade Acts.
1824	Act consolidating the Acts of 1807, 1814–15, 1818, 1822, 1823: purchasing, shipping, financing, insuring, fitting out slaving vessels or serving on them, and shipping goods to be used in the slave trade all illegal; slave trading a piracy. The penalty was death, but, according to Hugh Thomas, 'No prosecution was brought against a British subject under this head.'[7]
1828	Act amending and consolidating the 1824 Act.
1830	Alexander Findley, Lt Governor of the Colony of Sierra Leone and its Dependencies (including e.g. Cape Coast) issued Proclamation that it was illegal to aid and abet the trade in slaves in any way, including providing finance or supplying trade goods.
1833	Abolition of Slavery Act: all slaves in British colonies to

be registered by August 1834 to serve apprenticeships until 1838–40; all slaves in Britain freed. Slave holders in the Caribbean paid £20 million (*c.* £1000 million in 2005) in compensation. The freed slaves are not compensated.

1834–40   Slavery in South Africa abolished; £1,250,000 (between £5 and £6 million in 2005) compensation paid to the deprived owners in Cape Colony.

1837   Death penalty for participation in the trade in slaves replaced by transportation for life.

1839   Act for the Suppression of the Slave Trade: Royal Navy vessels empowered to stop and search Portuguese and stateless vessels; if found with slaves or slave-trading equipment, to be taken to the British Vice-Admiralty Court, which was empowered to confiscate the cargo and either take the vessel into 'Her Majesty's Service' or break it up.

1840   Legal status of slavery abolished in Cape Colony (South Africa): compensation of £1,250,000 paid to slave owners.

1843   Act for the More Effectual Suppression of the Slave Trade: reiterates the 1824 Act; Britons, wherever domiciled, forbidden to hold slaves or 'pawns'; joint stock companies established before the Act may sell or retain possession of slaves, as may those who inherited them.

1843   Legal status of 'slave' abolished in India, but holding slaves remained legal and domestic slavery remained untouched.

1845   'Aberdeen Act': equipment clause applies to Brazil and captured Brazilian vessels to be adjudicated by the British Vice-Admiralty Court.

1860   Holding slaves in India becomes a criminal offence.

1873   Holding of slaves by British subjects in East Africa created a criminal offence.

1874   In the Gold Coast colony, slave dealing abolished and slave children to be emancipated from 1 January 1875.

1876   Act for more effectively punishing offences against the slave trading laws.

1895   Legal status of 'slave' abolished in Egypt.

1901   Slavery abolished in Nigeria.

1924   Secretary of State for the Colonies forbids 'asssistance' by 'political officers' in the Gold Coast Northern Territories in recruiting labour for the privately owned gold mines.[8]

1928	Slavery abolished in Sierra Leone.
1932	Sierra Leone Forced Labour Ordinance permits thirty days' compulsory labour for 'personal or public services'.
1935	Sierra Leone Forced Labour Ordinance (II) forced labour for road work abolished.
1933	Ordinance passed in Nigeria applying the ILO Forced Labour Convention (see Treaties below) except for 'transport purposes', but Native Authority Ordinance 'allows native authorities to requisition native labour for public purposes and for any purpose approved by the Governor.'[9]
1934	Gambia Forced Labour Ordinance abolishes all forms of forced or compulsory labour.
1935	Gold Coast Colony Labour Ordinance and Ashanti Labour Ordinance: 'Provincial Commissioners may require native authorities to maintain their roads … compulsory labour is regarded as a temporary expedient.'[10]
1938	In Nigeria, pledging of 'pawns' outlawed.
1940	Gambia passes ordinance applying ILO Convention of Recruiting Indigenous Labour (see treaties below).
1946	Nigeria passes ordinance applying ILO Convention of Recruiting Indigenous Labour.
1948	Forced Labour Ordinance (see Treaties, below) passed by Gold Coast government but excepted compulsory labour by prisoners, in case of war and 'minor communal services'.[11]

International treaties signed by Britain with other countries

It is important, I think, to include the twentieth-century treaties which were supposed to impose controls on how 'native labour' was used in European colonies. Millions of people, including young children, still work under similar conditions in the twenty-first century.

1812	Treaty of Ghent: USA and Britain agree to work towards abolishing the trade in slaves.
1814	Treaty of Paris ending Napoleonic Wars includes clause against the slave trade.
1814	The Netherlands abolishes the slave trade; agrees to

establish Mixed (Dutch/English) Commission Court and despatch naval vessels.

1815   Britain promises to remit Portuguese £300,000 debt and indemnify owners of condemned Portuguese vessels (a total of £2,237,077 was paid to Spain and Portugal for their co-operation.[12]

1815   Importation of slaves to Brazil from north of the Equator made illegal.

1817   Anglo-French and Anglo-Portuguese treaties empower detention of ships with slaves on board by Royal Navy and establish Mixed Commission Courts.

1820   Spain agrees to abolish slave trading on payment of £400,000 by Britain as compensation for the 'losses sustained through the seizure of her vessels', etc.

1821   Importation of slaves to Cuba made illegal.

1830   Importation of slaves to Brazil from south of the Equator made illegal.

1831   France signs mutual search treaty with Britain.

1833   With France: sufficient to have slaving equipment on board for 'arrest' of vessels.

1835   Another treaty with Spain, as previous ones not put into practice: vessels equipped for slaving can be seized.

1839   With Portugal, similar, but crew not liable to punishment.

1841   Treaty with Belgium to suppress slave trade.

1842   Another treaty with Portugal making slave trading illegal and establishing Portuguese/British Mixed Commission Courts.

1862   With United States, which also permitted mutual search; being equipped for the trade is sufficient for 'arrest'. It was agreed to set up Mixed Commission (i.e. GB/USA) Courts in New York, Cape Town and Sierra Leone.

1890   Brussels Treaty signed by most European states and the USA, Turkey and Persia, to stop slave trading.

1926   League of Nations Slavery Convention binds signatories to progressively suppress slavery and condemns forced labour practised by the colonial powers.

1930   Forced Labour Convention signed by (some) members of the International Labour Organisation. This made the use of forced labour for private employers illegal but permitted its use 'for public purposes as an exceptional measure'.

1936   ILO Recruiting of Indigenous Workers Convention defines 'recruiting' as 'operations undertaken with the object of obtaining labour of persons who do not spontaneously offer their services'.

APPENDIX 2

Some slave traders on the
West African coast and in Liverpool

By the early nineteenth century there were many well-established slave traders on the West African coast. Some of those whose names were well known to the British Parliament investigating the 'nefarious trade', and to the African Squadron are listed below. These names are frequently mentioned as either receiving British goods or purchasing such goods from other traders, or of using British companies as their bankers. Hugh Thomas suggests that there is 'even a possibility that some London merchants (Forster & Co., for example), were indirectly concerned in the slave trade here in the early part of the century'.[1] According to Captain Adams of HMS *Gladiator*, in 1851 Forster & Smith was buying palm oil from the slave/legitimate trader Domingo Martinez.[2] Had Matthew Forster been supplying Martinez with goods to barter for slaves?

It is important to catch a glimpse of these traders from another perspective. Who were they? How did they live? What were their origins? By getting such a glimpse, we can envision the world of slave trading more easily.

Pedro Blanco, from Malaga, started off in life as a master of Cuban slaving vessels. He worked initially with Da Souza at Whydah. When he had made enough money he went Baltimore to buy some clippers and settled in the Gallinas in about 1828. There he replaced the previous trader there, John Kearney, 'a British ex-officer', who had just retired. He did so well that in a couple of years he established a number of branches along the coast. He had an agent in Sierra Leone, one of whose tasks was to buy condemned slaving vessels being auctioned by the Mixed Commission Courts.[3]

At Gallinas he had buildings on three islands: one for his home and office, one for his wives, each of whom had a separate house; and one as a trading post with barracoons for the enslaved. 'He supported ... quite a retinue of house servants, guards, etc., besides clerks and overseers in his barracoons.' His 17 office staff were all Europeans. 'His bills were accepted with as much facility as a bill upon the Lords of the Treasury by Baring Bros of London ... and other respectable bankers.' Two of his trading partners were the Zuluetas, Julian and Pedro, and there is some evidence of his using Zulueta & Co., in London, as well as Baring Bros, as his bankers.[4] One of his suppliers was William Hutton & Co. of Manchester.[5]

Blanco was partner in a Cuban firm, Blanco, Carvalla & Co., which supplied Julian de Zulueta with slaves.[6] He became the firm's sole owner in about 1839, when he settled in Cuba, leaving behind his agents at the Gallinas. He continued his slaving ventures from there until he moved to Barcelona, perhaps in the 1840s. When he retired he was said to be worth about £400,000.

Blanco's nephews, Fernando and Julio, were in the same business, supplying slaves to New Orleans and Havana.[7]

Richard Brew (1725–1776), an Irishman at first in the service of the Royal African Company, settled at Anomabu, near Cape Coast on the Gold Coast. A very successful trader, he died a wealthy man, leaving his home, 'Castle Brew', which included warehouses and slave barracoons, as well as 'twenty guns', presumably small cannon. *Sam Kanto Brew* followed in his grandfather's footsteps, and also established strong political and trading links with the Asante, for whom he 'sought alternative buyers for the slaves' after British trading became illegal. 'He had available a constant supply of slaves ... ready to ship out to vessels anchored some distance offshore for fear of capture.' The British apparently referred to him as a 'powerful mulatto slave trader'. He died in somewhat mysterious circumstances in 1823, on board the HMS *Cyrené*, which was deporting him from Cape Coast for having led the Governor's troops into an ambush by the Asante. His son, *Samuel Collins Brew* (1810–1881) was apparently also a trader in palm oil; one of his trading partners was Forster & Smith. He had several wives, 'some of them acting as his agents'. Did they hold slaves on his behalf, I wonder. Appointed a district commissioner and a magistrate, he was bankrupted in the early 1860s. Most of his assets went to Forster & Smith.[8]

Benjamin Campbell was a 'legitimate' trader: he supplied not only the barracoons but vessels with 'slave ship paraphernalia'.[9]

Théophile Canot was born in Florence in 1808; his real name was Conneau; his father was French. He joined the slave trade on a vessel from Havana in 1826. At first he traded from the Rio Pongo, sometimes buying vessels put up for sale by the courts in Freetown. He was captured on one of his slaving vessels by the French and imprisoned. On release he returned to the Coast and worked with Pedro Blanco. Lt Seagram of the African Squadron in 1840 persuaded Canot to give up slaving; he freed the 104 slaves he was holding at the time.[10] However, as he was a failure at legitimate trade, he returned to slaving, but was captured on an American slaver in 1847 and again sent for trial. He was released, returned to slaving, and was captured again. He then gave up slaving and settled in France, dying in 1860, as civil governor of New Caledonia.[11] His book, published under the name of Capt. Theophilus Conneau, *A Slaver's Log Book or 20 Years' Residence in Africa*, first published in 1854, is a goldmine of information, for example on his purchases from British traders and the ease with which his drafts were cashed in Sierra Leone.

Feliz Da (De) Souza, of Brazilian origins, originally went to Africa as a Portuguese government official, perhaps in the early 1790s. He then became a trader at Badagry. He helped in the overthrow of King Abandozan by his younger brother Gezo. To thank him, King Gezo appointed him his sole commercial agent at Whydah (or Ouidah) and gave him the title of Chacha.

    Buying and selling slaves on his own account as well as the King's, by the 1840s, he was the 'greatest slave trader in Whydah [and] shrewdest dealer on the African coast … [H]is mansion is like a palace ... [Da Souza] enjoys almost a monopoly of the coast trade. Blanco has been his only rival', according to slaver captain Richard Drake. Da Souza also knew where to buy vessels cheaply: 'an agent for da Sousa [spelling varies] spent several months of 1828 in Freetown buying prizes', reported an African Squadron captain.

However, another account states that as his fame spread he could never supply all the slaves required by the large number of vessels which came to Whydah laden with 'trade goods' and 'specie'. No account was kept of the cargoes, and general inefficiency is supposed to have prevailed. However, 'so lucrative was the profit in slaves' that he survived, until creditors began to arrive in Whydah. This resulted in King Gezo agreeing to his being supplanted by 'agents from the Havana and Brazils'. Da Souza was to 'receive a commission of a doubloon for every slave that was shipped'.[12]

Rev. Thomas Birch Freeman, a British-born Black Methodist missionary visited King Gezo in 1843 and met the man he called 'Antonio Da Souza'. He found him 'exceedingly polite and kind, and prepared to help by any means in his power'. He was a 'straightforward, open-dealing man', 'universally trusted and esteemed by all who knew him'.[13]

When he died in 1849 he was buried with great splendour, though he died 'almost a pauper, the consequence of having been over liberal in his presents, and having met some severe losses at sea. Besides the enormous expenses of his household, his wives alone amounting to 300, he lived in great magnificence, every article of table or domestic use was of solid silver'.[14]

In the 1820s an Englishman named *Edward Joseph*, also known as Jousiffe, was 'installed on the River Gambia [where] he carried on a tolerably good business'. According to Canot (Conneau, *A Slaver's Log Book*), in July 1827 one of Joseph's creditors in Sierra Leone informed the Governor there of this English slave trader; the Governor sent an expedition, as it was forbidden for Britons to trade in slaves. But Joseph escaped on 'a slaver for Havana, carrying with him sixty slaves and leaving his disconsolate wife' (p. 97). About two years later he was back on the Coast, working in partnership with Canot. In 1833 Capt. Leonard of HMS *Dryad* reported that a hundred kidnapped Liberated Africans were held 'in factories of an Englishman named

Joseph'.[15] Apparently the partnership dissolved as Canot recorded receiving 'a missive from my former English partner, a prisoner in Sierra Leone. He had been captured in a Spanish slaver, taken to Havana, thence to Jamaica [and] was now in Sierra Leone under sentence of being transported.... A draft on my employer (Pedro Blanco) was cashed in Sierra Leone, and a day after, my partner and jailor were on their way to Rio Pongo' (p. 263). If this jailor could be 'bought' how many others succumbed to such temptation?

The Squadron reported Joseph as dying at Rio Pongas (*sic*) around 1839.[16]

Isabel Gomes Lightburn sold slaves on the Rio Pongas. The daughter of an American father and an African mother, she and her sister and two brothers had been educated in England. Her barracoons were destroyed by the African Squadron in the early 1840s.[17]

It is not clear whether *Domingo Martinez* was born in Spain or Brazil, and where he lived prior to his arrival on the Coast in about 1830 as a crew member of a slaving vessel. This was captured and the crew was dumped in Whydah. Martinez then began to work with Da Souza and learned how to became a slave merchant. When he and Da Souza fell out in 1838, Martinez moved to Lagos. There he became the busiest slaver, reputedly amassing a fortune of some $2 million. He left for Brazil but could not settle there and returned to West Africa in 1846. He settled in Porto Novo, near Dahomey, where he built a mansion. He traded in both enslaved Africans and palm oil – and also supplied ammunition to many slave raiders. As the price of palm oil increased, he established a number of plantations and raised cattle. His trade was now worth about $200,000 (or about £40,000) a year. On Da Souza's death he took over his role as adviser to the Dahomean court. He now built a second mansion, as luxuriously furnished as the first. In 1849 Lt Forbes described him as:

> Domingo Jozé Martins, the richest merchant in the Bights (Brazilian), is a resident at Porto Novo, where he commands a monopoly of both slave and palm-oil trades, each of which he works to an enormous amount, as he is the only merchant in the Bights that ships a whole slave cargo ... Martins has a large consignment of British cotton on palm-oil account at Porto Novo. He has an establishment also at Whydah.[18]

In 1851 Brazil not only signed an Act to stop importing slaves, but actually enforced it. The African Squadron blockaded the Bights in an attempt to ensure that this was done. The King of Dahomey signed an anti-slaving treaty with the Royal Navy. Martinez's palm-oil shipments not only continued but escalated. He tried, with not much success, to rebuild his slaving enterprise, shipping the enslaved not to Brazil but to Cuba and the southern USA. However, changing circumstances led to more and more European traders establishing themselves on the Coast. The Marseilles trader Régis convinced the King to permit France to establish 'protection' over Dahomey. Martinez reputedly died in a fit of rage on being informed of this.[19]

Caetano Nozzolini, the son of an Italian sailor and a Cape Verdean woman, started his career as a slave trader at Bissau; by 1830 he was the governor of the Portuguese forts at Cacheu and Bissau on the Upper Guinea coast. He received the supplies he exchanged for slaves from an Afro-Englishman, Henry Tucker of Sherbro (see below), for which he paid with 'bills drawn on such respectable London houses as Baring Brothers'. Did he also trade with Matthew Forster's brother, who was trading on the Gambia river at that time?

After Captain Denman had burned the barracoons at Gallinas (see below), Nozzolini moved to the Rio Nunez in Guinea Bissau, and then to Cape Verde, from where he trans-shipped slaves brought from the Rio Pongo, Sherbro and Gallinas to vessels bound across the Atlantic. He was the 'undisputed lord of a slave-smuggling empire that spanned the Lusophone area of the Upper Guinea Coast'. In 1840 he employed not only 'coloured people' but 'two European agents to collect slaves' – their nationality is not known.[20]

John Ormond was the son of a slaver captain from Liverpool and the daughter of a Susu king (part of the Mandingo peoples, living between the Rio Pongo and Conakry on the Guinea coast.) Taken to England for some education by his father, he served in the Royal Navy for five years. His father disowned him, so he returned to Africa, where his mother officially recognised him as her son and thus a prince. Renowned for his cruelty, he died in 1791 after his slaves had risen against him.[21]

Ormond had built many barracoons, and a harem, and had a yearly income estimated at $200,000 (£40,000) One of his first clerks was Théophile Canot (see above), who was paid 'a negro a month'. His son, also named John but known as 'Mongo', by conquering many of his neighbours soon gained control of the trade in slaves. He exported slaves mainly to Cuba. Mongo John also traded in gold, alcohol and palm oil. He is said to have committed suicide in 1828.[22]

Henry Tucker, an 'Afro-Englishman', and his family traded in slaves at Sherbro and Gallinas. 'By the mid 1840s the Tuckers of Sherbro lost considerable influence thanks to the anti-slave trade treaties with British agents ... Nozzolini was their only competition once the Brazilian slave trade slowed in the 1850s.'[23]

Some of Liverpool's prominent men involved in slavery after 1807

Though in previous chapters there were some indications of the positions of power and authority assumed by traders in slaves, it is well worth looking a little more closely at some of the other traders in Liverpool. If the traders there held such positions, can we assume that traders in other cities held similar positions of influence? London was the banking and insurance centre of Britain: what influence did they have on banking and insurance policies? On the Bank of England?

When Pedro de Zulueta was in court (see Chapter 3), 'Sir John Pirie, the Baron de Rothschild, Mr Jones Lloyd, Mr Halifax, Mr Ricardo and a host of first bankers and merchants of the city of London gave the prisoner an extremely high character for honour, probity and amiability'.[24] This to me indicates the level of 'interest' in trade with Africa and the utmost desire of the new merchant/banking upper class to preserve its good character, no matter what it was involved in. What trading/banking and other policies did these men manipulate?

Jonas Bold was a member of the Africa Committee. Besides trading in slaves, he also owned privateers. He served on Liverpool's Common Council and was bailiff in 1796; mayor in 1802. Isaac Oldham, his son, continued trading with Africa, served on the town council and was bailiff in 1827. The Bolds were prominent importers of palm oil, mainly slave-produced in West Africa. Whether they also supplied trade goods to the slavers on the West African coast is not known.[25]

Edgar Corrie was a member of the Company of Merchants Trading to Africa. Corrie gave evidence to the Committee considering the Dolben Bill, which proposed some regulation of the trade in enslaved Africans. His very erudite and detailed evidence was on the 'four risques, a Failure in any of which will overset the best planned voyage'. This, I believe, is sufficient evidence for us to presume that he must have been a trader in enslaved Africans: how else would he have been able to give such evidence? In the 1780s he was a partner of John Gladstone, on whom see Chapter 2.

Another Gladstone, T. Stewart, formed a new partnership with William Corrie in the early nineteenth century.[26] In 1841 Corrie & Co. were among the founder members of the Cotton Brokers Association of Liverpool. Corrie is noted as having 'liked to take his flight in West Indian cotton and other commodities'.[27] But was he also an employer of slave labour? Did he also own coffee plantations in the days of slavery? Why else would he have published a pamphlet in 1808 on *The Subject of Duties on Coffee*? In this he argued that the 'distress' of West India planters was due to the heavy taxes imposed on their sugar and coffee, which he equated to 'planters paying war taxes'.

The *Heywood* clan, whose fortunes were founded by Arthur, 'had experience of the African trade, dabbled in privateering – had Letters of Marque' and continued their 'African interests' up to 1807. The Heywoods set up a bank in 1773, which by 1788 operated in both Liverpool and Manchester. The bank existed until 1883. They were also merchants, wool manufacturers and insurance brokers, and the first to import slave-grown cotton from the United States.

Benjamin Heywood was elected to the Liverpool Chamber of Commerce in the 1770s. A Heywood daughter married Robertson, son of Sir John Gladstone.[28] For services rendered (to whom, one wonders) Benjamin was created a baronet in 1838.

Charles Horsfall was an alderman on the town's Common Council, and mayor in 1832.[29] He owned a plantation in Jamaica; after 1807 his trade with the Americas increased. He was the chairman of the West Indian Association of Liverpool in the 1830s. Charles Horsfall was elected mayor in 1832 and sat on Liverpool Council, as did his sons Thomas and George. T.B. Horsfall was MP for Liverpool 1861–65.

The partnership of Horsfall & Tobin and then Horsfall & Sons was the largest Liverpool firm in the palm-oil trade. Bateson & Horsfall were prominent members of the Liverpool Cotton Brokers Association, so the Horsfalls must have had some kind of interest in slave-grown cotton (or, to be fair, cotton from India). Charles Horsfall tendered for the mail service to West Africa, but lost out to Macgregor Laird.[30]

Thomas Leyland (1752–1827) privateer, slave trader, merchant, member of the Chamber of Commerce, town councillor and bailiff, Leyland also served as Liverpool's mayor three times, in 1798, 1814 and 1820. In 1807, having dissolved previous banking partnerships, he set up Leyland & Bullin, which existed until 1901. *Richard Bullin* had been Leyland's slave-trading partner and served as Liverpool's mayor in 1821. Until 1835 Liverpool Corporation banked with L & B; it then transferred to Heywood's Bank. Leyland left an estate of £600,000 (*c.* £28 million in 2005).[31]

The *Rathbones* were a Quaker family and therefore supposedly opposed to slavery.[32] Two Rathbones were active abolitionists. Yet William Rathbone III, a timber merchant, imported timber from Barbados, and exported sugar, coffee and tobacco to the Baltic in the mid- to late nineteenth century – presumably all slave-produced. In about 1785 William Rathbone IV began trading in cotton; his sons formed a new partnership known as Rathbone Bros & Co., to act as cotton commissioners in America, and also acted as shipping agents for America. William Rathbone V was Mayor of Liverpool in 1837–8. William Rathbone VI, who spent 18 months in training with Baring Bros, enlarged the cotton business of the firm, and traded in coffee from Brazil. Cotton, of course, was all slave-produced.

The *Tarletons* – Edward, John (1739–1775) and Clayton (1762–1797), traders in enslaved Africans, were Mayor of Liverpool in 1712, 1764 and 1792, respectively. In the list of slaving vessels leaving Liverpool for the West Coast in 1799 their slaving vessels are named as the *Swift* and the *Abigail*. In their slaving ventures the family worked in partnership with the Backhouses; and also with William Rigg, in the firm of Tarleton & Rigg, which owned the *Resource*. Rigg was to serve as bailiff during the mayorality of Thomas Molyneux, a close business associate of Thomas Leyland.[33]

The Tarletons owned estates on the islands of Grenada, Dominica and Carriacou. They banked with the Heywoods. John, the ex-mayor, who died in 1775, left £30,000 (*c.* £1.9 million in 2005), to be evenly distributed between his wife and five children. It is therefore not surprising that the family could afford to spend £3420 (*c.* £120,000 in 2005) in 1810 buying a commission for Thomas (1776–1836) in the army. Thomas seems to have been much involved with the family's West Indian plantations.

John as MP for Liverpool led the city's delegation to Prime Minister Pitt's Slave Trade Committee in 1788. Naturally he opposed abolition. His son Banastre (1754–1833), created a general for services rendered in the American War of Independence, was elected to Parliament representing Liverpool in 1790, and served with one brief deselection, until 1812. Naturally, as an MP he opposed abolition in all the debates. He was created a baronet in 1815.[34]

Sir John Tobin, a Manxman, began his seafaring life on privateers. Probably after he and his brother had amassed sufficient prize-money, they settled in Liverpool, continued privateering and learned about the slavery business by working on slaving vessels.[35] They learned quickly and well; by the 1790s they had their own slaving vessels, and were raking in vast sums of money.[36] In 1799 his *Young William* was listed as sailing on a slaving voyage from Liverpool. The *May*, another Tobin vessel, was exempted from paying dock and town dues, which must say something about his influence in the city.

John, knighted (for what services?) in 1820, served as an alderman on the Liverpool Common Council and then as mayor in 1819. Tobin's daughter and son John married into the Aspinall family – another successful slave-trading clan. Patrick, another son, was also in the slave-trade business and owned plantations in the West Indies. James

Aspinall Tobin also served on Liverpool Council and as mayor in 1854.[37]

Sir John is said to have given up slaving after 1807; he certainly did move into the palm-oil trade with another (supposedly) ex-slaver, Thomas Horsfall.[38] Thomas Tobin was asked to give evidence to the Parliamentary Slave Trade Committee of 1848. It will be recalled that in response to the question, 'Did the slaves generally regard their exportation with great apparent horror?' Tobin replied: 'Not at all.' 'They did not lose their natural cheerfulness?' 'No.' 'You regarded that transportation of slaves from Africa to our colonies as an exchange from an inferior to a superior state of society?' 'I did.'[39]

Samples of information reaching the British government and Parliament

Visconde de Sé da Bandeira (who had introduced into the Portuguese Chamber of Peers a bill for the Abolition of Slavery in India), in his *The Slave Trade and Lord Palmerston's Bill*, published in London in 1840, wrote that

> British capital, British goods and British speculators [are] employed in the [slave] traffic, carrying it on to a great extent in the immediate vicinity of the British Colonies ... [Slave traders] supply themselves with goods from Sierra Leone with which they purchase slaves and the Spanish factories at Gallinas have purchased through their agents at Sierra Leone vessels condemned by the Mixed Commission with the intention of employing them afresh in the transportation of slaves.[1]

Slave trade at Gallinas

As outlined in Chapter 3, Pedro de Zulueta was believed by the jury when he claimed he did not know that by sending his ships to the Gallinas he was supplying slave traders. Yet, before and after the court case, the government knew that there was no other trade on the Gallinas (and had also been informed of some of Zulueta's other vessels involved in the trade in slaves).

- PP 1848, *Slave Trade Papers, Class A*, p. 295: from the *Report of the Sierra Leone Commissioners*, 9 February 1848: 'The principal barracoons ... are at the Gallinas and Solyman rivers, where between 2000 and

3000 slaves are kept in readiness for shipping.'[2]

- PP 1849, vol. IX(1), *Reports from Committees: To Consider Best Means Great Britain can Adopt for the Final Extinction of the African Slave Trade.* 5 February, f. 171: Lt Cmdr Forbes: 'at the Gallinas there is no trade but the slave trade'.

- PP 1849, vol. IX(2), 16 May 1849, q. 1883 to Sir Charles Hotham, ex-commodore of the West African Squadron: 'slavery in the Gallinas – almost exclusively for Cuba?' 'Yes.'

That lowering the duty on sugar increased the trade in slaves

- PP 1849, *Slave Trade Papers*, Class B, p. 131, Report of the Commissioners at the Cape of Good Hope, 22 November 1847: 'The operation of the sugar laws of Great Britain, as we have before observed, stimulated the trade to a lamentable extent.'[3]

- PP 1849, vol. IX, *Reports from Committees: To Consider Best Means Great Britain can Adopt for the Final Extinction of the African Slave Trade,* 30 May questions 959–1050, Steven Lushington MP: 'impossible to entertain a doubt' that the reduction in duty has 'stimulated the slave trade ... [though] I am the strongest advocate of Free Trade, the slave trade ... [is] a violation of all the principles of justice and humanity.'

- PP 1849, vol. IX(2) (as above), 25 April, q. 207: 'Did the alteration in sugar duties result in an increase in the trade in slaves?' Ex-Minister to Brazil, Lord Howden: 'Yes.'

- PP 1849, vol. IX(2) (as above), 5 July 1849, q. 3850: same question put to to J. Macqueen, who replied 'Yes, the Sugar Bill has been a great impetus to the slave trade and must continue to be so.'

The use of British capital in slave-worked enterprises

- *Hansard*, House of Commons, 1815, vol. 30, 18 April, col. 658, J.F. Barham MP: 'large amounts of British capital employed in Brazilian ships in this [slave] trade'. He is about to propose a bill to forbid the use of capital. The bill was lost in the House of Lords 1 June 1815.

- The British Consul at Cape Verde reported another method of participation: 'On 16th October 1839 ... the *Taraensa*, a steam vessel arrived, bound for Brazil. It is the sixth vessel of the kind that has called here from Liverpool for the supply of coals, belonging to the same company. [F]rom reports, I am led to understand that they assist the landing of slaves from vessels coming to the coast of Brazil from the coast of Africa.'[4]

- PP 1839–40, *Slave Trade Papers*, #18, Class A, p. 218, British Consul in Rio de Janeiro to Lord Palmerston, 6 May 1838: 'As regards British capital ... the various undertakings going on in this country, which are every day multiplying, and which are for the most part the result of British enterprise, are all dependent on slave labour ... Candonga Mining Co. goes into the market for its slave labour.'

- *Hansard*, House of Lords, 1841, vol. 59, 20 September, cols 608–10, Lord Brougham: '[I]t was to be greatly regretted that British capital and British skill were still found engaged in that infernal traffic.... Several British mining companies were established in the Brazils and Cuba ... worked chiefly by slaves, and British capital was employed by British subjects in the purchase of newly imported slaves from Africa.'

- *Report of the Committee of the African Civilization Society*, 1842, 'Employment of British Capital in the Slave Trade': 'This very important subject has been strenuously urged on the attention of Her Majesty's Government from various quarters, and there is reason to hope that some further measures of prevention will be devised to remedy so crying an evil.'[5]

- *Proceedings of the General Anti-Slavery Convention, held in London 1843*: 'in the report of the Directors of the Cobre Copper Company (in Cuba), in which many Englishmen, to their disgrace, are proprietors ... who hold 400 wretched human being in bondage.'[6]

- PP 1849 XIX, *Reports from Committees – Slave Trade*, 30 May, ff. 92–3, Stephen Lushington MP: 'It would be impossible to keep out British capital from engaging in the slave trade ... I know that it has been engaged in the slave trade even where it has been prohibited by our laws ... British capital has gone ... to the island of Cuba.'

The use of British merchandise in the slave trade

- PP 1839–40, *Slave Trade Papers*, Class A, p. 218, British Consul in Rio de Janeiro to Lord Palmerston, 6 May 1838: 'it is chiefly with British goods that the African market was supplied through this country'.

- The Attorney-General, Sir Frederick Pollock, had pronounced in 1842 that trading with known slavers was not illegal.[7]

- *British and Foreign Anti-Slavery Society, 5th Report, 1844, Resolutions*: 'That although a British merchant may furnish supplies to the most notorious slave-traders in the world, the evidence by which a charge of aiding and abetting the slave-trade can be substantiated against him is of such a nature that it is extremely difficult, if not impossible, to prosecute such an offender to conviction.'[8]
- 'We cannot recommend that a provision so difficult to be carried out [the stopping of 'provisioning' of slave vessels], so vexatious and yet so ineffectual for its object, should be made the subject of legislation.' (House of Commons Committee on British Possessions in West Africa, quoted in *African Repository* 21/6 (June 1845), p.184).
- PP XXII, 1847–8, *Slave Trade Committees*, Minutes of Evidence, 15 May 1848, Macgregor Laird questioned: 'You mean that the connexion with the slave trade and the employment of slaves is indirect ... arising from the supply of merchandise or from discounting bills of exchange?' Reply: 'Messrs Overend, Gurney and company do more in this way, on the arrival of every Brazilian or West Indian mail than any other men in London.'
- PP 1850, vol. IX, *Select Committee 1849*, q. 210, Lord Howden, ex-British Minister in Brazil: 'There is British capital employed in mining quite ostensibly. The great mines in Brazil, called Congo Socco, belonged to an English company ... I believe it belongs to one still.'

The use of British banks/bankers

- *Hansard*, House of Lords, 1841, vol. 59, 20 September, cols. 608–10, Lord Brougham: 'British banking companies had been formed in those countries [the Brazils and Cuba] ... were consignees of goods from British merchants which goods they must know were used ... only as barter for the purchase of slaves.'
- PP 1842, vol. XI, *Reports from Committees – West Coast of Africa*, p. 631, 18 July 1842, Thomas Whitfield, just returned from Africa, questioned: 'Have you seen bills drawn by Pedro Blanco on houses in England?' 'Yes, on Baring Bros.'
- PP XIX 1849, *Reports from Committees – Slave Trade*, 30 May: Stephen Lushington MP: 'articles indispensably requisite for the slave trade have been sent to various parts of Africa, and paid for either by bills on Spain or upon London' (f. 94).

Notes

Introduction

1. For Africans in India, see R.R.S. Chauhan, *Africans in India: From Slaves to Royalty*, New Delhi: Asian Publications Services, 1995; Shihan de S. Jayas-uriya et al., *The African Diaspora in the Indian Ocean*, Trenton NJ: African World Press, 2003; K.K. Prasad, *In Search of an Identity: An Ethnographic Study of the Siddis in Karnataka*, Bangalore: Jana Jagrati Prakashana, 2005. (My thanks to Cliff Pereira for these.)
2. David Eltis, 'The British contribution to the nineteenth-century trans-atlantic slave trade', *Economic History Review* 32/2 (1979), p. 211.

Chapter 1

1. Elizabeth I freed indigenous slaves in her lands in 1574. See G.W. Prothro, *Select Statutes and other Constitutional Documents ... Elizabeth and James I*, Oxford: Clarendon Press, 1898, pp. 173–4. On the export of Irish men and children, see W.R. Brownlow, *Lectures on Slavery and Serfdom in Europe*, London: Burns & Oates, 1892, pp. 401–9.
2. Spain, for example, began to import Africans to its silver mines in Mexico in the middle of the sixteenth century; the trade was abolished in 1817, by when around 200,000 African had been imported.
3. See, e.g., BL: Add. Mss 38416, Liverpool Papers, vol. 227.
4. *A Letter from Lord Denman to Lord Brougham on the Final Extinction of the Slave Trade*, London: Hatchard, 1848, p. 9.
5. Frank J. Klingberg, *The Anti-Slavery Movement in England* (1926), Hamden CT: Archon Books, 1968, p. 86.
6. Peter Leonard, *Record of a Voyage to the Western Coast of Africa in HMS Dryad, 1830–1832*, Edinburgh: William Tait, 1833, p. 237n.

7. David Eltis, 'Export of slaves from Africa 1821–1843', *Journal of Economic History* 37/2 (1977), p. 425.

8. See Paul Edwards, 'The early African presence in the British Isles', in Ian Duffield and Jagdish Gundara (eds), *Essays on the History of Blacks in Britain*, Aldershot and Brookfield VT: Avebury, 1992, pp. 9–29; Marika Sherwood, 'Black people in Tudor England', *History Today*, October 2003; 'Blacks in Tudor England', *BASA Newsletter* 38 (January 2004), 39 (April 2004), 40 (September 2004); Miranda Kaufman; '"The speedy transportation of blackamoores": Caspar Van Senden's search for Africans and profit in Elizabethan England', and Imtiaz Habib, 'Was Sir Peter Negro Black?', *BASA Newsletter* 46 (September 2006).

9. Hugh Thomas, *The Slave Trade*, London: Picador, 1997, pp. 155–6; S.T. Bindoff, *Tudor England* (1950), Harmondsworth: Penguin, 1972, pp. 252–3; James A. Rawley, *London: Metropolis of the Slave Trade*, Columbia: University of Missouri Press, n.d. (*c.* 2003).

10. Thus, contrary to popular belief, only the export of men and women from Britain into slavery, *not slavery in Britain*, was declared illegal by Chief Justice Mansfield.

11. James Elmes, *Thomas Clarkson: A Monograph* (1854), Miami: Mnemosyne Publishing, 1969, pp. 37–9; Prince Hoare, *Memoirs of Granville Sharp Esq*, vol. 1, London: Henry Colburn, 1827, p. 371.

12. For a list of names, see e.g. Peter Fryer, *Staying Power*, London: Pluto Press, 1984, p. 108; *BASA Newsletter* 44 (January 2006), p. 38.

13. This is available as a reprint by Mnemosyne Publishing, Miami, 1969.

14. Elmes, *Thomas Clarkson*, p. 73.

15. *Letters of the Late Ignatius Sancho, an African*, London, 1782.

16. Derrick Knight, *Gentlemen of Fortune*, London: Frederick Muller, 1978, p. 74.

17. James E. Inikori, *Africans and the Industrial Revolution in England*, Cambridge: Cambridge University Press, 2002, pp. 458–9, 464–5.

18. *Hansard*, House of Commons 1815, vol. 34, cols 168–77; *Substance of the Debate in the House of Commons 5 May 1823 ...* [re] *the Mitigation and Gradual Abolition of Slavery*, London, 1823.

19. See Knight, *Gentlemen of Fortune*, for much more on the Beckfords; Fryer, *Staying Power*, p. 48.

20. See Ellen Gibson Wilson, *Thomas Clarkson*, London: Macmillan, 1989. On 29 April 1830 Clarkson was honoured by being 'admitted to the freedom of the city' by the Corporation of London (Elmes, *Thomas Clarkson*, pp. 293–4). He died on 26 September 1848. On women's participation, see Clare Midgley, *Women Against Slavery*, London: Routledge, 1992.

21. Klingberg, *The Anti-Slavery Movement in England*, p. 146.

22. See, e.g., E.M. Howse, *Saints in Politics*, London: George Allen & Unwin, 1953; Charles Buxton (ed.), *Memoirs of Sir Thomas Fowell Buxton*, London: John Murray, 1882; R.H. Mottram, *Buxton the Liberator*, London: Hutchinson, n.d. (*c.* 1946); John Pollock, *Wilberforce*, Tring: Lion Publishing, 1977. Reginald Coupland, in his *Wilberforce* (London: Collins, 1945), indicates that Wilberforce's initial and ongoing interests in Parliament focused on 'Vice and Immorality', which included 'blasphemous and indecent publications'; he sought to be the 'guardian of the religion and morals of the people' by, for

example, suppressing 'indecorous rustic festivities' (Coupland, *Wilberforce*, p. 50).

23. Robin Blackburn, *The Overthrow of Colonial Slavery*, London: Verso, 1988, p. 472 n55; Joseph Wechsberg, *The Merchant Bankers*, New York: Pocket Books, 1966, p. 267. Compensation would have been especially welcomed by those planters whose extravagant lifestyle in Britain was leading them into bankruptcy. Generally, the plantations were run inefficiently with no thought to the welfare of the labourers or the introduction of any form of machinery. Most were affected by the increasing importation of sugar from India into the UK.

24. William Dickson, *Mitigations of Slavery*, London: Longman, 1814, p. 452.

25. Leslie Bethell, 'The mixed commissions for the suppression of the transatlantic slave trade in the 19th century', *Journal of African History* 7/1 (1966), pp. 79–93.

26. On India, see William Adam, *Slavery in India*, presented at (and printed by) the 1840 Anti-Slavery Convention.

27. Bethell, 'The mixed commissions', p. 82.

28. Christopher Fyfe, *A History of Sierra Leone*, Oxford: Oxford University Press, 1962, pp. 196–7.

29. Eric Williams, *Capitalism and Slavery* (1964), London: Andre Deutsch, 1975, pp. 88–9, 93, 99, 105; S.G. Checkland, 'John Gladstone as trader and planter', *Economic History Review* 7/2 (1954), pp. 216–29; J.L. Hammond and M.R.D. Foot, *Gladstone and Liberalism* (1952), London: English Universities Press, 1967.

30. David Eltis, *Economic Growth and the Ending of the Transatlantic Slave Trade*, Oxford: Oxford University Press, 1987, p. 249 Table A8, p. 252; Philip A. Curtin, *The Atlantic Slave Trade*, Madison: University of Wisconsin Press, 1969, pp. 283, 234; Paul E. Lovejoy, 'The volume of the Atlantic slave trade: a synthesis', *Journal of African History* 23 (1982), pp. 473–501.

31. Letter from Capt. Henry J. Matson, *The Times*, 14 August 1849, p. 3. Matson had commanded the very successful anti-slaver the *Waterwitch*. His *Remarks on the Slave Trade* was published in 1848.

32. Alan R. Booth, 'The US Africa Squadron', *Boston: University Papers in African History*, vol. 1, 1964, p. 111; Christopher Lloyd, *The Navy and the Slave Trade*, London: Longmans, Green, 1949, pp. 68, 124; Eltis, *Economic Growth*, p. 93.

33. Lloyd, *The Navy and the Slave Trade*, pp. 79–81.

34. On the Kru in Africa, see e.g. George E. Brooks, *The Kru Mariner in the Nineteenth Century*, Newark: Liberian Studies Association, 1972; on the Kru in Britain, see Diane Frost, *Work and Community among West African Migrant Workers in the Nineteenth Century*, Liverpool: Liverpool University Press, 1999.

35. Eltis, *Economic Growth*, pp. 3–4.

36. Richard B. Allen, *Slaves, Freedmen, and Indentured Laborers in Colonial Mauritius*, Cambridge: Cambridge University Press, 1999, pp. 14–15. It was Fowell Buxton who pushed the legislation through Parliament. For a description of Buxton Fowell's part in pressing the House to appoint a Select Committee to enquire into this, see R.H. Mottram, *Buxton the Liberator*, London: Hutchinson, n.d., pp. 70–72. Detailed evidence on the Mauritius slave trade was

gathered by yet another 'unsung' hero of abolitionism, Sir George Stephen (Klingberg, *The Anti-Slavery Movement in England*, p. 242).

37. Rhodes House: Mss Br. Emp s.18, Correspondence of John Tredgold, Box C8/52.

38. Rhodes House: Br. Emp. s.18, c158/216, Letter from Mr Joseph Angus, enclosing letter from T.H. Lewis. Correspondence with Local Record Office, Colchester (April and May 2005), which very kindly sent me the advertisements in the *Essex & Suffolk Times*, 15 August 1840, and *Essex County Standard*, 14 August 1840.

39. According to Dr Tom Wareham, Curator of Maritime and Community Histories, Museum in Docklands, there is no research on London's involvement in the trade in slaves or slavery.

40. African Institute, *7th Report*, 1815, p. 5.

41. Joseph C. Dorsey, *Slave Traffic in the Age of Abolition, 1815–1859*, Gainesville: University Press of Florida, 2003, p. 154. Mrs Isabel Lightburn was the daughter of an African mother and a European father; all her children were educated in England; the two daughters married Englishmen; the sons returned to the family trade on the river. Many of the slave traders on the coast were the children of such unions.

42. D. Eltis, 'The British trans-atlantic slave trade after 1807', *Maritime History* 4/1 (1974), p. 3; Thomas, *The Slave Trade*, p. 570.

43. David Eltis and James Walvin (eds), *The Abolition of the Atlantic Slave Trade*, Madison: University of Wisconsin Press, 1981, pp. 188–91; PP 1847–48, vol. XXII, *Slave Trade Committee*, Minutes of Evidence, Appendix: Consul Porter from Bahia to Lord Palmerston, 31 December 1847.

44. Eltis, 'The British trans-atlantic slave trade after 1807', p. 5.

45. TNA: FO84/1218, *Slave Trade Spain*, January–December 1864, ff. 233–40, 252, 264–5; Crawford to Russell, 10 May 1864.

46. Consul G.W. Slocum to Daniel Webster, Secretary of State, 1 May 1842, *House Executive Document #43, 29th Congress, 1st Session 1845–6*. This document, together with others relating to the trade in slaves, was presented to Congress in December 1845. The US Consuls in Rio were often staunch abolitionists and brought heavy (but ineffective) pressure on the US government to take more positive action to stop US (illegal) participation in the 'nefarious' trade.

47. Capt. Fair, RN, *A Letter to the Hon. W.T.H. Fox Strangeways, Under Secretary at the Foreign Office, on the Present State of the Slave Trade*, London: Ridgway, 1830.

48. Fyfe, *A History of Sierra Leone*, p. 184.

49. Williams, *Capitalism and Slavery*, p. 132.

50. David Eltis, 'The British contribution to the nineteenth-century trans-atlantic slave trade', *Economic History Review* 32/2 (1979), pp. 211–27.

51. Leland J. Jenks, *The Migration of British Capital to 1875*, London: Nelson, 1971, p. 44.

52. Eltis, 'The British contribution', p. 214.

53. Williams, *Capitalism and Slavery*, p. 242 n50.

54. D.C.M. Platt, *Latin America and British Trade 1806–1914*, London: A. & C. Black, 1972, Appendix I and II; H.R. Fox-Bourne, *English Merchants*, vol. 1, London:

R. Bentley, 1866, pp. 385–9.

55. Thomas Fowell Buxton, *The African Slave Trade and Its Remedy*, London: John Murray, 1840, p. 55n.

56. PP 1847–48, vol. XXII, *Slave Trade Committee*, 30 March 1848, p. 1684.

57. Eltis, 'The British contribution', p. 219.

58. *Minutes of the Proceedings of the General Anti-Slavery Convention of the BFASS, 12/6/1840*, London: Johnston & Barrett, 1840, p. 29.

59. Quoted in *Report of the Committee of the African Civilization Society, 21/6/1842, Exeter Hall*, London: John Murray, 1842, Appendix BB.

Chapter 2

1. A Genuine 'Dicky Sam', *Liverpool and Slavery: An Historical Account of the Liverpool–African Slave Trade* (1884), Liverpool: Scouse Press, 1985, p. 137. See also, e.g., Gail Cameron and Stan Crooke, *Liverpool, Capital of the Slave Trade*, Liverpool: Picton Press, 1992.

2. Eric Williams, *From Columbus to Castro* (1970), London: Andre Deutsch, 1983, p. 149.

3. Ibid., p. 118, list for 1750.

4. Ibid., p. 5.

5. Ibid., pp. 111, 103. According to the data from the Bank of England, the value of the pound halved between 1790 and 1800.

6. Ray Costello, *Black Liverpool*, Liverpool: Picton Press, 2001, p. 12.

7. Ellen Gibson Wilson, *Thomas Clarkson: A Biography*, London: Macmillan, 1989, p. 37.

8. H. Smithers, *Liverpool and its Commercial Statistics*, Liverpool: Thomas Kaye, 1825, p. 453.

9. David M. Williams, 'Abolition and the re-deployment of the slave fleet 1807–1811', *Journal of Transport History* II/2 (1973), pp. 103–15. Eleven vessels were redeployed to the Canaries and Azores, most probably carrying 'trade goods' to slavers awaiting them there. See Chapter 5, Africa.

10. B.K. Drake, 'Continuity and flexibility in Liverpool's trade with Africa and the Caribbean', *Business History*, 1976, pp. 85–97; p. 90.

11. PP 1852–53, vol. XCIX, *Return of sugar etc imported*. In the 1850s, about 60 per cent of the imported tobacco was exported. PP 1839, vol. XLVI, p. 175; B.R. Mitchell, *British Historical Statistics*, Cambridge: Cambridge University Press, 1988, 'External Trade', Table 7.

12. PP 1839, vol. XLVI, *Accounts & Papers*, p. 175. Greenock in Scotland was the second major port receiving slave-grown cotton; e.g. it received 5.5 million lb in 1838. According to F.W. Spackman (*An Analysis of Occupations of the People* [1847], New York: Augustus M. Kelley 1969, p. 55), in 1815, 92.5 million lb of raw cotton was imported; in 1844, 554.2 million lb.

13. Pamphlet in Liverpool Local History Archives, H382 SOM; Williams, 'Abolition and the re-deployment of the slave fleet 1807–1811', n26; PP 1865, *Accounts & Papers*, vol. L, 'General Imports 1864 – Cotton'; Cameron and Crooke, *Liverpool*, p. 31; Thomas Barnes, *History of the Commerce and Town of Liverpool*, London: Longman, Brown & Green, 1852, pp. 760, 778. In that year, 242 of the 754 ships cleared for the USA sailed to Southern ports (ibid.,

p. 773). Smithers, *Liverpool and its Commercial Statistics*, p. 254, states that in 1824 of the cotton imported 94 per cent came from slave-worked countries. The exports to Brazil included about 116 million yards of calicoes (Barnes, *History*, p. 807).

14. Every author gives a different figure. For example, D.A. Farnie (*The English Cotton Industry and the World Market 1815–1896*, Oxford: Clarendon Press, 1979, p. 10) states that the 'contribution of cotton manufactures to domestic exports of GB' was 53 per cent in 1784–1819; and 35 per cent in 1819–61. See also Spackman, *An Analysis of Occupations of the People*, p. 92.

15. The Rathbones were importing timber from Jamaica in the eighteenth century and also sold sugar, salt, coffee, lead, tobacco and ginger – some undoubtedly slave-grown. The company moved into cotton in 1785 and formed a new partnership, Rathbone Bros & Co. for this purpose; by 1846 they had 'a consignment business' with America, and American cotton. The company was associated with Barings. Lucie Nottingham, *Rathbone Brothers: From Merchant to Banker 1742–1992*, London: Rathbone Brothers, 1992, pp. 10, 22, 36, 50, 57. Captain Tucker of the Anti-slave Trade Squadron on the West African coast informed the government on 30 July 1841 that he had 'arrested' a vessel named the *Rathbone* for assisting a slave vessel. I presume this was owned by Rathbone Bros (TNA: FO84/616).

16. E. Chambré Hardman Archives, www.mersey-gateway.org, 'sugar and cotton'; John Saville, *The Consolidation of the Capitalist State*, London: Pluto Press, 1994, p. 12.

17. See, e.g., material in Liverpool Record Office: Hq 338/476 CUT, Cotton Exchange Cuttings.

18. Barnes, *History*, pp. 809.

19. Ibid., pp. 807, 809; *Gore's Liverpool Directory* 1842, 1848, 1851. The members listed were James Peter, James Powell and John North (1842) and J.B. Moore, C. Saunders and John North (1848 and 1851).

20. TNA: FO84/616, Domestic Various 1845: 'Memorandum of British Subjects and Capital Engaged in the Slave trade 1834–1845', f. 256.

21. W.S. Lindsay, *History of Merchant Shipping*, vol. 4, London: Sampson Low, Marston, Low and Searle, 1874, pp. 317–33. I looked at entries for 1820, for the 28th day of every second month; at the 2nd day of every second month for 1832; and for the 15th day of every second month in 1850. Cotton, linens and 'hardware' are the most frequently listed exports. (There are no particular reasons for my choice of years or dates.)

22. Drake, 'Continuity and flexibility', pp. 91–3; A.G. Hopkins, 'Economic imperialism in West Africa: Lagos, 1880–92', *Economic History Review* 21/3 (1968), p. 585.

23. Drake, 'Continuity and flexibility', p. 117, quoting *Hansard*, 17 May 1848.

24. Cloth exports rose from 2.5 million yards in 1830 to 17 million yards in 1850: Martin Lynn, 'Liverpool and Africa in the nineteenth century', *Transactions of the Historic Society of Lancashire and Cheshire* 147 (1998), pp. 27–54. Barry K. Drake, 'Liverpool's African commerce before and after the abolition of the slave trade', M.A. thesis, University of Liverpool, 1974, pp. 146–7, 263. Gavin White, 'Firearms in Africa', *Journal of African History* 12/2 (1971), pp. 173–84; p. 180. See also R.A. Kea, 'Firearms and warfare on the Gold and Slave Coasts

from the sixteenth to the nineteenth centuries', *Journal of African History* 12/2 (1971), pp. 185–213; the *Export Merchant Shippers of London Directory* for 1873, which shows that liquor, guns and cottons remained the staple exports.

25. Martin Lynn, 'Trade and politics in 19th century Liverpool', *Transactions of the Historic Society of Lancashire and Cheshire* 142 (1993), pp. 99–120; letter from Martin Lynn, 8 May 1997, quoting data from Susan Martin, *Palm Oil and Protest* (Cambridge: Cambridge University Press, 1988).

26. See, e.g., Martyn Lynn, *Commerce and Economic Change in West Africa: The Palm Oil Trade in the Nineteenth Century*, Cambridge: Cambridge University Press, 1997, pp. 51–2; David Northrup, 'The compatibility of the slave and palm oil trades in the Bight of Benin', *Journal of African History* 17/3 (1976), pp. 353–64.

27. Hugh Thomas, *The Slave Trade*, London: Picador, 1997, pp. 570–71.

28. 'Pawns' are usually described as people temporarily enslaved because of debts. This description is questionable – see Chapter 5, 'Africa'.

29. Liverpool Local History Archives, 920 Roscoe Papers, #859, Clarkson to Roscoe, 12 June 1809.

30. Roscoe Papers, #2496, Roscoe to Macaulay, 10 February 1812. It should be noted that not all the vessels I tried to trace through *Lloyd's* could be found in that supposedly infallible register of British shipping. The correspondence begins with a letter from Macaulay in March 1809, asking Roscoe to become a member of the Committee of the African Institute's Directors, appointed to 'watch over the execution of the Abolition laws'.

31. On Roscoe, see e.g. Anne Holt, *Walking Together*, London: Allen & Unwin, 1838; H. Roscoe, *The Life of William Roscoe*, London: T. Cadell, 1833.

32. Liverpool Local History Archives, 920 Roscoe Papers, #2475, 8 July 1809; #2478, 10 November 1809; E. Chambré Hardman Archives, 'Did slave trading continue after abolition?', www.mersey-gateway.org.

33. Liverpool Local History Archives, 920 Roscoe Papers, #2478, Macaulay to Roscoe, 10 November 1809; #2479, Macaulay report to the Directors of the Anti-Slavery Society, 7 November 1809, encl. letter from Clarkson of August 1809; #2480, Macaulay to Roscoe, 8 December 1809. For the names of more vessels, see *Edinburgh Review* 18 (1811), pp. 305–25.

34. It is interesting to note that there is no vessel by this name listed in *Lloyd's Register* 1836–42, yet the *Register* is supposed to list all ships registered in the UK. Did this ship change hands and names somewhere? This is also reported in the *Anti-Slavery Reporter*, 23 September 1840, p. 247.

35. *Report from the Select Committee on the West Coast of Africa*, London: House of Commons, 5 August 1842, pp. 318–20; PP 1840, vol. XX, *Slave Trade Papers*, Class A: Correspondence with British Commissioners Relating to the Slave Trade, pp. 17 et seq.; PP 1841, vol. XI, *Slave Trade Papers*, pp. 17–20. The common practice of disembarking and re-embarking cargo is noted here.

36. Report on the *Guiana* in PP 1841, vol. XI, *Slave Trade Papers*, Commissioners R. Doherty and W.E. Lewis in Sierra Leone to Lord Palmerston, 27 August 1840.

37. *Cornwall and Scilly Historic Environment Record*, NGR SV 82660 07380; *Lloyd's List*, 2 February 1843; National Maritime Museum: Newspaper Cuttings, 3 October 1977.

38. TNA: FO84/712: Slave Trade Sierra Leone 1848, #34, James Hook to Lord Palmerston, 12 December 1848; PP 1849, vol. XIX, *Reports from Committees*: 'To consider the best means for the final extinction of the slave trade', questions 189–192; report from Mixed Commission Court Acting Judge James Hook, 31 December 1848, in the Appendix. Christopher Fyfe, *A History of Sierra Leone*, Oxford: Oxford University Press, 1962, p. 247.

39. TNA: TS25/238, Treasury Solicitor's department, April 1846.

40. See BFASS, *Slave-Traders in Liverpool – Extracts from the Slave Trade Correspondence*, April 1862; Marika Sherwood, 'Perfidious Albion: Britain, the USA and slavery in the 1840s and 1860s', *Contributions in Black Studies* 13/14 (1995), pp. 174–200.

41. Liverpool Local History Archives, 920 Roscoe Papers, #2479 letter from Clarkson, August 1809, encl. in Macaulay report of 7 November 1809; #2493, Macaulay to Roscoe, 28 October 1811; #2494, Macaulay to Roscoe, 14 November 1811; #861, draft of letter form Roscoe to Clarkson, 13 January 1811; Eric Williams, *Capitalism and Slavery* (1944), London: Andre Deutsch, 1975, p. 171.

42. Roscoe, *The Life*, vol. 2, p. 477; Liverpool Local History Archives, 920 Roscoe Papers, #2476, draft of letter by Roscoe, n.d.; #2477, deposition by Ioze, 28 July 1809.

43. Taken from Derrick Knight, *Gentlemen of Fortune*, London: Frederick Muller, 1978, pp. 66–80; Thomas, *The Slave Trade*, pp. 248, 296, 531; *Gore's Liverpool Directory*, 1829; Lynn, 'Trade and politics'; A Genuine 'Dicky Sam', *Liverpool and Slavery*, pp. 120–29. For other well-known names profiting from the slave trade and slavery, see Williams, *Capitalism and Slavery*, pp. 87–105.

44. Tony Lane, *Gateway to Empire*, London: Lawrence & Wishart, 1987, pp. 32, 117; Marika Sherwood, *Pastor Daniels Ekarte and the African Churches Mission*, London: Savannah Press, 1994, p. 6.

45. Sherwood, *Pastor Daniels Ekarte*, p. 9.

46. I shall not describe Gladstone's very active role in destroying the power of the East India Company and in setting up a banking system for India. See Tony Webster, 'Liverpool and the Eastern trade, 1800–1850', paper presented at the conference Liverpool and Empire, Liverpool, April 2006.

47. Nothing is known of the fate of one of the Whites, but the other, John Smith, a missionary, was tried and sentenced to death. The King commuted the sentence but Smith, an ill man, died before the order expelling him reached Demerara. Jack Gratus, *The Great White Lie*, London: Hutchinson, 1974, pp. 169–71.

48. Ibid., pp. 166–72; Robin Blackburn, *The Overthrow of Colonial Slavery*, London: Verso, 1988, pp. 429–31.

49. Smithers, *Liverpool and its Commercial Statistics*, p. 448.

50. PP 1837/8, vol. LII, *Slavery and the State Papers*, pp. 2–9. The Calcutta firm of Gillanders, Arbuthnot & Co. was experienced in recruiting Indian labour for Mauritius. D. Dabydeen and B. Samaroo (eds), *India in the Caribbean*, London: Hansib, 1987, pp. 28–9; Hugh Tinker, *A New System of Slavery*, London: Hansib, 1993, p. 63.

51. Blackburn, *The Overthrow of Colonial Slavery*, p. 464.

52. Tinker, *A New System of Slavery*, p. 69.

53. Howard Temperley, *British Anti-Slavery 1833–1870*, London: Longman, 1972, pp. 125–6; *Anti-Slavery Reporter*, 24 February 1841, p. 59.

54. *The Correspondence between John G. Gladstone Esq. MP and James Cropper Esq. On the Present State of Slavery in the British West Indies and in the United States of America…with Appendix*, Liverpool: West India Association, 1824, pp. 17, 71; *Facts Relating to Slavery in the West Indies and America … addressed to Sir Robert Peel by John Gladstone of Liverpool*, 1830. This is the second edition, published in London, Liverpool, Bristol, Edinburgh and Glasgow. Gladstone was certainly spreading his opinions around the country!

55. S.G. Checkland, 'John Gladstone as trader and planter', *Economic History Review* 7/2 (1954), pp. 216–29; www.en/wikipedia.org.wiki/John_Gladstone; *Fortunes Made in Business – by Various Writers*, vol. 2, London: Sampson Law, 1884, pp. 109–78; Barnes, *History*, pp. 608–9, 618; Philip Magnus, *Gladstone* (1954), London: John Murray, 1963, p. 2. Magnus describes the revolt of the slaves on Gladstone's Demerara plantation and his belief that 'the difficulties regarding emancipation are insurmountable'. Twenty-seven of the slaves were executed. Gladstone's coat of arms 'included a savage's head, affronté, distilling drops of blood' (pp. 2–3). On the bribery charges against Thomas, see Checkland, 'John Gladstone as trader and planter', p. 235; M. Stenton, *Who's Who of British MPs 1832–1885*, Hassocks: Harvester Press, 1976.

56. M.M. Schofield, 'Shoes and ships and sealing wax: 18th century Lancashire exports to the colonies', *Transactions of the Historic Society of Lancashire and Cheshire* 135 (1984), pp. 61–82; the report is on p. 76.

57. Derrick Knight, *Gentlemen of Fortune*, London: Frederick Muller, 1978, p. 70; Thomas, *The Slave Trade*, p. 296.

58. Spackman, *Occupations of the People*, p. 47.

59. Andrew Porter, '"Gentlemanly capitalism" and empire', *Journal of Imperial and Commonwealth History* 18/3 (October 1990), pp. 265–5; the quotation is from p. 278; Sherwood, *Pastor Daniels Ekarte*, p. 5.

60. The other main 'cotton' cities were Ashton, Bolton, Bury, Oldham, Preston and Stockport. According to Thomas Ellison (*The Cotton Trade of Great Britain* [1886] London: Frank Cass, 1968, p. 52), in 1800 only 56 million lb had been imported. The total number of mills in England was 3959; of these 3165 were in Lancashire, Cheshire and Yorkshire (Barnes, *History*, p. 760).

61. Arthur Redford, *Manchester Merchants and Foreign Trade 1794–1858*, Manchester: Manchester University Press, 1934, p. 99; Ellison, *The Cotton Trade*, Table 1. The British cotton industry also partially destroyed the 2000-year-old cotton manufacturing industry in India. Initially this was done by imposing a 78 per cent duty on Indian calicoes imported into Britain and then by ongoing manipulations of both the duty paid on British cottons imported into India and that on raw cotton imported into England. See, e.g., R. Palme Dutt, *Guide to the Problem of India*, London: Victor Gollancz, 1942, pp. 49–51; C.C. Eldridge (ed.), *British Imperialism in the Nineteenth Century*, London: Macmillan, 1987, pp. 75, 77, 79–80; M. de P. Webb, *India and the Empire*, London: Longman, 1908, pp. 100–106; R.J. Moore, *Liberalism and Indian Politics 1872–1922*, London: Edward Arnold, 1966, pp. 17, 19, 70.

62. Frederick Engels, *The Condition of the Working Class in England* (1892), St Albans: Granada, 1976, pp. 171–2; there are excellent descriptions of the

cotton towns on pp. 75–105. There is huge disagreement regarding the numbers directly employed in the cotton industry. For example, *British Historical Statistics* (Cambridge: Cambridge University Press, 1988), which devotes pp. 330–56 to cotton, gives 413,000 workers for 1825, 408,000 for 1835, 333,000 for 1845, 398,000 for 1855 and 401,000 for 1867. The estimates of S.D. Chapman (*The Cotton Industry*, London: Macmillan, 1972, p. 60) are 110,000 'domestic workers' in the cotton industry in 1795 and 348,000 in 1833; R. Robson (*The Cotton Industry in Britain*, London: Macmillan, 1959, p. 342) gives over 400,000 'spinning and weaving operatives' from 1829 onwards.

63. Lancashire population figures from B.R. Mitchell, *British Historical Statistics*, Cambridge: Cambridge University Press, 1988, pp. 30–31; Sydney J. Chapman, *The Cotton Industry*, Manchester: Manchester University Press, 1904, p. 112; Norman Longmate, *The Hungry Mills*, London: Temple Smith, 1978, p. 49; Virginia Berridge and Griffith Edwards, *Opium and the People*, London: Allen Lane, 1981, pp. 97–106. A contemporary researcher calculated that 'in every seven years, 14,000 children die in Manchester over and above the natural proporion' (W. and R. Chambers, *The Cotton Metropolis (1849–1850)*, Manchester: R. Shipperbotton, 1972, p. 15). The government only began to take action as the numbers of opium-related deaths among children increased.

64. L.C.A. Knowles, *Industrial and Commercial Revolutions in Britain during the Nineteenth Century* (1921), London: Routledge, 1966, p. 59; Tony Barley, *Myths of the Slave Power*, Liverpool: Coach House Press, 1992, p. 72. Authors give different figures for the numbers employed. Ellison (*The Cotton Trade*, p. 66) gives 486,600 for 1841 and 646,000 for 1861, and for children under 13 in the industry in 1874, 66,900 (p. 327). According to George Henry Wood (*The History of Wages in the Cotton Trade*, London: Sherratt & Hughes, 1910, pp. 123, 136), by 1859 there were 451,000 factory workers and between 5000 and 10,000 hand loom weavers in the cotton industry; the proportion of children under 13 at that time was 8.8 per cent; this rose to 13.9 per cent in 1874. See also Richard Burn, *Statistics of the Cotton Trade*, London: Simpkin, Marshall, n.d. (*c.* 1847); D.A Farnie, *The English Cotton Industry 1815–1896*, Oxford: Clarendon Press, 1979, p. 24.

65. Longmate, *The Hungry Mills*, p. 56. The total population of Lancaster was *c.* 1.7 million. The increase in population was fairly rapid at this time: e.g. it rose from 18 million in 1853 to 21.5 million by 1867.

66. The growth in industrialisation affected poverty levels as the 'average number of paupers' in Britain dropped from just over 1 million in 1849 to 992,640 in 1868. The preferred 'remedy' for dealing with paupers was forced migration for those who were counted as living in 'undeserved pauperism' (James Greenwood, *The Seven Curses of London*, London: Stanley Rivers, 1869, pp. 421, 431, 455). Emigration had long been seen as a cure, a palliative; in 1840 a commission to encourage it had been set up; from 1846 to 1855, between 2 and 3 million had emigrated from the UK; between 1871 and 1931, about 4 million. Terry Colman, *Passage to America*, Harmondsworth: Penguin, 1976, pp. 21–2; *Royal Commission on Population*, London: HMSO, 1949, p. 122.

67. Ellison, *The Cotton Trade*, pp. 122, 126, 130; Ralph Davis, *The Industrial Revolution and British Overseas Trade*, Leicester: Leicester University Press, p. 17. G.

Jones (*Merchants and Multinationals*, Oxford: Oxford University Press, 2000, p. 39) gives a figure of £52 million for 1860 (£2277.6 million in 2005).

68. Redford, *Manchester Merchants*, p. 243.

69. D.A. Farnie, *The English Cotton Industry and the World Market 1815–1896*, Oxford: Clarendon Press, 1979, p. 24; Robson, *The Cotton Industry in Britain*, p. 334; Arthur W. Silver, *Manchester Men and Indian Cotton 1847–1872*, Manchester: Manchester University Press, 1966, p. 5.

70. Library of Congress, *Guide to the Records of Ante-bellum Southern Plantations*, Series I, Louisiana, and Series J, Louisiana, Pt 5.

71. Harold D. Woodman, *King Cotton and His Retainers*, Lexington: University of Kentucky Press, 1968, pp. 17–18, 18n.

72. Stanley Broadbridge, 'The Lancashire cotton "famine" 1861–65', in Lionel M. Munby, *The Luddites and Other Essays*, London: Michael Katanka Books, 1971, pp. 143–4; Woodman, *King Cotton*, p. 18; Phillip Ziegler, *The Sixth Great Power: Barings 1762–1929*, London: Collins, 1988, pp. 131, 201, 288. Barings, as bankers, had also 'floated' shares for the Manchester Ship Canal in 1894, and for the Mersey Docks and Harbours Board.

73. My very grateful thanks to Devon Lee of the Manuscripts Department of the Library at the University of North Carolina at Chapel Hill.

74. All the data is from W.D. Rubinstein, 'British Millionaires, 1809–1949', *Bulletin of the Institute of Historical Research* 47 (1947), pp. 202–9.

75. This pamphlet is available in the Canterbury Cathedral archives.

76. Sir George Stephen, *Anti-Slavery Recollections*, London: Hatchard, 1854, p. 42.

77. Redford, *Manchester Merchants*, pp. 99–100, 101–3, 106.

78. Ibid., p. 106.

79. TNA: FO84/616, Domestic Various 1845: Memorandum of British Subjects and Capital Engaged in the Slave Trade 1834– 1845, e.g. f. 274.

80. In, e.g., NA: CO96/12, 'Gold Coast 1847', there is a special section for 'Mr Hutton'.

81. Barrie M. Ratcliffe, 'Commerce and Empire: Manchester Merchants and West Africa 1873–1895', *Journal of Imperial & Commonwealth History* 7/3 (May 1979), pp. 293–320; Thomas, *The Slave Trade*, p. 690. On the Congo, see e.g. Adam Hochschild, *King Leopold's Ghost*, London: Macmillan, 2000.

82. Francis E. Hyde, *Liverpool and the Mersey*, Devon: David & Charles 1971, p. 98; Broadbridge, 'The Lancashire cotton "famine" 1861–65', p. 155.

83. Longmate, *The Hungry Mills*, pp. 21–2.

84. Ibid., pp. 272–4, quoting the *Liverpool Daily Post*.

85. Mary Ellison, *Support for Secession: Lancashire and the American Civil War*, Chicago: Chicago University Press, 1972, p. 48.

86. From Sherwood, 'Perfidious Albion', pp. 174–200, which lists many of the innumerable publications on the British involvement with the Confederates. The quotation is from Thomas E. Taylor, *Running the Blockade*, London: John Murray, 1896, p. 185.

87. Union and Emancipation Society, *Earl Russell and the Slave Power*, Manchester, 1863; *Report of a Public Meeting in the Free Trade Hall, Manchester on 'War Ships for the Southern Confederacy'*, Manchester, 1863. These and other informative publications by the society are available at the British Library.

88. James D. Bulloch, *The Secret Service of the Confederate States in Europe, or How the Confederate Cruisers Were Equipped* (1884), New York: Modern Library, 2001, p. 76. This book gives all the details of Bulloch's achievements – and hence of the many British companies' infringements of the neutrality laws and support for the Southern slave states.

89. George Chandler, *Liverpool Shipping*, London: Phoenix House, 1960, p. 35; Longmate, *The Hungry Mills*, pp. 233, 235; email from Malcolm McRonald, 28 November 2005; some of these other ships are listed in Ellison, *Support for Secession*, pp. 168–72.

90. Bulloch, *The Secret Service of the Confederate States in Europe*, pp. 252–4.

91. Longmate, *The Hungry Mills*, p. 230.

92. Ibid., p. 55; David Hollett, *The Alabama Affair*, Wilmslow: Sigma Press, 1993, p. 54. See also Frank J. Merli and Thomas W. Green, 'Great Britain and the Confederate Navy 1861–1865', *History Today* 14/10 (October 1964), pp. 687–95.

93. Tony Barley, *Myths of the Slave Power*, Liverpool: Coach House Press, 1992, p. 42.

94. Hollett, *The Alabama Affair*, p. 53; *Illustrated London News*, 19 December 1863, p. 647.

95. Hollett, *The Alabama Affair*, p. 276.

96. Ibid., pp. 248–52; Ellison, *Support for Secession*, p. 190; Chandler, *Liverpool Shipping*, p. 35. See also Philip S. Foner, *British Labour and the American Civil War*, New York: Holmes & Meier, 1981.

97. *New York Herald-Tribune*, 14 October 1861; from www.marx.org/archive/marx/works/1861/10/14.htm.

98. Hyde, *Liverpool and the Mersey*, p. 240.

99. Peter Mathias, *The First Industrial Nation* (1969), London: Methuen, 1983, p. 239; numbers for 1844 in Spackman, *An Analysis*, p. 159.

100. Spackman, *An Analysis*, Appendix, pp. 5, 18–19, 44–5. The data is for 1844 for the counties of Chester, Lancaster and York West Riding. I have not included the separate figures for 'weavers' as these include silk and woollen workers.

101. Spackman, *An Analysis*, p. 60.

102. Ibid., Appendix p. 172.

Chapter 3

1. I know of only one book on the tobacco trade: T.M. Devine, *The Tobacco Lords*, Edinburgh: Edinburgh University Press, 1975; reprinted 1990. Sadly this only covers the period until 1790.

2. Kingston Committee, *The Jamaican Movement for Promoting the Enforcement of Slave Trade Treaties and the Suppression of the Slave-Trade*, London: Charles Gilpin, 1850, pp. 418–28.

3. Douglas J. Hallam, *The First Two Hundred Years: A Short History of Rabone Chesterman Ltd*, Birmingham: Rabone Chesterman, 1984. My thanks to Fiona Tait for telling me of this book.

4. My thanks, yet again, to archivist Fiona Tait, who, after reading the draft on Rabone Bros, scoured the archives for more material and found Ms 2536,

two pamphlets on Rabones: *The Rabone Peterson Group of Companies. Now in the third century of continuous export trading*, and *Rabone, Petersen & Company Ltd.* No dates of publication or authors' names are given. The information I've used is from the chapter entitled 'Over 200 years of trading', in the first publication.

5. Email correspondence with Plymouth West Devon Records Office, July 2005.

6. Birmingham Archives: Ms 3782/1/9, Boulton & Fothergill Letter Book 1770–1773, Rabone & Crinsoz, 23 January 1771. Crinsoz was naturalised in 1771; he was probably Swiss-born. In 1784 he was declared bankrupt. Whether this was his own firm or that of Rabone & Crinsoz I have not checked. NA: T1/568/150A-151, Victualling – Admiralty.

7. By this did he mean that the company used to 'charter their own vessels' for the Cuban trade, as noted in the pamphlet on the firm? So why not build them? And have them built so they could be used for a multiplicity of purposes?

8. British Library, 5156.c.54: A Letter to Lord Viscount Palmerston by Thomas Lloyd Esq., dated Birmingham, 4 August 1850. The *Triumfante* is listed as sailing from/to Havana in July 1850 and May 1851. TNA: FO84/401, ff. 198–200, Turnbull to Aberdeen, 15 March 1842; ff. 203–4, Turnbull to Aberdeen, 11 May 1842. In his original letter to Lord Aberdeen, sent from Havana, Thomas Lloyd complains bitterly of Turnbull: 'I have suffered every species of arrogance and vexation from his ungentlemanly, overbearing and un-businesslike conduct'. As Lloyd goes on to mention 'the state of competition which our manufactures are subject to from the Americans', could it have been the possible loss of profits that led him to complain of 'unbusinesslike' behaviour? TNA: FO84/447, Lloyd to Aberdeen, 12 March 1842.

9. TNA: FO84/357, ff. 165–73, Turnbull to Lord Palmerston, 24 May 1841. A report by Edward Schenley, dated 4 May 1841, is enclosed by Turnbull. This states that he had twice been on board 'and never seen a vessel better calculated to carry a large cargo of slaves … her hatches, even in their present state, are not such as a merchant vessel destined for legal traffic ought to possess'. The Spanish 'supercargo's' name is given here as Menchaca.

10. William West, *Directory of Warwickshire*, 1830, Birmingham Section; www.ibrax.com

11. Probably at least from the early twentieth century, Rabones had an agent in Chile, Townsend & Cia (www.patbrit.com/eng/Econ/PABrits.html).

12. Emails from Peter Drake, Local History Librarian, Birmingham Central Library, 29 March and 1 April 2006. Peter referred me to a book by Samuel Lloyd, *The Lloyds of Birmingham* (Birmingham: Cornish Bros, 1909), which states that Thomas Lloyd was deputy chair of Lloyds Banking Co. Ltd in 1865 (Appendix II); this became Lloyds & Co., a public company, which, after acquiring other banks, moved to London in 1884.

13. Birmingham Library, Local History section, ref. 306.

14. Eric Hopkins, *The Rise of the Manufacturing Town: Birmingham and the Industrial Revolution*, Thrupp: Sutton Publishing, 1998, p. 48.

15. Jenny Uglow, *The Lunar Men*, London: Faber & Faber, 2002, p. 414; www.

search.revolutionaryplayers.org.uk/egnine/resource/exhibition: '3. Commerce, slavery and anti-slavery'.

16. S. Timmins (ed.), *The Resources, Products and Industrial History of Birmingham and the Midland Hardware Districts*, London: R. Hardwicke, 1866, pp. 391, 418–20; Hugh Thomas, *The Slave Trade*, London: Picador, 1997, p. 325.

17. There is a little correspondence dating from 1859 preserved in the Unilever Archives: Gambia: Miscellaneous papers, 1858–1869. By 1859 Forster & Smith's local agent was William Goddard. He seems also to have used his own agents there, F.S. Ingram and Francis T. Evans.

18. George E. Brooks, *Yankee Traders, Old Coasters and African Middlemen: A History Of Legitimate Trade in West Africa in the 19th Century*, Boston MA: Boston University Press, 1970. p. 153.

19. Ibid., p. 168. Elder Dempster, who controlled West African shipping some fifty years later, used the same tactics. See Marika Sherwood, 'Elder Dempster and West Africa 1891–1940: the genesis of underdevelopment', *International Journal of African Historical Studies* 30/3 (1997).

20. M. Lynn, 'The British palm oil trade with West Africa 1833–1855', ICS Seminars in Imperial and Colonial Economic History, 1976/7. The league of importers is headed by members of the slaving families Tobin and Horsfall. The price markup, according to Lynn, was 100 per cent in the nineteenth century: letter from M. Lynn, Queen's University, Belfast, 8 May 1997.

21. Edward Reynolds, *Trade and Economic Change on the Gold Coast 1807–1874*, Harlow: Longman, 1974, p. 90; PP 1839–40, *Slave Trade Papers Class B*, pp. 36–9, Consul Tolmé, 10 May 1839, to Foreign Secretary.

22. F. Boyle, *Through Fanteeland to Coomassie*, London: Chapman Hall, 1874, pp. 31–3.

23. Roderick Braithwaite, 'Matthew Forster of Bellsise', *Camden History Review* 19 (1995), pp. 13–16; the quotation is from p. 14.

24. Roderick Braithwaite, *Palmerston and Africa*, London: British Academic Press, 1996, p. 74. Unless stated otherwise, this account of Forster & Smith is taken from Braithwaite's work.

25. The Liverpool Board chairman, J.C Ewart, Liverpool MP, removed Forster from the chairmanship of the London board of the Liverpool & London Insurance Co. in 1859. Why this was remains obscure. See *The Times*, 15 November 1859 (anonymous, but obviously by Forster), *A Statement of Facts relating to Mr Matthew Forster's Removal from the London Board of the Liverpool and London Insurance Company, Addressed to the Shareholders*, London, n.d.

26. Berwick-upon-Tweed Record Office, BRO/10/1/23 re sale of stocks in the Berwick Salmon Fisheries by Robert Guthrie to Matthew Forster; *Newcastle Journal*, 3 July 1841, in Braithwaite, *Palmerston and Africa*, p. 80.

27. *The Times*, 31 August 1852, p. 7; 6 September 1852, p. 8; 18 April 1853, p. 5; 8 February 1854, p. 10; 15 November 1858, p. 5.

28. *The Times*, 23 February 1847, p. 6.

29. Braithwaite, *Palmerston and Africa*, p. 80, quoting the *Newcastle Journal* of 3 July 1841. Forster's business record begs further investigation. For example, he was on the London board of the Liverpool and London Insurance Company, which was accused in 1858 of not sharing investment information with all board members. *The Times*, 15 and 21 November 1858, p. 5;

21 December 1859, p. 7.

30. He sat on the Decimal Coinage Committee. Was this perhaps because of his interest in gold? *The Times*, 12 April 1853, p. 4.

31. On this history, see e.g. G.E. Metcalfe, *Maclean of the Gold Coast*, Oxford: Oxford University Press, 1962.

32. F. Pedler, *The Lion and the Unicorn in Africa*, London: Heinemann, 1974, pp. 39–40. On aspects of the history of the Ahanta nation in South-Eastern Gold Coast, see C.W. Welman, *The Native States of the Gold Coast*, London: Dawson, 1969, Part II.

33. Brooks, *Yankee Traders*, p. 268.

34. Robin Law, *Ouidah: The Social History of a West African Slaving 'Port' 1727–1892*, Oxford: James Currey, 2004, p. 170; *Report from the Select Committee on the West Coast of Africa*, Hansard, House of Commons, 5 August 1842, p. 320.

35. Pedler, *The Lion and the Unicorn in Africa*, pp. 33, 288.

36. Ibid., pp. 42–3; the story is told somewhat differently in E. Reynolds, *Trade and Economic Change on the Gold Coast 1807–1874*, pp. 140 ff. I tend to believe Reynolds.

37. Christopher Fyfe, *A History of Sierra Leone*, Oxford: Oxford University Press, 1962, p. 239. Charles Heddle was the son of an African mother and an Orkadian army doctor who had committed suicide before his son's birth. By 1834 he was an established merchant, at first in Gambia then in Sierra Leone, where he became one of the most eminent citizens. He was an early 'correspondent' of Forster & Smith.

38. Thomas, *The Slave Trade*, p. 683.

39. Brooks, *Yankee Traders*, pp. 267–8; Graeme J. Milne, *Trade and Traders in Mid-Victorian Liverpool*, Liverpool: Liverpool University Press, 2000, p. 61, quoting the evidence of Tobin to the Parliamentary West African Committee, 1865, 1.5234.

40. Rhodes House: Mss. Br. Emp. S.444, vol. 29, ff. 33, etc. There is also correspondence in vols 17, 27, 30 and 31.

41. Email correspondence with Victor Gray, archivist, Rothschild & Co., April 2005.

42. Forster's letters were never short; one I looked at was twelve pages! He was such a constant correspondent that in many government files (e.g. CO96/12 1847; CO96/17, 1849) there are sections labelled either 'Matthew Forster' or 'Forster & Smith'.

43. See, e.g., TNA: CO96/12, 'Gold Coast 1847' and CO96/17, 'Gold Coast 1949', 'Forster & Smith' sections.

44. TNA: CO87/7, Gambia, 1832: Letters from Forster, 21, 24 and 26 April; 17 August. CO267/117: Sierra Leone and African Ports 1832: Forster to Viscount Goodrich, 9 January. The pamphlet is also at Rhodes House Library, Buxton Correspondence, vol. 29, ff. 313–20.

45. Forster & Smith to the Colonial Secretary, 9 January 1832, in R. Montgomery Martin, *History of the British Colonies*, vol. 4, London: James Cochrane, 1835, p. 610.

46. *The Times*, 30 August 1839, p. 7.

47. Braithwaite, 'Matthew Forster of Bellsize', p. 16; and Braithwaite, *Palmerston and Africa*. The author is a descendant of Joseph Braithwaite.

48. For example, *A Second Letter to the Rt. Hon. Lord John Russell on the Plans of the Society for the Civilisation of Africa, by Sir George Stephen*, London: Saunders & Otley 1840.

49. TNA: CO267/170, Forster to Lord Stanley, 28 September 1841.

50. *Anti-Slavery Reporter*, 20 April 1842, p. 61; 2 November 1842, p. 192.

51. Dr Madden's report can be seen in TNA: CO267/171. See also his *The Slave Trade and Slavery: The Influence of British Settlements on the West Coast of Africa, in Relation to Both: Illustrated by Extracts from the Letters of Dr R.R. Madden in the Morning Chronicle, the United Service Gazette, etc.*, London: James Madden, 1843.

52. On Da Souza, see e.g. Law, *Ouidah*.

53. See, e.g., TNA: CO267/178, Treasury to James Stephen of the Colonial Office, 17 November 1842; letter from [illegible signature] to Stephen and Lord Stanley, 16 December 1842; CO167/177, evidence by Capt. William Tucker 29 March 1841 and correspondence in the 'Foreign Office' and 'Law Officers' sections; CO267/167, correspondence between the Colonial Office, the Admiralty, naval officers, Privy Council for Trade, the Foreign Office and Matthew Forster, July to November 1841.

54. TNA: CO267/170, Sierra Leone and African Forts 1841: letters from Forster & Smith, e.g. 29 June, 19 July, 25 and 26 August, 24 and 28 September, 23 November, 4 and 22 December; Law, *Ouidah*, p. 204.

55. TNA: CO267/178, Sierra Leone and African Forts vol. 4, 1842: extract from letter from John Jackson enclosed in Hutton to G.W. Hope (?), 8 December 1842.

56. TNA: FO84/616, Domestic Various 1845: 'Memorandum of British Subjects and Capital Engaged in the Slave Trade 1834–1845'.

57. Thomas, *The Slave Trade*, p. 679.

58. See, e.g., TNA: CO96/17, Matthew Forster to the Colonial Secretary, 30 April 1849.

59. Forster to Colonial Office, 3 May 1826, in Braithwaite, *Palmerston and Africa*, p. 77.

60. Forster to Thomas Buxton, 11 November 1839, in Braithwaite, *Palmerston and Africa*, p. 79.

61. TNA: CO96/17, 'Mr Forster' section, extract from letter from B. Cruickshank Esq. to M. Forster Esq. MP, Anamaboe, 29 September 1849.

62. *The Times*, 27 October 1848, p. 7.

63. *The Times*, 27 October 1848, p. 7; 18 March 1857, p. 9; 25 April 1853, p. 3; 20 August 1860, p. 7.

64. Thomas, *The Slave Trade*, pp. 41, 280, 676. According to the *Anti-Slavery Reporter* (23 February 1842, p. 26), about 150 slave trade vessels from Cadiz and Barcelona sailed to Cuba annually.

65. Prospectus of the Peninsular Steam Navigation Co., 1834. In 1866 Zulueta resigned his directorship because of frequent absences in Spain. His eldest son, Don Brodie Manuel de Zulueta y Willcox, Conde de Torre Diaz, is listed among the members of the Spanish Chamber of Commerce in London in 1889. Tamini, *Anglo–Spanish–Portuguese–Brazilian Directory*, London, 1889.

66. Evidence of Pedro de Zulueta to the Select Committee on West Africa, PP 1842, vol. XI, p. 679; Kent's *Original London Directory*, 1827; *Merchant Shippers*

of London, London, 1868; Pigot & Slater's *Commercial Directory*, London, 1843; Boyd Cable, *A Hundred Years of the P&O*, London: Nicholson & Watson, 1937.

67. The government appointed Capt. Hill as Governor of the Gold Coast colony in March 1843, but he had to spend so much of his time giving evidence in the court case regarding the sale of the *Augusta* that he resigned in August 1845. His claim for his salary and travel costs backwards and forwards from the Gold Coast was still unresolved in 1850. See TNA: CO96/17 and 96/21, under 'H'.

68. Evidence of Capt. Hill, PP 1842, vol. XI, pp. 447–9; 503–6, evidence of Judge Macaulay, PP 1842, vol. XI, pp. 679–84.

69. On Martinez, see David A. Ross, 'The career of Domingo Martinez in the Bight of Benin 1833–1864', *Journal of African History* 6/1 (1965), pp. 79–90; there is much on Pedro Blanco in Thomas, *The Slave Trade*, who also suspects that Zulueta & Co. was an agent of Blanco's (p. 690). That Blanco used Zulueta & Co. as his banker was well known.

70. Evidence of Zulueta, PP 1842, vol. XI, pp. 679–84.

71. Ghana Archvies, Accra: ADM5/3/3: pp. 1–6, enc. letter from George Maclean to Lord John Russell, Secretary of State for the Colonies, August 1839.

72. For the *Arrogante*, see PP 1840, vol. XLVI, pp. 465–7, Slave Trade Correspondence, Class B, 1839; Rhodes House: Br. Emp. Mss s.444, Thomas Buxton Slave Trade Papers, vol. 27, ff. 257–60.

73. See letter by 'Legion' in *The Morning Chronicle*, 31 October 1843; *Moore's Reports of Cases Heard by the Privy Council*, vol. II, 1837–38; Rhodes House: Br. Emp. Mss s.444, Thomas Buxton Slave Trade Papers, vol. 32, f. 427. The *Cazador* was sold to the slave trader del Campo by a man named Arthur Anderson, owner of the forerunner of the P&O company. It is not known whether Arthur was related to the well-known Anderson brothers, slave traders in the estuary of the Sierra Leone River until at least 1807.

74. Johnson U.J. Asiegbu, *Slavery and the Politics of Liberation 1787–1861*, London: Longman, 1969, p. 121.

75. *House of Lords Journal 1841*, p. 150, 23 March 1841.

76. For the banking connection, see e.g. TNA: CO267/139, Maer to Lord Glenelg, 14 July 1835; on Pedro Blanco's use of British merchants and bankers, see e.g. TNA: 267/139, Lord Glenelg to Governor Campbell of Sierra Leone, 25 October 1835; Madden's accusation is in PP 1842, vol. XII, *Report from the Select Committee on the West Coast of Africa*, Appendix.

77. *Anti-Slavery Reporter*, 4 October 1843, pp. 181–2.

78. The delays are chronicled in the *The Anti-Slavery Reporter* from September to October 1843.

79. *The Times*, 28 October 1843 p. 6.

80. The court case was widely reported in the daily papers such as *The Times*, the *Morning Chronicle*, the *Morning Herald* and also in the *Illustrated London News*, 4 November 1843. All supported Zulueta. For another perspective, see *The Anti-Slavery Reporter*, 1 November 1843, pp. 193–208; 15 November 1843, pp. 212–14; 13 December 1943, pp. 225–32; and the *Fifth Report of the British and Foreign Anti-Slavery Society, May 1844*, pp. 149–52. For a transcript of some of the trial, see http://memory.loc.gov/cgi-bin/query, State Trials 1820–1858,

New Series, vol. 6, Trial of Pedro de Zulueta. See also *Old Bailey Sessions Papers*, October 1843, pp. 1038–52. Zulueta published his own self-exculpating version, *Trial of Pedro de Zulueta Jun. On a Charge of Slave Trading*, London: Wood & Co., 1844 (reprinted Negro Universities Press, 1969), which was much criticised in *The Anti-Slavery Reporter* of 6 March 1844, especially for its many omissions.

81. *Annual Register* for 1843, pp. 395–8. Joseph Ewart's brother William also served as MP for Liverpool. Joseph was also a shipowner. Cable, *A Hundred Year History of the P & O*, p. 65.

82. P & O also got the Suez to Bombay mail contract in 1853. Arthur Redford, *Manchester Merchants and Foreign Trade 1794–1858* (1934), Manchester: Manchester University Press, 1973, p. 199.

83. See Marika Sherwood, 'Britain, the slave trade and slavery, 1808–1843', *Race & Class* 46/2 (2004), pp. 54–77. Only *The Patriot* (2 and 9 November 1843) reported the judge's concluding remarks.

84. *The Times*, 10 November 1849, re the San Jose Mine, Cuba; see 3 March 1853, 30 May 1867 etc. for court functions.

85. Most of the information on Barings is from Philip Ziegler, *The Sixth Great Power: Barings 1762–1929*, London: Collins, 1988; Ralph H. Hidy, *The House of Baring in American Trade and Finance*, Cambridge MA: Harvard University Press, 1949. See also Joseph Wechsberg, *The Merchant Bankers*, New York: Pocket Books, 1966, pp. 78–100; Youssef Cassis, *City Bankers 1890–1914* (1984), Cambridge: Cambridge University Press, 1994, p. 34; Anthony Sampson, *The Money Lenders*, London: Coronet, 1982, p. 38.

86. Ziegler, *The Sixth Great Power*, p. 209.

87. Hidy, *The House of Baring*, p. 55.

88. Thomas, *The Slave Trade*, pp. 683–4.

89. Anything that made a profit seemed to be of interest to the Barings. For example, they bought the Liverpool agency of the Old Line (Black Ball) packets in 1834 as there was a great demand by passengers – mostly the impoverished – for berths to New York.

90. Ziegler, *The Sixth Great Power*, p. 90. Alexander was MP for Taunton 1806–26, Callington, 1826–31; Thetford 1831–32 and North Essex 1833–35. How much bribing the electors cost him has not been recorded, but it was generally known that he was the 'owner of the constituencies of Callington and Thetford'. Hidy, *The House of Baring*, p. 47.

91. PP 1842, vol. XI, *Reports from Committees: West Coast of Africa*, p. 631, 18 July 1842, q. 9714–17; *Hansard*, House of Commons, vol. 31, 5 May 1815, col. 174.

92. Information on the Rothschild family from: Cassis, *City Bankers*; Amos Elon, *Founder: Mayer Amschel Rothschild and His Time*, London: HarperCollins, 1998; F.W. Fetter and D. Gregory, *Monetary and Financial Policy*, Dublin: Irish University Press, 1973; Niall Ferguson, *The House of Rothschild 1798–1848*, London: Penguin Books, 2000; Wechsberg, *The Merchant Bankers*; Stanley Weintraub, *Charlotte and Lionel: A Rothschild Love Story*, New York: Free Press, 2003.

93. Wellington, who banked with Rothschild, voted against the 'emancipation' of Jews in Parliament in 1830. Ferguson, *The House of Rothschild*, p. 180. Victor Gray of the Rothschild Archive states that Wellington did *not* bank with Rothschild.

94. According to Victor Gray (email, 26 May 2006), who also quotes a number of books, the loan was for £15 million. But this was the amount the government first offered the planters. They demanded £30 million; finally £20 million was agreed. If Rothschild only lent £15 million, who lent the other £5 million?

95. Hidy, *The House of Baring*, p. 377; Ziegler, *The Sixth Great Power*, p. 201.

96. Wechsberg, *The Merchant Bankers*, p. 271; my thanks to Victor Gray for the correct insurance company names.

97. L.H. Jenks, *The Migration of British Capital to 1875*, London: Jonathan Cape, n.d. (*c.* 1927), Appendix C.

98. Email from Victor Gray, Rothschild Archive, 15 April 2005.

99. Hidy, *The House of Baring*, p. 333.

100. Jehanne Wake, *Kleinwort Benson*, Oxford: Oxford University Press, 1997, p. 73.

101. According to Ferguson (*The House of Rothschild*, p. 369), Rothschild 'give first place in their operations to public finance, and rarely conducted commercial business in a country without also lending to its government'. The Philippine islands were a Spanish colony at this time.

102. Were the Rothschilds reluctant to participate in this venture of Cecil Rhodes because he had forced 'his greatest rival, Barney Barnato ... the East End Jew ... to amalgamate his interests with those of Rhodes'? M.E. Chamberlain, *The Scramble for Africa*, London: Longman, 1974, p. 75.

103. Wechsberg, *The Merchant Bankers*, p. 271; Elizabeth Longford, *Jamesons Raid*, London: Panther, 1984, pp. 30, 162, 233; David E. Torrance, *The Strange Death of Liberal Empire*, Liverpool: Liverpool University Press, 1996, pp. 30, 31, 93; Geoffrey Wheatcroft, *The Randlords*, New York: Simon & Schuster 1987, pp. 121, 250; the Rand Mines shares were held by the London and Paris firms (p. 133). In his email of 19 April 2006, Victor Gray states that Rothschild fell out with Rhodes over his expansionist policies, but this disagreement appears not to have affected their relationship.

104. Chamberlain, *The Scramble for Africa*, pp. 37–8. The company formed in 1858 to construct the canal had been dominated by France, and Britain was fearful of French expansionism. The status of the labourers toiling on the construction is debatable, to put it politely.

105. For some of the petitions, see *Hansard*, House of Lords, vol. 96, 7 and 22 February 1848. It should be noted that the issue of 'Jewish disabilities' was debated in Parliament many times. Among those voting for their retention – i.e. the exclusion of Jews as members of Parliament – was the son of abolitionist William Wilberforce, then Bishop of Oxford. Weintraub, *Charlotte and Lionel*, p. 111.

Chapter 4

Conversion rates of reales/dollars/pounds and nineteenth-century pounds to 2005 values from material kindly sent by Kath Begley of the Bank of England, February 2005.

1. PP 1843, vol. LII, *Trade: Shipping*, f. 78, Cuba: imports. On women campaigners, see Claire Midgley, *Women against Slavery: The British campaigns 1780–1870*,

London: Routledge, 1995.

2. 1787 figure from Robin Blackburn, *The Making of New World Slavery*, London: Verso, 1997, p. 403.

3. Figures from Franklin W. Knight, *Slave Society in Cuba During the Nineteenth Century*, Madison: University of Wisconsin Press, 1970, pp. 22, 94. The official figures indicate that from 1841 the White population had increased by 30 per cent while the free Black population had decreased by 7 per cent and that of slaves had fallen from 436,491, a decrease of just over 30 per cent. I would therefore doubt the figures collected for both free and enslaved Blacks, though the death rate was undoubtedly much higher for slaves than for Whites.

4. The quotation is from Robert L. Paquette, *Sugar is Made with Blood*, Middletown CT: Wesleyan University Press, 1988, p. 146. Howard Temperley, *British Anti-Slavery*, London: Longman, 1972, p. 235. In 1848 America offered to buy Cuba from Spain; part of the argument was based on the assumption that Britain might seize the island 'for the debt due to British bond holders'. L.H. Jenks, *Our Cuban Colony*, New York: Vanguard Press, 1928, p. 12.

5. Figure for 1787 from Blackburn, *The Making of New World Slavery*, p. 403; others from Lucia Lamounier, 'Between slave and free labour', in M. Turner (ed.), *From Chattel Slaves to Wage Slaves*, London: James Currey, 1995.

6. See, e.g., D.R. Murray, 'Statistics of the slave trade to Cuba, 1790–1867', *Journal of Latin American Studies* 3/2 (1971), pp. 138–9. In 1841 the British Consul in Havana believed that in some areas less than 50 per cent of slaves were registered.

7. Knight, *Slave Society in Cuba*, p. 22; Murray, 'Statistics of the slave trade to Cuba', p. 149.

8. *Anti-Slavery Reporter* 23/2 (1842), p. 26.

9. 1847 and 1852 prices from Lamounier, 'Between slave and free labour'; 1860 price from Knight, *Slave Society in Cuba*, p. 29, converted from $ at the rate of $5 = £1; 1870s from A. Gallenga, *The Pearl of the Antilles* (1873), New York: Negro Universities Press, 1970, p. 78. Antonio Gallenga, an Italian by birth, supporter of Italian and French revolutions, resident in England for some of his life and correspondent of *The Times* (London), was also a prolific author. Why he visited Cuba, probably in the late 1860s, is not known. Though a revolutionary, he clearly also held racist views, as, for example, he refers to enslaved Africans as 'black cattle' and 'African savages' (pp. 79, 87); the children of intermarriages are 'mongrels' (p. 77).

10. David Eltis, *Economic Growth and the Ending of the Transatlantic Slave Trade*, Oxford: Oxford University Press, 1987, pp. 218–19; D. Eltis, Table 4 in documents circulated at seminar at Institute of Commonwealth Studies, 20 March 1995.

11. H.H.S. Aimes, *A History of Slavery in Cuba*, New York: G. Putnam, 1907, p. 49.

12. David Eltis, 'The British contribution to the nineteenth-century transatlantic slave trade', *Economic History Review* 32/2 (1979), p. 220; David Eltis, 'The export of slaves from Africa 1821–1843', *Journal of Economic History* 37/2 (1977), p. 419.

13. Murray, 'Statistics of the slave trade to Cuba', p. 147; BFASS, *The Slave Trade*

to Cuba: An Address to Marshal Espartéro, London: BFASS, 1861, p. 6.

14. See, e.g., Frederick Drake, 'Secret history of the slave trade to Cuba, written by an American Naval Officer, Robert Wilson Schufeldt, 1861', *Journal of Negro History* 55/3 (1970), pp. 218–35. Among the British merchants supplying slaves was Baker & Dawson, whose agent in Havana was Philip Atwood.

15. Commissary Judge to Lord John Russell, possibly from Slave Trade Papers 1862, Class B, pp. 7, 19, quoted in BFASS, *Horrors of the Slave Trade,* pamphlet, n.d. (*c.* 1858–60). Conversion rate from email from Bank of England, 19 December 2005.

16. Luis Martínez-Fernández, 'The Havana Anglo-Spanish Mixed Commission for the suppression of the slave trade and Cuba's *emancipados*', *Slavery & Abolition* 16/2 (1995), p. 207.

17. Eltis, 'The British contribution', p. 213; Stephen Cave, Esq, *A Few Words on the Encouragement Given to Slavery and the Slave Trade by Recent Measures*, London: John Murray, 1849, p. 33.

18. Gallenga, *The Pearl of the Antilles*, pp. 42, 46.

19. R.F. Jameson, *Letters from Havana During the Year 1820*, London: John Miller, 1821, p. 17; John Howison, *Foreign Scenes and Travelling Recreations*, Edinburgh: Oliver Boyd, 1825, pp. 129, 143.

20. Alexander von Humboldt, *The Island of Cuba: A Political Essay* (1856), Kingston, Jamaica: Ian Randle, 2001, p. 56.

21. A Physician (J.G.F. Wurdemann), *Notes on Cuba*, Boston MA: James Munroe, 1844, pp. 63, 153, 185, 342.

22. B.M. Norman, *Rambles by Land and Water ... Cuba & Mexico,* New York: Paine & Burgess, 1845, p. 79; Aimes, *A History of Slavery in Cuba*, p. 130; Arthur F. Corwin, *Spain and the Abolition of Slavery in Cuba*, Austin: University of Texas Press, 1967, p. 140.

23. Paquette, *Sugar is Made with Blood*, pp. 45, 47, 159, 223; Hugh Thomas, *The Slave Trade*, London: Picador, 1997, pp. 541–2, 647; Hugh Thomas, *Cuba*, London: Eyre & Spottiswoode, 1971, p. 137; Johanne Wake, *Kleinwort Benson*, Oxford: Oxford University Press, 1997, p. 73.

24. Just how free these *emancipados* were is examined in Martínez-Fernández, 'The Havana Anglo-Spanish Mixed Commission', pp. 205–25.

25. Luis Martínez-Fernández, *Fighting Slavery in the Caribbean: The Life and Times of a British Family in Nineteenth Century Havana*, New York: M.E. Sharpe, 1998, pp. 58–63, 115; A Genuine 'Dicky Sam', *Liverpool and Slavery*, (1884), Liverpool: Scouse Press, n.d., ch. 14; *Anti-Slavery Reporter*, 14 July 1841, p. 145. The BFASS sent a memorial to Lord Palmerston protesting about slave-holding by British 'functionaries' in Cuba and Brazil. See *Anti-Slavery Reporter*, 29 July 1840, p. 180.

26. Paquette, *Sugar is Made with Blood*, pp. 152, 155.

27. TNA: FO72/634, f. 276; Consul Charles Clarke at Santiago de Cuba to Consul Crawford in Havana, 12 December 1843.

28. Arthur Redford, *Manchester Merchants and Foreign Trade*, Manchester: Manchester University Press, 1934, p. 98.

29. Gallenga, *The Pearl of the Antilles*, p. 79.

30. Thomas, *The Slave Trade*, pp. 647–8; *Anti-Slavery Reporter*, 23 February 1842, p. 26; TNA: FO72/585: Turnbull's 'Review of the Trade of the Island of

Cuba', 27 January 1841. Turnbull notes that there are 'problems' with Cuban statistics.

31. PP 1847, vol. LX, f. 32; PP 1843, vol. LII, f. 78.

32. http://en.wikipedia.org/wiki/Kleinwort_Benson; Johanne Wake, *Kleinwort Benson*, Oxford: Oxford University Press, 1997.

33. The company survived until 1936, when it was absorbed by the British Overseas Bank Ltd. See, e.g., www.freshford.com/huthhome1.htm.

34. Joseph Wechsberg, *The Merchant Bankers*, New York: Pocket Books, 1966, pp. 78–100; Youssef Cassis, *City Bankers 1890–1914* (1984), Cambridge: Cambridge University Press, 1994, p. 34.

35. Philip Ziegler, *The Sixth Great Power: Barings 1762–1929*, London: Collins, 1988, p. 209.

36. PP 1847, vol. LX, *Exports & Imports January – July*, f. 120; Knight, *Slave Society in Cuba*, p. 44.

37. Irving Stone, 'British direct and portfolio investment in Latin America', *Journal of Economic History* 37/3 (1977), pp. 690–722, Tables 2 and 6.

38. Thomas, *The Slave Trade*, p. 647.

39. Von Humboldt, *The Island of Cuba*, p. 194; David Turnbull, *Travels in the West*, London: Longman, 1840, p. 190.

40. Knight, *Slave Society in Cuba*, pp. 32–4.

41. Irving Stone, *The Global Export of Capital from Great Britain 1865–1914*, London: Macmillan, 1999, pp. 262–4; T. Nelson, *Remarks on the Slavery and the Slave Trade of the Brazils*, London: Hatchard, 1846.

42. Knight, *Slave Society in Cuba*, p. 37; Herbert S. Klein, *African Slavery in Latin America and the Caribbean*, Oxford: Oxford University Press, 1986, p. 98; Jennifer Tan, 'Steam and sugar: the diffusion of the stationary steam engine to the Caribbean sugar industry', *History of Technology* 19 (1997), p. 1209; Thomas, *Cuba*, pp. 156–7; L.H. Jenks, *The Migration of British Capital to 1875* (1927), London: Jonathan Cape, n.d. (*c.* 1962), p. 30.

43. Turnbull, *Travels in the West*, pp. 116–17.

44. *Annual Report 184*, p. 134.

45. The Anti-Slavery Society estimated that in the early 1840s about 150 vessels left Cadiz and Barcelona annually on slaving voyages.

46. Joseph J. Gurney, *A Winter in the West Indies,* London: John Murray, 1840, p. 218.

47. Jenks, *Our Cuban Colony*, p. 35; TNA: FO72/634 ff. 146–173: Consul Clarke to Consul Crawford in Havana, 27 April 1843.

48. *Anti-Slavery Reporter*, 11 August 1841, p. 171.

49. Turnbull, *Travels in the West*, p. 3–16; Thomas, *Cuba*, pp. 140–41; Eltis, 'The British contribution', p. 213; duty calculated from PP 1846, vol. XLIV, Trade, f. 129, copper imports.

50. Eltis, *Economic Growth*, p. 145. The firm of Sir J.W. Lubbock & Co. of Liverpool shipped 'steam boat engines' to Cadiz, for the vessels *Relampago* (in 1845), *Ligero* (1852) and *Hercules* (1844, 1846, 1850); for the *El Rapido* (1843–57) of Seville; and the *Trojano* belonging to the Cadiz firm of Pinto Perez & Co. Were these by any chance used as slavers? (Tan, 'Steam and sugar', p. 1185.)

51. Eltis, 'The British contribution', p. 220; Eltis, 'The export of slaves', p. 419.

52. Knight, *Slave Society in Cuba*, pp. 56, 134. www.fs-iav@fsancho-sabio.es. This

is the website of the Sancho el Sabio Institution, the Alava Basque Library, housed in the Zulueta Palace in Vitoria-Gasteiz, Spain.

53. Gallenga, *The Pearl of the Antilles*, pp. 97–102, 114; 37, 39.

54. Thomas, *The Slave Trade*, p. 280. For a description of the Spanish slave trade at this time, see Leslie B. Rout, *The African Experience in Spanish America*, Cambridge: Cambridge University Press, 1976, ch. 2. In the late eighteenth century two contracts to supply slaves were granted by Spain to Peter Baker and John Dawson of Liverpool and an Irishman, Edward Barry (p. 59).

55. Jos. T. Crawford to Earl Russell, 12 December 1863, in PP 1865, vol. LVI, *Slave Trade*, p. 40. Were these vessels built in Cadiz or perhaps in the UK and only fitted out in Spain?

56. Thomas, *The Slave Trade*, pp. 645–7; Eltis, *Economic Growth*, pp. 150, 202.

57. Eltis, *Economic Growth*, p. 149.

58. Lamounier, 'Between slave and free labour'.

59. Richard H. Dana, *To Cuba and Back*, Boston MA: Ticknor & Fields, 1959, p. 211; Martínez-Fernández, *Fighting Slavery in the Caribbean*, p. 9.

60. *Anti-Slavery Reporter*, 5 May 1841, p. 85; House Executive Documents, 36th Congress, 2nd Session, 1860–1861, vol. 1095, Document #47, US Consul in Havana, 10 August 1856. On the question of Liberated Africans, see Johnson U.J. Asiegbu, *Slavery and the Politics of Liberation 1787–1861*, London: Longman, 1969.

61. *Relations of the British and Brazilian Governments*, London: Chapman & Hall, 1865, p. 13.

62. BFASS, *Epitome of Anti-Slavery Information*, London: A. Ward, 1842; Nelson, *Remarks on the Slavery and the Slave Trade of the Brazils*, p. 65; Roger E. Conrad, *World of Sorrow*, Baton Rouge: Louisiana State University Press, 1986, p.171.

63. L. Bethell, *The Abolition of the Brazilian Slave Trade*, Charlottesville: Virginia University Press, 1970, p. 390; Philip D. Curtin, *The Atlantic Slave Trade*, Madison: University of Wisconsin Press, 1969, pp. 207, 216, 236, 240; Eltis, *Economic Growth*, pp. 243–4.

64. Conrad, *World of Sorrow*, pp. 111–12.

65. Thomas (*The Slave Trade*, ch. 30) has good descriptions of the 'nefarious', both legal and illegal, trade to Cuba and Brazil. But Lord Hugh has very little to say about British complicity.

66. J. Candler and W. Burgess, *Narrative of a Recent Visit to Brazil*, London: Society of Friends, 1853, p. 25.

67. TNA: FO84/95, ff. 82–3, Ponsonby to Earl Aberdeen, 27 (or 29?) June 1829; FO84/616, ff. 157–78: Rio Commissioner to Foreign Office 29 March 1835 and 18 July 1838.

68. W.D. Christie, *Notes on Brazilian Questions* (1865), London: Macmillan, 1985, pp. 13–16.

69. Conrad, *World of Sorrow*, pp. 127–33.

70. *Anti-Slavery Reporter*, 8 September 1841, p. 185.

71. House Executive Document, 30th Congress, 2nd Session, pp. 44–6, Wise to J.C. Calhoun, 12 January 1845; pp. 14, 148, depositions by British seamen.

72. Journal of the US House of Representatives, 28th Congress, 2nd Session 1844–45, doc.#148, ff. 102–8, Henry Wise to Geo. W Gordon, US Consul in Bahia, 25 October 1844.

73. House Executive Document 30th Congress, 2nd Session, Doc. #61, pp. 44-6, Wise to Calhoun, 12 January 1845.

74. Alan K. Manchester, *British Pre-eminence in Brazil*, Chapel Hill: University of North Carolina Press, 1933, p. 258.

75. Stone, *The Global Export of Capital*, pp. 102-4; Irving Stone, 'British Direct and Portfolio Investment in Latin America', *Journal of Economic History* 37/3 (1977), pp. 690-722; government bonds from A.K. Cairncross, *Home and Foreign Investment 1870-1913*, Cambridge: Cambridge University Press, 1953, p. 185; conversion rates supplied by the Bank of England.

76. Jenks, *The Migration of British Capital to 1875*, Appendix C; Christie, *Notes on Brazilian Questions*, p. lxix. Christie had been Ambassador to Brazil.

77. Manchester, *British Pre-eminence in Brazil*, p. 327; R.G. Greenhill and Rory M. Miller, 'Liverpool and South America, 1850-1930', paper given at the conference Liverpool and Empire, April 2006.

78. P.L. Cottrell, *British Overseas Investment in the Nineteenth Century*, London: Macmillan, 1975, pp. 41-2, 127.

79. Eltis, *Economic Growth*, p. 59; Leslie Bethell, *The Abolition of the Brazilian Slave Trade*, Cambridge: Cambridge University Press, 1970, pp. 388-90.

80. Bethell, *The Abolition of the Brazilian Slave Trade*, p. 225; quoted in George Pendle, *A History of Latin America*, Harmondsworth: Penguin, 1971, p. 71.

81. Manchester, *British Pre-eminence in Brazil*, pp. 258, 322.

82. Ibid., pp. 325-6; Liverpool Maritime Museum Archives: MS3147/5, Boulton and Watt, f. 790.

83. Manchester, *British Pre-eminence in Brazil*, p. 315; Cottrell, *British Overseas Investment in the Nineteenth Century*, pp. 41-2; Christie, *Notes on Brazilian Questions*, p. 129.

84. BFASS (1842), p. 13; Nelson, *Remarks on the Slavery and the Slave Trade of the Brazils*, p. 26; Cottrell, *British Overseas Investment in the Nineteenth Century*, pp. 35-6; Candler and Burgess, *Narrative of a Recent Visit to Brazil*, p. 35; TNA: FO84/501, ff. 196-7: Imperial Brazilian Mining Co. to the Foreign Secretary, 16 June 1843.

85. *Anti-Slavery Reporter*, 7 October 1840, p. 257; 22 October 1840, p. 266; 18 November 1840, p. 289; TNA: FO84/616, ff. 157-78: Rio Commissioner to Foreign Office, 29 March 1835 and 18 July 1838.

86. www.projects.ex.ac.uk/cornishlatin.

87. Manchester, *British Pre-eminence in Brazil*, pp. 323-4; Anthony Burton, *The Railway Empire*, London: John Murray, 1994, pp. 110-19. Among the engineers and companies were William Bragge, Daniel Fox, William Webb, James Brunlees; the Fairbairn company of Manchester, Robert Sharpe & Sons, Vignoels, whose son Hutton V was sent out as resident engineer. Cottrell, *British Overseas Investment*, pp. 41-2; Christie, *Notes on Brazilian Questions*, p. lxix.

88. Manchester, *British Pre-eminence in Brazil*, pp. 316, 320; Cottrell, *British Overseas Investment in the Nineteenth Century*, p. 65.

89. F.W. Spackman, *Occupations of the People* (1847), New York: Augustus M. Kelley, 1969, Appendix, pp. 170-71.

90. *Journal of the House of Representatives*, 28th Congress, 2nd Session, 1844-45, ff. 112-26, Henry A. Wise, Minister Plenipotentiary and Envoy Extraordinary

for the United States to the Court of Brazil to British Consul Hamilton
Hamilton in Rio, 1844.

91. Ibid.

92. Ibid.

Chapter 5

1. A. Adu Boahen, *African Perspectives on Colonialism*, Baltimore: Johns Hopkins
   University Press, 1987, p. 96. On the Berlin Conference, see e.g. M. Crowder,
   West Africa under Colonial Rule, London: Hutchinson, 1968, ch. 3.

2. See, for example, Humphrey J. Fisher, *History of Muslim Black Africa*, London:
   Hurst & Co., 2001; Ronald Segal, *Islam's Black Slaves*, London: Atlantic Books,
   2001; Paul E. Lovejoy (ed.), *Slavery on the Frontiers of Islam*, Princeton NJ:
   Markus Wiener, 2004.

3. See Shihan de S. Jayasuriya and R. Pankhurst (eds), *The African Diaspora in
   the Indian Ocean*, Trenton NJ: Africa World Press, 2003; Joseph E. Inikori,
   The Chaining of a Continent, Mona, Jamaica: ISER, 1992.

4. On resistance in Africa, see Sylviane A. Diouf, *Fighting the Slave Trade*,
   Athens: Ohio University Press, 2003; and some of the essays in Michael
   Crowder (ed.), *West African Resistance: The Military Response to Colonial Occupa-
   tion*, New York: Africana Publishing, 1971.

5. By 1814 treaties had been signed with Austria, Denmark, the Netherlands,
   Portugal, Russia and Sweden. Others followed, equally ineffective.

6. David Eltis et al., *The Transatlantic Slave Trade: A Database on CD Rom*, Cambridge: Cambridge University Press, 1999. On the problems of arriving at
   the numbers of slaves exported, see e.g. Paul E. Lovejoy, 'The volume of
   the Atlantic slave trade: a synthesis', *Journal of African History* 23 (1982), pp.
   473–501.

7. For both French and English use of forced labour, see e.g. Crowder, *West
   Africa under Colonial Rule*, pp. 183–4, 208–9.

8. Suzanne Miers and Richard Roberts (eds), *The End of Slavery in Africa*,
   Madison: University of Wisconsin Press, 1988, pp. 43, 45. There are innu-
   merable books on British imperialism; see, e.g., Denis Judd, *Empire*, London:
   HarperCollins, 1996; Bernard Porter, *The Lion's Share*, London: Longman,
   1975; R. Robinson and J. Gallagher, *Africa and the Victorians* (1961), New
   York: Anchor Books, 1968; Walter Rodney, *How Europe Underdeveloped Africa*,
   London: Bogle L'Ouverture, 1973. H.L. Wesseling, *Divide and Rule*, Westport
   CT: Praeger, 1996.

9. For a brief (27 pp.) but excellent summary, see Walter Rodney, *West Africa
   and the Atlantic Slave Trade* (1967), Dar-es-Salaam: East African Publishing
   House, 1970.

10. The Sultan of Zanzibar imported Baluchi men from today's Pakistan to
    serve as his soldiers. Email from historian Cliff Pereira, 19 June 2006.

11. Zanzibar had been ruled by Omani sultans until 1801 when it became
    independent of Oman. It became a British protectorate in 1890. Frederick
    Cooper, 'Conditions analogous to slavery', in Frederick Cooper et al., *Beyond
    Slavery*, Chapel Hill: University of North Carolina Press, 2000, p. 120. In the
    Quaker 'Minute of Meeting for Sufferings 3 December 1897', it is noted that
    there was an 'almost complete failure of the Decree of Emancipation in the

Zanzibar Protectorate ... [we] will be sending a deputation to the Foreign Office with the British & Foreign Anti-Slavery Society'. See also Joseph Pease, *How We Countenance the Slave Trade in East African British Protectorates*, London: BFASS, 1895. For the struggle to end the trade there, see Daniel Liebowitz, *The Physician and the Slave Trade*, New York: W.H. Freeman, 1998. On the East African slave trade, see e.g. Edward Alpers, *Ivory and Slaves*, Berkeley: University of California Press, 1975; Pascoe G. Hill, *Fifty Days On Board a Slave Vessel* (1848), Baltimore: Black Classic Press, 1993.

12. See, e.g., George E. Brooks, *Yankee Traders, Old Coasters and African Middlemen*, Boston MA: University Press, 1970, pp. 111–12, quoting the evidence of Capt. Matson of the RN in PP 1850, vol. IX (590), pp. 198 ff., where he states that American vessels could outsail the British Squadron – 'superannuated tubs...[some] not refitted for the coast ... [O]thers lacked the whale boats necessary to attack becalmed slavers out of range of gunshot ... steamers in speed no match for the clippers'. See Christopher Fyfe, *A History of Sierra Leone*, Oxford: Oxford University Press, 1962; D. Eltis, 'The British Trans-Atlantic Slave Trade after 1807', *Maritime History* 4/1 (1974), p. 4.

13. *An Exposition of the African Slave Trade, from the Year 1840, to 1850, Inclusive* (1851), New York: Books for the Libraries Press, 1871, p. 91, quoting from British Parliamentary Papers.

14. Capt. F.W. Butt-Thompson, *Sierra Leone*, London: H.F. & G. Witherby, 1926.

15. L. Bethell, 'The Mixed Commissions for the suppression of the transatlantic slave trade in the nineteenth century', *Journal of African History* 7/1 (1966), pp. 84, 89. Between 1817 and 1821 only 24 vessels were captured, of which 20 were condemned; between 1834 and 1837, 97 vessels were taken for adjudication to the Mixed Commission Court. See Christopher Lloyd, *The Navy and the Slave Trade*, London: Longman, 1949, p. 124; Thomas Fowell Buxton, *The African Slave Trade and Its Remedy*, London: John Murray, 1840, p. 283. The numbers liberated annually averaged about 1000 until 1825, from when they rose to about 3000 for the next ten years. Lloyd, *The Navy and the Slave Trade*, pp. 275, 61.

16. Ibid., p. 62.

17. Brooks, *Yankee Traders*, p. 18.

18. This use of intermediate docks was extended to Cape Verde, the Canary Islands, Fernando Po, Isle de Los (until it became British in 1818): besides the 'trade goods', slavers picked up the manacles, chains, food and water casks and timber (to increase the number of decks) which had been deposited there by 'licit' traders. Brooks, *Yankee Traders*, p. 169; Peter Leonard, *Record of a Voyage to the Western Coast of Africa in HMS Dryad, 1830–2*, Edinburgh: William Tait, 1833, p. 139; Rhodes House: Mss. Br. Emp. s18, C8/52, Correspondence of John Tredgold, evidence of William Laidlow, 1843.

19. D. Eltis and J. Walvin (eds), *The Abolition of the Atlantic Slave Trade*, Madison: University of Wisconsin Press, 1981, p. 162.

20. Captain Theophilus Conneau, *A Slaver's Log Book or 20 Years' Residence in Africa* (1854), London: Robert Hale, 1977, p. 246.

21. For Capt. Matson's very public criticism of the vessels assigned to the African Squadron, see his letters in *The Times*, 14 August 1849, p. 3; 17 August 1849, p. 6.

22. Mannix and Cowley, *Black Cargoes*, pp. 238–9; Johnson U.J. Asiegbu, *Slavery and the Politics of Liberation 1787–1861*, London: Longman, 1969, pp. 119–25, 167; Fyfe, *A History of Sierra Leone*, p. 220; Lloyd, *The Navy and the Slave Trade*, pp. 93–6.

23. Between 1810 and 1846 a total of just over £1 million (*c.* £50 million in 2005) was paid out in 'bounty money'. By 1847 the total number of enslaved Africans liberated at the various Mixed Commission Courts and the Vice-Admiralty Courts was 116,862. PP 1847–8, vol. LXIV, *Accounts and Papers 1847–1848, Slave Trade*, f. 1, p. 479.

24. From the 1840s, as it was held that the system was open to abuse, it was only 'meritorious service' that was rewarded, and from 1854 all prize moneys had to be paid into a central account, which the Lords of the Admiralty then distributed. See Lloyd, *The Navy and the Slave Trade*, pp. 83–5.

25. PP 1849–50, vol. IX(2) House of Lords Select Committee 1849–1850: *The Best Means Great Britain Can Adopt for the Final Extinction of the African Slave Trade*, App. F, p. 825.

26. Brooks, *Yankee Traders*, pp. 109, 113.

27. *The African Repository* 21/6 (June 1845), pp. 181–2.

28. Conneau, *A Slaver's Log Book*, p. 178.

29. Brooks, *Yankee Traders*, p. 109 n33. The dollar was fixed at 5 shillings in 1822, so $5000 is £1250. See Fyfe, *A History of Sierra Leone*, p. 142.

30. Macaulay had been governor from 1793 to 1799. Sierra Leone had been founded to resettle what was considered to be too many Blacks in the UK, some of whom did wish to return to Africa. Other immigrants included African Americans who had fought for the British in the American War of Independence and had been settled on unproductive lands in Nova Scotia. On his return to the UK Macaulay became secretary of the Sierra Leone Company, which was in charge of the settlement until it was taken over by the Crown. Land for the settlement had been 'purchased' from the people living there, but the notion of *selling* land was not known in West Africa at that time. See Fyfe, *A History of Sierra Leone*. On some immigrants from the West Indies, see my 'Jamaicans and Bajans in the Province of Freedom: Sierra Leone 1802–1841', *Caribbean Studies* 13/2–3 (1998).

31. David R. Murray, *Odious Commerce*, Cambridge: Cambridge University Press, 1980, p. 47.

32. Fyfe, *A History of Sierra Leone*, pp. 153, 166.

33. The East Africa Squadron 'dumped' Liberated Africans in Mumbai and Karachi. Email from historian Cliff Pereira, 19 June 2006.

34. Asiegbu, *Slavery and the Politics of Liberation*, p. 24; David Northrup, 'The compatibility of the slave trade and palm oil trades in the Bight of Biafra', *Journal of African History* 17/3 (1976), p. 357 n18. Nevertheless, many were liberated: for example, Northrup states that 17,622 captives were landed from 1831 to 1840 (p. 357); see also *An Exposition of the African Slave Trade*, p. 111.

35. By 1813, 665 men had been enlisted in the Royal Africa Corps and the West India Regiments. The Admiralty office could not provide the government with numbers serving in the Royal Navy. PP 1826, vol. XXXIII, *Slave Trade Captures 1802–1825*.

36. See Asiegbu, *Slavery and the Politics of Liberation*, chs 4 and 5; table p. 189.

37. See F. Deaville Walker, *Thomas Birch Freeman*, London: SCM, *c.* 1929, for mentions of some who returned to Abeokuta.

38. The territory that became Sierra Leone was proclaimed a British Protectorate in 1896. Some Africans fought against this. Acting District Commissioner Wallis believed that the reality behind the Hut Tax War of 1898 was the desire to 'throw off the British yoke entirely' due to the 'desire to be able to perpetuate slavery and their exports'. (The Hut Tax had been imposed in order to pay the costs of the administration imposed by Britain.) C. Braithwaite Wallis, *The Advance of our West African Empire*, London: T. Fisher Unwin, 1903, pp. 204, 207.

39. Northrup, 'The compatibility of the slave trade', p. 364.

40. Cooper, 'Conditions analogous to slavery', pp. 107—50; the quotations are from p. 114.

41. See, for example, Francine Shields, 'Those who remained behind: women slaves in nineteenth century Yorubaland', in Paul E. Lovejoy (ed.), *Identity in the Shadow of Slavery*, London: Continuum, 2000, pp. 183—201

42. Capt. Colomb RN, *Slave Catching in the Indian Ocean*, London: Longman, Green & Co., 1873, pp. 483—5, 488.

43. C.W. Newbury, 'Credit in early nineteenth century West African trade', *Journal of African History* 13/1 (1972), pp. 81—95.

44. PP 1842, vol. XII, *Slave Trade Papers*, Reports from Committees: West Coast of Africa, pp. 496—7; Lynn Pan, *Alcohol and Colonial Africa*, Helsinki: Finnish Foundation for Alcohol Studies, vol. 22 (1975), pp. 7—11; A. Olurunfemi, 'The liquor traffic dilemma in British West Africa: the Southern Nigerian example, 1895—1918', *International Journal of African Historical Studies* 17/2 (1984), pp. 229—41; Ayodeji Olukoju, 'Race and access to liquor', *Journal of Imperial and Commonwealth History* 24/2 (May 1996), pp. 218—41; see also letter from Bishop Tugwell in *The Times*, 28 September 1897. Britain also reaped profits from this trade once official colonies were established in West Africa: e.g. in the late 1890s, between 55 and 65 per cent of revenue from the colonies was from the duty on spirits. There appears to be little research on the liquor trade (and its effects) prior to the nineteenth century, or on the work of the British Native Races and Liquor Traffic Committee, founded in 1895.

45. See, e.g., Robin Law, 'Horses, firearms and political power in pre-colonial West Africa, *Past and Present* 72 (August 1976), pp. 112—32; C.W. Newbury, 'Credit in early nineteenth century West African trade', *Journal of African History* 13/1 (1972), pp. 81—95. These wars are well documented; see, for example, R. Law and S. Strickrodt, *Ports of the Slave Trade (Bights of Benin and Biafra)*, University of Stirling, 1999. For gun exports in the eighteenth century, see Joseph E. Inikori, *Africans and the Industrial Revolution in England*, Cambridge: Cambridge University Press, 2002, pp. 457—66. Inikori points out (p. 464) that the major gun manufacturers of Birmingham, the Galtons, also traded in slaves.

46. Cherry Gertzel, 'Relations between African and European traders in the Niger Delta 1880—1896', *Journal of African History* 3/2 (1962), pp. 361—6.

47. According to Patrick Manning, *Slavery and African Life*, Cambridge: Cambridge University Press, 1990, the British 'came to an understanding with the old elite and acted directly and indirectly to prevent slaves liberating

themselves' (p. 161).

48. Waibinte E. Wariboko, 'New Calabar', in Law and Strickrodt, *Ports of the Slave Trade*, pp. 153–68. Guns were some 30 per cent of British exports to Africa until 1836 (ibid., p. 119 n71).

49. Benedict G. Der, *The Slave Trade in Northern Ghana*, Accra: Woeli Publishing, 1998, p. 7.

50. See Jacob Songsore, *Regional Development in Ghana*, Accra: Woeli Publishing, 2003.

51. On the kola trade, see e.g. Edmund Abaka, *Kola is God's Gift: The Kola Industry of Asante and the Gold Coast c. 1820–1950*, Oxford: James Currey, 2005; Paul E. Lovejoy, *Caravans of Kola: The Hausa Kola Trade 1700–1900*, Zaria: Ahmadu Bello University Press, 1980.

52. Gareth Austin, 'Between abolition and Jihad: the Asante response to the ending of the Atlantic slave trade, 1807–1896', in R. Law (ed.), *From Slave Trade to Legitimate Commerce*, Cambridge: Cambridge University Press, 2002, p. 97; Philip D. Curtin, *The Atlantic Slave Trade*, Madison: University of Wisconsin Press, 1969, p. 150. The French exported about a million slaves from Gold Coast between 1711 and 1800 (ibid., p. 170). There are many revisions of the data on numbers of slaves exported and the sources of the slaves. See, e.g., Paul E. Lovejoy, 'The volume of the Atlantic slave trade: a synthesis', *Journal of African History* 23 (1982), pp. 473–501.

53. Ghana Archives, Accra: ADM1/1/9, Pt. 1, Despatches from the Secretary of State to the Government, p. 20, Canning to Admiralty, 11 September 1843, my emphasis. Hutton and other merchants in Britain advised Lord Stanley in 1843 of the importance of 'gifts': 'was essential to the prosperity of our settlements to maintain friendly relations with the Kings of Ashantee… But in dealing with a power so ignorant as that of the Ashantee [it] is usual to send Messengers to the King accompanied with presents for the King'. Ibid., p. 17: J. Reid, M. Hutton and J.G. Nicholls to Lord Stanley, 18 September 1843.

54. Matthew Forster pressured the government to take over the Danish forts, presumably to ensure his virtual monopoly of trade along the Coast. Lord Palmerston agreed and paid £10,000 for the forts. See correspondence in TNA: CO96/14 (1848); CO96/15 (1849) and CO96/17 (1850). On the Danish territories, see Ray A. Kea, 'Plantations and labour in the south-east Gold Coast from the late 18th to the mid-19th century', in Law, *From Slave Trade to Legitimate Commerce*, pp. 119–43.

55. Akosua Perbi, 'A history of indigenous slavery in Ghana from the 15th to the 19th century', Ph.D. dissertation, University of Ghana, 1997, p. 324.

56. The quotation is from H. Dalton, 'The development of the Gold Coast under British administration 1874–1901', M.A. thesis, University of London, 1957, p. 270.

57. For an excellent summary of the wars with the Asante, see J.K. Flynn, 'Ghana-Asante (Ashanti)', in Crowder (ed.), *West African Resistance*, pp. 19–52. The quotations about guns is from T.J. Bowen, *Adventures and Missionary Labors in Several Countries in the Interior of Africa from 1849 to 1856* (1857), New York: Negro Universities Press, 1969, p. 319.

58. On the export trade from the Gold Coast, see e.g. R. Dumett and M.

Johnson, 'Britain and the suppression of slavery', in Miers and Roberts (eds), *The End of Slavery in Africa*, pp. 71–98; Perbi, 'A history of indigenous slavery in Ghana'; Freda Wolfson, 'British Relations with the Gold Coast 1843–1880', Ph.D. dissertation, University of London, 1950; Marion Johnson, 'The slaves of Salaga', *Journal of African History* 27 (1986), pp. 341–62; Trevor R. Getz, *Slavery and Reform in West Africa*, Athens: Ohio University Press, 2004, esp. ch. 2. Der, *The Slave Trade in Northern Ghana*, estimates that about half a million slaves were exported from the Northern Region; he emphasises that this does not include the numbers killed in the innumerable wars fought to procure slaves (p. 32).

59. Getz, *Slavery and Reform in West Africa*, pp. 171–3; Perbi, 'A history of indigenous slavery in Ghana', pp. 246, 259, 273; G. Mikell, *Cocoa and Chaos in Ghana*, New York: Paragon, 1989, p. 29; Johnson, 'The slaves of Salaga', p. 354; Kwame Arhin, *West African Traders in Ghana in the 19th and 20th Centuries*, London: Longman, 1979, e.g. pp. 52–5; Akosua Adoma Perbi, *A History of Indigenous Slavery in Ghana*, Accra: Sub-Saharan Publishers, 2004. This excellent and ground-breaking book has no index!

60. Kofi Affirifah, *The Akyem Factor in Ghana History 1700–1875*, Accra: Ghana Universities Press, 2000, pp. 200–201; Dumett and Johnson, 'Britain and the suppression of slavery', p. 74; Johnson, 'The slaves of Salaga', p. 253. Robert's father, James Bannerman, was of Danish and African descent.

61. Wolfson, 'British Relations with the Gold Coast', p. 81. TNA: CO 267/178, Hutton to Lord Stanley, 20 April 1842, quoted in Brooks, *Yankee Traders*, p. 260; Robin Law, *Ouidah: The Social History of a West African Slaving 'Port' 1727–1892*, Oxford: James Currey, 2004, p. 33.

62. Michael Mason, 'Captive and client labour and the economy of the Bida emirate 1857–1901', *Journal of African History* 14/3 (1973), pp. 459, 461; Perbi, *A History of Indigenous Slavery in Ghana*, pp. 55–6.

63. See, e.g., Mason, 'Captive and client labour', pp. 453–71; David Northrup, 'Nineteenth-century patterns of slavery and economic growth in Southeastern Nigeria', *International Journal of African Historical Studies* 12/1 (1979), p. 10. For definitions of 'slave', and methods of procuring them and the use of domestic slaves along the Gallinas river, which was eventually incorporated in the British colony of Sierra Leone, see Adam Jones, *From Slaves to Palm Kernels*, Wiesbaden: Franz Steiner, 1983.

64. Martin Lynn, *Commerce and Economic Change in West Africa: The Palm Oil Trade in the Nineteenth Century*, Cambridge: Cambridge University Press, 1997, pp. 13, 113. Counting the numbers of casks of oil imported, in 1835 the ex-slavers Tobins and Horsfall & Co. imported 39 per cent of the total coming into Britain. M. Lynn, 'The British Palm Oil Trade with West Africa 1833–1855', ICS Seminars in Imperial and Colonial Economic History, 1976/7.

65. Sir Alan Pim, *The Financial and Economic History of the African Tropical Territories*, Oxford: Clarendon Press, 1940, p. 39. Pim, a Quaker, was a Colonial Office adviser and had been a Government of India officer. He was an extraordinary government official, proposing quite radical social and economic reforms.

66. Northrup, 'Nineteenth-century patterns of slavery', p. 8 n20; Lynn, *Commerce and Economic Change in West Africa*, p. 21.

67. Robert. S. Smith, *The Lagos Consulate 1851–1861*, Berkeley: University of California Press, 1979, p. 72, quoting official correspondence in TNA: FO84 series.

68. Ibid., p. 107.

69. According to Patrick Manning (*Slavery and African Life*, Cambridge: Cambridge University Press, 1990), the British 'came to an understanding with the old elite and acted directly and indirectly to prevent slaves liberating themselves' (p. 161).

70. Suzanne Miers, *Britain and the Ending of the Slave Trade*, London: Longman, 1975, pp. 301–2; Rina Okonkwo, 'The Lagos Auxiliary of the Anti-Slavery Society: a re-examination', *International Journal of African Historical Studies* 15/3 (1982), pp. 42–5. A.J.H Latham (*Old Calabar*, Oxford: Clarendon Press, 1973) describes 'canoe house' as ' a compact and well organised trading and fighting corporation, capable of manning and maintaining a war canoe of slaves' which could be under the authority of a slave (p. 34).

71. Jonathan Derrick, *Africa's Slavery Today*, London: Allen & Unwin, 1985, pp. 160–64; Miers and Roberts (eds), *The End of Slavery in Africa*, pp. 43–7. For WWII, see D. Killingray and R. Rathbone (eds), *Africa and the Second World War*, London: Macmillan, 1986; D. Killingray, 'Military and labour recruitment in the Gold Coast during WWII', *Journal of African History* 23 (1982), pp. 83–95; Kenneth P. Vickery, 'The Second World War revival of forced labour in the Rhodesias', *International Journal of African Historical Studies* 22/3 (1989), pp. 423–37; L.L. Bessant, 'Coercive development: land shortage, forced labour and colonial development in colonial Zimbabwe', *International Journal of African Historical Studies* 25/1 (1992), pp. 39–65.

72. Perbi, *A History of Indigenous Slavery in Ghana*, p. 80.

73. J. Duncan (ex-Life Guard and Niger Expedition), *Travels in Western Africa in 1845 and 1846*, London: Richard Bentley, 1847, p. 69, quoted in Perbi, *A History of Indigenous Slavery in Ghana*, p. 70.

74. 'Pawns' had also been used as a guarantee for the supply of slaves. The British trader gave trade goods to the African trader in exchange for slaves. The African trader had to deposit 'pawns' – sometimes his relatives – until he produced the number of slaves that had been agreed with the British trader. See Paul E. Lovejoy and David Birmingham, 'Trust, pawnship and Atlantic history: the institutional foundations of the Old Calarbar slave trade', *American Historical Review*, April 1999, pp. 333–55.

75. Dumett and Johnson , 'Britain and the suppression of slavery', p. 94.

76. Getz, *Slavery and Reform in West Africa*, pp. 40, 60.

77. P. Haenger, *Slavery and Slave Holders on the Gold Coast*, trans. J.J. Shaffer and Paul E. Lovejoy, Basel: P. Schlettwein, 2000, p. 68; Susan B. Kaplow, 'Primitive accumulation and traditional social relations in the nineteenth century Gold Coast', *Canadian Journal of African Studies* 12/1 (1978), pp. 19–36; Perbi, *A History of Indigenous Slavery in Ghana*, p. 159.

78. Getz, *Slavery and Reform in West Africa*, p. 64; Brodie Cruickshank, *Eighteen Years on the Gold Coast of Africa* (1853), London: Frank Cass, 1966, p. 234; Johnson, 'The slaves of Salaga', pp. 356–7; Ghana Archives, Accra, ADM5/5/3: Select Committee on the West Coast of Africa.

79. See two articles by Kwabena Opare Akurang-Parry, 'Slavery and abolition

in the Gold Coast: colonial modes of emancipation and African initiatives',
Ghana Studies 1 (1998), pp. 11–34; quotations from pp. 28, 30; and '"We shall
rejoice to see the day when slavery shall cease to exist": the *Gold Coast Times*,
the African intelligentsia, and abolition on the Gold Coast', *History in Africa*
31 (2004), pp. 19–42.

80. Miers and Roberts (eds), *The End of Slavery in Africa*, p. 105.

81. An interesting book, but which deals more with South than West Africa, is
A.T. Nzula et al., *Forced Labour in Africa* (1933), London: Zed Books, 1979.

82. Ghana National Archives, Tamale: NRG8/4/3: Informal Diary, Navrongo-
Zouaragu, 14 November 1919; NRG8/4/10, Informal Diary, Navrongo-
Zouaragu, 25 and 30 October 1920; NRG8/4/4, Informal Diary, Salaga, 13
December 1919, 27 November 1920; NRG8/48 Informal Diary, Salaga, 8 and
9 October 1920.

83. Roger G. Thomas, 'Forced labour in British West Africa: the case of the
Northern Territories of the Gold Coast 1906–1927', *Journal of African History*
14/1 (1973), pp. 70–103; Dumett and Johnson, 'Britain and the suppression of
slavery', p. 94; Songsore, *Regional Development in Ghana*, pp. 66–72.

84. There are references to these reports in most of the sources listed here.
See, e.g., Perbi, 'A history of indigenous slavery in Ghana', pp. 259 ff., 324;
Ghana National Archives, Accra, ADM1/1/88, Pt.1, copy of R.E. Firminger
to the Secretary of State for the Colonies, 30 April 1889, recounting his
observations while a government official in the Gold Coast.

85. Mikell, *Cocoa and Chaos in Ghana*, p. 43 n48.

86. For an overview of some of these, see Raymond E. Dumett, 'Pressure
groups, bureaucracy, and the decision-making process: the case of slavery
abolition and colonial expansion in the Gold Coast', *Journal of Imperial and
Commonwealth History* 9/2 (1981), pp. 193–215.

87. Miers and Roberts (eds), *The End of Slavery in Africa*, pp. 102–3.

88. Minute by Earl Grey, Colonial Office, July 1848, in G.E. Metcalfe, *Great
Britain and Ghana: Documents of Ghana History 1807–1957*, London: Nelson &
Sons, 1964, p. 206.

89. Perbi, 'A history of indigenous slavery in Ghana', pp. 280, 282.

90. Cooper, *Beyond Slavery*, pp. 112, 132–3.

91. Ghana National Archives, Tamale, NRG8/2/204, memo by 'ARS' 22 September 1927. These records are considerably deteriorated, so I do not know
whether the Colonial Secretary was asking all his District Commissioners
this question, or only the ones in the North. I did not have time to search
Slater's records in Accra or for the records of the Northern Territories
Council.

92. Ghana National Archives, Accra, CSO2123/17/2, file 41/33: Ormsby Gore to
Colonial Governors, 29 August 1936.

93. Ghana National Archives, Accra, CSO2123/17/2, file 41/33: *The Echo*, 23
August 1937 and 29 March 1937; Sekondi Police Superintendent to Western
Province Commissioners, 13 September 1937; Gov. Hodson to Ormsby Gore,
27 November 1937; Geo. E. London, Acting Governor to Secretary of State
Malcolm Macdonald, 20 August 1938.

94. Caroline Sorensen-Gilmour, 'Networks of slave supply', in Law and Strickrodt, *Ports of the Slave Trade*, p. 93; A.G. Hopkins, 'Economic imperialism in

West Africa: Lagos, 1880–92', *Economic History Review* 21/3 (1968), pp. 580–606; the quotation is from p. 584. See also Jonathan Derrick, *Africa's Slaves Today*, London: Allen & Unwin 1975, esp. ch. 8; S. Miers and I. Kopytoff, *Slavery in Africa*, Madison: University of Wisconsin Press, 1977.

95. Leonard, *Record of a Voyage to the Western Coast of Africa*, p. 105.

96. [Horatio Bridge], *Journal of An African Cruizer, by an Officer of the US Navy*, London, 1845. See also Northrup, 'The compatibility of the slave trade', p. 359, quoting Macgregor Laird complaining of this preference for slavers.

97. K. Onwuka Dike, *Trade and Politics on the Niger Delta 1830–1845*, Oxford: Clarendon Press, 1956, p. 53, quoting from TNA: CO82/6, Nicolls to Hay, 29 October 1833.

98. Lynn, *Commerce and Economic Change in West Africa*, pp. 19, 26, 83, 97. In 1830 Liverpool imported 96 per cent of the total of palm oil coming into the UK, but this dropped to 71 per cent by 1855; many of the early vessels used to carry the oil had been slavers (ibid., pp. 26–7).

99. Brooks, *Yankee Traders*, pp. 199, 222.

100. Lynn, *Commerce and Economic Change in West Africa*, pp. 22, 32–2.

101. Brooks, *Yankee Traders*, p. 105.

102. See, e.g., Manning, *Slavery and African Life*. For the effects in East Africa, see e.g. Edward Alpers, *Ivory and Slaves in East Central Africa*, London: Heinemann, 1975.

103. Unless otherwise stated, these are from Buxton, *The African Slave Trade and Its Remedy*, pp. 83–9.

104. Walker, *Thomas Birch Freeman*, pp. 151–2.

105. Ibid., p. 160.

106. Ibid., p. 192.

107. Bowen, *Adventures and Missionary Labors in Several Countries*, pp. 113–14.

108. Gouldsbury's report, 27 March 1876, in M. Johnson, *Salaga Papers*, vol. 1, Institute of African Studies, University of Ghana (n.d.), SAL/21/1 (un-numbered f. 38).

109. Rev. Samuel Johnson, quoted in Hopkins, 'Economic imperialism in West Africa', p. 590.

110. Der, *The Slave Trade in Northern Ghana*, p. 32; Songsore, *Regional Development in Ghana*, pp. 67–70.

111. Getz, *Slavery and Reform in West Africa*, pp. 181–2, 191; Northrup, 'The compatibility of the slave trade', p. 361.

112. See Kaplow, 'Primitive accumulation and traditional social relations'.

113. Manning, *Slavery and African Life*, p. 99.

114. Given the reduction in prices, the *amount* of goods increased even more than is indicated by the increase in value. I've used 'Real value', which is usually calculated at a higher rate than 'official value'. G. Liesegand et al. (eds), *Figuring African Trade*, Berlin: Dietrich Reimer Verlag, 1986, p. 60.

115. G.I. Jones, *From Slave Trade to Palm Oil*, Cambridge African Monographs 13 (1989), p. 56; my emphasis. Jones had served as a government official in Nigeria before becoming a lecturer in Social Anthropology at Cambridge University.

116. M. Perham (ed.), *Mining, Commerce and Finance in Nigeria*, London: Faber, 1948, p. 4.

117. The export of cotton cloth increased from 358,000 yards in 1814 to almost 17,000 yards in 1850 and reached 72,000 yards by 1880. Jones, *From Slave Trade to Palm Oil*, p. 56, quoting the evidence given by Thomas Tobin of the slave-trading family to the House of Commons, in PP 1847–8, vol. XXII, Third Report.

118. Jones, *From Slave Trade to Palm Oil*, states that rum and brandy were diluted between 25 per cent and 33 per cent (p. 58).

119. Perham, *Mining, Commerce and Finance in Nigeria*, p. 230.

120. TNA: FO/84/1001: Memorandum #76, dated 20 August 1856, quoted in Newbury (1972), p. 90.

121. Claude Meillassoux, *The Anthropology of Slavery*, Chicago: Chicago University Press, 1991, p. 318.

Chapter 6

1. *Anti-Slavery Reporter*, 1 December 1847, quoting the report received from Anti-Slavery Society at Exeter, 23 November 1847.

2. Paul Edwards and James Walvin, *Black Personalities in the Era of the Slave Trade*, London: Macmillan, 1983, p. 19; Douglas Lorimer, *Colour, Class and the Victorians*, Leicester: Leicester University Press, 1978, pp. 202–6. See also Christine Bolt, *Victorian Attitudes to Race*, London: Routledge, 1971. The basic text on the history of people of African descent/origins in Britain is Peter Fryer, *Staying Power: The History of Black People in Britain*, London: Pluto, 1984.

3. However, the British West Indian colonies could continue to sell slaves to each other until 1825.

4. From Jane Longmore, '"Cemented by the Blood of a Negro"? The impact of the slave trade on Liverpool', paper presented at the Liverpool and Transatlantic Slavery Conference, 15 October 2005.

5. Olaudah Equiano, *The Interesting Narrative and Other Writings*, London: Penguin, 1995; James Walvin, *An African's Life*, London: Cassell, 1998; letter from Equiano in *Birmingham Gazette*, 28 June 1790, thanking all those who attended his lecture and subscribed to his book; Nini Rodgers, 'Equiano in Belfast', *Slavery and Abolition* 18/2 (1997), pp. 73–89. On the abolitionists, see C.L. Brown, *Moral Capital: Foundations of British Abolitionism*, Chapel Hill: University of North Carolina Press, 2006 (my thanks to Isaac Land for this reference).

6. All the information on women's participation in anti-slavery is from Clare Midgley, *Women Against Slavery*, London: Routledge, 1992. For class and religious issues, see Seymour Drescher, *Capitalism and Antislavery*, London: Macmillan, 1986, especially chs 6 and 7.

7. On Sam Sharpe's Rebellion, and others, see Richard Hart, *Slaves Who Abolished Slavery*, Kingston, Jamaica: ISER, University of the West Indies, 1985.

8. Midgley, *Women Against Slavery*, pp. 67, 44.

9. On the women, see Louis Billington, 'British humanitarians and American cotton, 1840–1860', *American Studies Journal* 11/3 (1977), pp. 320–23.

10. I must thank Dr Mark Ledwidge for obtaining a copy of this for me from

the John Rylands Library of Manchester University.

11. See Billington, 'British humanitarians and American cotton', pp. 313–34.

12. Unless otherwise noted, this section is taken from Frank J. Klingberg, *The Anti-Slavery Movement in England* (1926), New Haven CT: Yale University Press, 1968, chs 8, 9 and 10. Wilberforce in the House of Commons, 17 March 1807, quoted in Jack Gratus, *The Great White Lie*, London: Hutchinson, 1973, pp. 123, 127.

13. *Autobiographical Memoirs of Thomas Fletcher of Liverpool, written 1843*, Liverpool: for private circulation, 1893.

14. For example, in Winchelsea, Sussex, out of a population of 817, 11 could vote for the two MPs representing the town; in Old Sarum in Wiltshire, 'owned' by the Earl of Caledon, 7 electors out of a total population of 148 were also represented by two MPs. See, e.g., E.P. Thompson, *The Making of the English Working Class* (1963), Harmondsworth: Penguin, 1968, pp. 887–909; there is much useful information on the web – search 'rotten boroughs'.

15. Izhak Gross, 'The abolition of Negro slavery and British parliamentary politics 1832–3', *The Historical Journal* 32/1 (1980), pp. 63–85; the figure is from p. 65.

16. Klingberg, *The Anti-Slavery Movement in England*, p. 285.

17. Gratus, *The Great White Lie*, pp. 244–9; James Williams, *Narrative of the Cruel treatment of James Williams, a Negro Apprentice in Jamaica...*, Glasgow: Aird & Russell, 1837.

18. On the many aspects of the sugar duty issue and debates between the interested parties, see e.g. Philip D. Curtin, 'The British sugar duties and West Indian prosperity', *Journal of Economic History* 14/2 (1954), pp. 157–64; Arthur Redford, *Manchester Merchants and Foreign Trade 1794–1858* (1934), Manchester: Manchester University Press, 1973, pp. 144–9; C. Duncan Rice, '"Humanity sold for sugar!" The British abolitionist response to free trade in slave-grown sugar', *The Historical Journal* 13/3 (1970), pp. 402–18; Robert L. Schuyler, 'The abolition of British imperial preference, 1846–1860', *Political Science Quarterly* 33/1 (March 1918), pp. 77–92.

19. There is a good collection of pamphlets published in the 1820s in the Canterbury Cathedral archives.

20. F.W. Spackman, *Occupations of the People* (1847), New York: Augustus M. Kelley, 1969, p. 111.

21. In 1841 Britain imported 134 million lb of coffee from Brazil; much was re-exported. G.W. Alexander, *Letters of the Slave Trade, Slavery and Emancipation*, London: Charles Gilpin, 1842, p. 172.

22. See, e.g., Parliamentary Debates reported in *The Times*, 8 May 1841, p. 10; *Journal of the House of Lords* for 1844. When the House of Commons passed the Sugar Bill in 1846 the Society petitioned the House of Lords to refuse their assent. The petition was signed by the ever-active Thomas Clarkson. *Journal of the House of Lords*, 27 June 1846, p. 1135.

23. See the petition in *The Times*, 21 July 1846, p. 6.

24. Lt Henry Yule, *The African Squadron Vindicated*, London: James Ridgway, 1850, p. 8.

25. Howard Temperley, *British Antislavery 1833–1870*, London: Longman, 1972, p. 140.

26. The differences in duty were large: on colonial, 14 shillings per cwt; on foreign (free labour), 23 shillings; on foreign (slave labour), 63 shillings. The equalisation of sugar duties led to a reduction in imports from the British West Indies, e.g. from about 180,000 tons in 1833 to 110,000 tons in 1841. *The Times*, June 1848, p. 5. This in turn led to unemployment, strikes and pressures on Parliament. The response was to permit the West Indian colonies to drop the regulations imposing preferential duty on – and the restriction to purchase only – British goods. On the twists and turns of these debates, see e.g. C. Duncan Rice, '"Humanity sold for sugar!" The British abolitionist response to free trade in slave-grown sugar', *The Historical Journal* 13/3 (1970), pp. 402–18; Robert L. Schuyler, 'The abolition of British imperial preference, 1846–1860', *Political Science Quarterly* 33/1 (March 1918), pp. 77–92; Temperley, *British Antislavery*.

27. John Fitzgerald, *Man-Stealing by Proxy: Slavery and the Slave Trade by the Purchase of Slave-grown Cotton*, London: Dalton, 1850, p. 19. Fitzgerald quotes much from the innumerable Parliamentary Reports.

28. *The Times*, 25 July 1846, p. 4; 20 July 1846, p. 6.

29. H. Richard, *Memoirs of Joseph Sturge*, London: S.W. Partridge, 1864, pp. 384–8; the quotation is from pp. 395–6.

30. *Mercury*, 13 June 1848, p. 373.

31. See *Cambridge History of the British Empire*, vol. 2, ch. 6.

32. Redford, *Manchester Merchants and Foreign Trade*, p.243.

33. Karl Marx, *Articles on India*, Bombay: Peoples' Publishing House, 1943, p. 8.

34. My thanks to Cliff Pereira for this.

35. Martin was a member of the Legislative Council in China and had been Treasurer in Hong Kong.

36. Daniel H. Buchanan, *The Development of Capitalistic Enterprise in India*, London: Frank Cass, 1966, pp. 36–8.

37. *Journal of the House of Lords*, 4 August 1842, p. 508. The *Journal* notes many petitions from all over England, to emancipate 'those held in bondage in British possession in the East'.

38. *The Times*, 19 June 1850. The 1840 Anti-Slavery Convention, which considered the issue of slavery in India at some length, was presented with an estimate of between 5 and 8 million slaves in India and Ceylon under British government. William Adam, 'Slavery in India', in *General Anti-Slavery Convention 1840*, p. 1.

39. This suggestion comes from my colleague Cliff Pereira.

40. All from R. Palme Dutt, *A Guide to the Problem of India*, London: Victor Gollancz, 1942, pp. 48–51.

41. Sir George Stephen, *Anti-Slavery Recollections*, London, 1854, p. 42.

42. Andrew Porter, '"Gentlemanly capitalism" and empire', *Journal of Imperial and Commonwealth History* 18/3 (October 1990), pp. 265–95; the quotation is from p. 278.

43. Arthur W. Silver, *Manchester Men and Indian Cotton 1847–1872*, Manchester: Manchester University Press, 1966, p. 21.

44. Redford, *Manchester Merchants and Foreign Trade*, p. 106.

45. PP 1847–8, vol. XXII, *Slave Trade Committees, Minutes of Evidence*, Horsfall, 18 May 1848, questions 4775–928; Tobin, 30 May 1848, questions 5622–777.

46. Redford, *Manchester Merchants and Foreign Trade*, pp. 102 103.

47. *Anti-Slavery Reporter*, 11 June 1844, p. 113.

48. *Hansard*, House of Commons, 1845 vol. 82, 22 July, col. 957.

49. *Hansard*, House of Commons, 1846, vol. 84, 9 March, col. 810; 1847, vol. 90, 19 February, col. 247.

50. J. Wechsberg, *The Merchant Bankers*, New York: Pocket Books, 1966, p. 267.

51. Youssef Cassis, *City Bankers*, Cambridge: Cambridge University Press, 1994, pp. 207, 231–2.

52. Ibid., p. 77; *Barclays Bank (Dominion, Colonial and Overseas): A Banking Centenary*, for private circulation, n.d. (*c.* 1937), pp. 24–8; www.adb.online.anu.edu/biog. Cassis has a very interesting table on p. 226, giving an example of the interconnectedness of the holdings of bankers in the nineteenth century: e.g. men of the Lubbock family were directors of five banks, eight insurance companies and five investment trusts.

53. See Joseph E. Inikori, *Slavery and the Rise of Capitalism*, Mona, Jamaica: University of the West Indies, 1993.

54. *Journals of the House of Lords*, 1842, 2 and 4 August, pp. 505, 508. *Hansard*, House of Commons, vol. 168, 1862, 17 July, col. 425: question by Sir Francis Baring to Colonial Office.

55. Printed in PP 1843, vol. IV, #393.

56. TNA: FO84/501, ff. 196–204.

57. I have to thank my colleague Dr Caroline Bressey for this information. The documentation also indicates the buying and selling of British companies to each other, possibly in order to cover up slave-owning.

58. *Proceedings of the General Anti-Slavery Convention, held in London 1843*, p. 193. In 1830 the election 'expenses' of Mr Ewart, a merchant, were estimated to have been £65,000; the total number of electors in Liverpool was 4401. W.A. Munford, *William Ewart MP: Portrait of Radical*, London: Grafton, 1960, p. 52.

59. *Hansard*, House of Commons, 1845, vol. 81, 24 June, col. 1158; 1848, vol. 96, cols 1101–7.

60. *Hansard*, House of Commons, 1847, vol. 94, 9 July, cols 125–41.

61. *Hansard*, House of Lords, 1847–48, p. 813.

62. PP 1847–8, vol. XXII, *Slave Trade Committees, Minutes of Evidence*, 23 March 1848, q.489.

63. The quotation is from David R. Murray, *Odious Commerce*, Cambridge: Cambridge University Press, 1980, p. 121.

64. Quoted in Jean D'Costa and Barbara Lalla (eds), *Voice in Exile*, Tuscaloosa: University of Alabama Press, 1989, pp. 68–9; Murray, *Odious Commerce*, p. 121.

65. The quotation is from David R. Murray, 'Richard Robert Madden: his career as a slavery abolitionist', *Studies: An Irish Quarterly* 1 (Spring 1972), p. 49.

66. Howard Jones, *Mutiny on the Amistad*, Oxford: Oxford University Press, 1988, p. 109.

67. Dr Madden was actually on six months' leave; his appointment to Cuba had not terminated.

68. On Maclean, see G.E. Metcalfe, *Maclean of the Gold Coast*, London: Oxford

University Press, 1962; the accusation regarding the sale of guns etc. to the *Dos Amigos* is also in the *Anti-Slavery Reporter*, 17 January 1841, p. 29.

69. Dr Madden's handwritten report can be seen in TNA: CO267/171.

70. *Hansard*, House of Commons, 29 September 1841, cols 1004–5.

71. See, e.g., TNA: CO267/170, Slave Trade & African Forts, 1814 – Correspondence, and Commissioner Dr Madden, which includes copies of some of Forster's correspondence with Dr Madden and other government departments.

72. TNA: CO267/17: Draft of letter, 16 December 1842, in Treasury Section.

73. Matthew Forster's 'procured' witnesses are listed in the 'Expenses of Witnesses' report in PP 1842, vol. XI, *Select Committee on the West Coast of Africa.* Who, I wonder, asked a Dr José Cliffe to give evidence? He was an 'American, settled in Brazil, who had [possibly] fled the United States to avoid conviction as a slave trader'. He was also an owner of slaves. *A Letter from Lord Denman to Lord Brougham...* London: Hatchard, 1848, p. 25.

74. For example, the Committee agreed to his suggestion to omit from the published report 'the names of those implicated in abuses in the Government of Sierra Leone [who] have had no opportunity of defending themselves before the Committee' (PP 1842, vol. XI, *Select Committee on the West Coast of Africa,* 2 August 1842). The Committee could have checked Dr Madden's allegations with the many reports sitting on Parliament's library shelves.

75. Thomas More Madden (ed.), *The Memoirs from 1798 to 1886 of Richard Robert Madden,* London: Ward & Downers, 1891, p. 113.

76. Society for the Extinction of the Slave Trade and for the Civilization of Africa, *Present State of Africa,* n.d., p. 10.

77. *Anti-Slavery Reporter,* 2 November 1842, pp. 173 ff., 180.

78. Quoted in Madden, *The Memoirs from 1798 to 1886 of Richard Robert Madden,* p. 115. Other papers named as supporting Dr Madden or questioning the government are the *United Services Gazette,* the *Morning Chronicle,* the *Freeman's Journal* and *Planet.*

79. TNA: CO267/178, Hutton to GW Hope, 8 December 1842. The letter is marked 'private' and 'don't wish to be known as the party conveying this information'. Hutton was a Coast merchant. Why did he forward this letter? Was he in some sort of private conflict with the rival firm for Forster & Smith?

80. Macgregor Laird, *The Effect of an Alteration in Sugar Duties on the Condition of the People of England and the Negro Race,* London: Effingham Wilson, 1844, pp. 21–2.

81. Search of Old Bailey website; telephone conversation (22 May 2006) with Dr Ian Duffield, the expert in transportation, who has scoured the transportation records to New South Wales and Van Dieman's Land.

82. Letter from Capt. Matson in *The Times,* 14 August 1849, p. 3. Matson is repeating the evidence he had given to Parliament. Prize money continued to be paid to the African Squadron; for example, £13,488 was paid between 6 January and 15 April 1841 (TNA: HCA35/53, ff. 216–17)

83. TNA: CO267/172, Foreign Office to Sir James Stephen, Colonial Office, 7 May 1842; deposition by Capt. Tucker, 1 September 1841; Walter Lewis to Lord Palmerston, 22 January 1841.

84. Sir George Stephen, *Anti-Slavery Recollections*, London: Hatchard, 1854, p.101.

Conclusion

1. There was, and is, no mandatory or compulsory follow-up to Select Committees findings. The volumes just sit comfortably on Parliament's library shelves.

Appendix 1

1. Philip Curtin, *Economic Change in Precolonial Africa*, Madison: University of Wisconsin Press, 1975, pp. 188–9.
2. Quoted in ibid., p. 243.
3. Joseph Pease, *How We Countenance Slavery in the West African British Protectorates*, London: BFASS, 1895, p. 13.
4. Capt. Lugard, 'Slavery under the British Flag', *Nineteenth Century* 39 (1896), pp. 335–55; quotation is from p. 353.
5. Johnston, 1913, quoted in M.E. Chamberlain, *The Scramble for Africa*, London: Longman, 1974, p. 106.
6. Sir Harry Johnston, *The Backward Peoples and Our Relations with Them*, Oxford: Oxford University Press, 1920, p. 23.
7. Hugh Thomas, *The Slave Trade*, London: Picador, 1997, p. 590.
8. Lord Hailey, *An African Survey*, Oxford: Oxford University Press, 1945, p.643.
9. Ibid., pp. 619–20.
10. Ibid., p. 620.
11. ILO, *African Labour Survey*, Geneva, 1958, pp. 296–8.
12. R. Montgomery Martin, *The British Colonies*, vol. IV: *Africa and the West Indies*, London: London Printing & Publishing Co., 1851–57, p. 172.

Appendix 2

1. Hugh Thomas, *The Slave Trade*, London: Picador, 1997, p. 683.
2. Capt. Adams to Commodore Fanshawe, 24 March 1851, in Tim Coates (ed.), *King Guezo of Dahomey, 1850–1852*, London: Stationery Office, 2001, p. 139.
3. Thomas, *The Slave Trade*, p. 690.
4. PP 1839, vol. XLIX, *Slave Trade*, Class A [188], p. 155; PP 1842 vol. XI, *Reports from Committees – West Coast of Africa*, p. 631, question 9717, evidence of Thomas Whitfield, 18 July 1842.
5. Richard Drake, *Revelations of a Slave Smuggler – being the autobiography of Capt. Rich'd Drake* [1860], Northbrook IL: Metro Books, 1972, pp. 72, 92. Drake's uncle, Richard Willing, changed his name to Villeno after 1807; Joseph C. Dorsey, *Slave Traffic in the Age of Abolition 1815–1859*, Gainesville: University Press of Florida, 2003, pp. 26, 154; Daniel P. Mannix and Malcolm Cowley, *Black Cargoes*, New York: Viking Press, 1962, pp. 231–2; Adam Jones, *From Slaves to Palm Kernels*, Wiesbaden: Franz Steiner, 1983, pp. 42–3, 78–9; Thomas, *The Slave Trade*, p. 690.

6. PP 1839, vol. XLIX, *Slave Trade*, Class A [188], p. 155.

7. Thomas, *The Slave Trade*, p. 644; Fyfe, *A History of Sierra Leone*, p. 220.

8. The history of the Brew family is taken from Margaret Priestley, *West African Trade and Coast Society: A Family Study*, London: Oxford University Press, 1969.

9. Mannix and Cowley, *Black Cargoes*, pp. 236-8.

10. Report of John Jeremie, Commissioner at Sierra Leone to Lord Palmerston, 31 December 1840, http://home.planet.nl/~pbdavis/SL1840.htm.

11. Drake, *Revelations of a Slave Smuggler*, p. 96; Mannix and Cowley, *Black Cargoes*, p. 232; R. Law and S. Strickrodt, *Ports of the Slave Trade (Bights of Benin and Biafra)*, University of Stirling, 1999, p. 59. See also Adam Jones, 'Theophile Conneau at Galinhas and New Sestos, 1836-1841: a comparison of sources', *History in Africa* 8 (1981), pp. 89-105.

12. Thomas Hutton to (his uncle in London) Mr Hutton, from Cape Coast, 7 August 1850, in Coates (ed.), *King Guezo of Dahomey*, pp. 96-7.

13. F. Deaville Walker, *Thomas Birch Freeman*, London: SCM, *c.* 1929, p. 164.

14. Dorsey, *Slave Traffic in the Age of Abolition*, p. 154; Christopher Fyfe, *A History of Sierra Leone*, Oxford: Oxford University Press, 1962, pp. 196, 220; Lt Forbes to Lord Palmerston, 5 November 1849, in Coates (ed.), *King Guezo of Dahomey*, p. 36.

15. Peter Leonard, *Record of a Voyage to the Western Coast of Africa in HMS Dryad, 1830-1832*, Edinburgh: William Tait, 1833, p. 80.

16. Gov. John Jeremie to Lord Palmerston from Sierra Leone, 31 December 1840, http://home.planet.nl/~pbdavis/SL1840.htm; For much on Ormond and Edward Joseph, see Capt. Theophilus Conneau, *A Slaver's Log Book or 20 Years' Residence in Africa* (1854), London: Robert Hale, 1977.

17. Law and Strickrodt, *Ports of the Slave Trade*, pp. 90-92.

18. Lt F.E. Forbes, on HMS *Bonetta*, 5 November 1849 (to Lord Palmerston?), in Coates (ed.), *King Guezo of Dahomey*, p. 36.

19. Dorsey, *Slave Traffic in the Age of Abolition*, p. 153; Brooks, *Yankee Traders*, p. 194; David A. Ross, 'The career of Domingo Martinez in the Bight of Benin 1833-1864', *Journal of African History* 6/1 (1965), pp. 79-90.

20. Gov. John Jeremie to Lord Palmerston from Sierra Leone, 31 December 1840, http://home.planet.nl/~pbdavis/SL1840.htm.

21. Fyfe, *A History of Sierra Leone*, p. 66. Thomas, *The Slave Trade*, pp. 683-4; Mannix and Cowley, *Black Cargoes*, p. 230; Fyfe, *A History of Sierra Leone*, pp. 66, 133, 185. The value of dollar was fixed at 5 shillings in 1822 (ibid., p. 142). (The accounts of the Ormonds by these two writers do not always tally.)

22. Dorsey, *Slave Traffic in the Age of Abolition*, pp. 153-60; 122, 134; Thomas, *The Slave Trade*, p. 686; John Hughes, *Liverpool Banks and Bankers 1760-1837*, Liverpool: Henry Young, 1906, pp. 138-45.

23. Dorsey, *Slave Traffic in the Age of Abolition*, p. 155.

24. *Illustrated London News*, 4 November 1843.

25. The list for 1807 is in Gail Cameron and Stan Crooke, *Liverpool, Capital of the Slave Trade*, Liverpool: Picton Press, 1992, p. 61. It is, I suppose, possible that Corrie was only involved in 'legitimate trade'.

26. Sheryllyne Haggerty, 'Perceptions not Profits', paper presented at a conference, available on www.hslc.org.uk; S.G. Checkland, *The Gladstones*,

Cambridge: Cambridge University Press, 1971, pp. 13–14.

27. Hughes, *Liverpool Banks and Bankers*, pp. 95–103.

28. Eric Williams, *Capitalism and Slavery* (1964) London: Andre Deutsch, 1975, pp. 46, 99.

29. On the Tobins and Horsfalls, see Martin Lynn, 'Trade and Politics in 19th century Liverpool: the Tobin and Horsfall families', *Transactions of the Historic Society of Lancashire and Cheshire* 142 (1993), pp. 99–120. See also Graeme J. Milne, *Trade and Traders in Mid-Victorian Liverpool*, Liverpool: Liverpool University Press, 2000, p. 173.

30. Milne, *Trade and Traders*, pp. 169–79.

31. Williams, *Capitalism and Slavery*, p. 100.

32. Lucie Nottingham, *Rathbone Brothers*, London: Rathbone Bros, 1992; Thomas Barnes, *History of the Commerce and Town of Liverpool*, London: Longman, Brown & Green, 1852, p. 491. It was William IV and William VI who were known as active abolitionists.

33. A Genuine 'Dicky Sam', *Liverpool and Slavery* (1884), Liverpool: Scouse Press, 1985, pp. 120–29; F.E. Sanderson, 'Liverpool Abolitionists', in R. Anstey and P.E.H. Hair (eds), *Liverpool: The African Slave Trade and Abolition*, Liverpool: Historic Society of Lancashire and Cheshire, 1989, p. 226.

34. There are some Tarleton papers at the Liverpool Record Office. Sadly some of the microfilm is almost unreadable. See also the *Cheshire Sheaf*, July 1930.

35. www.isle-of-man.com/manxnotebook/fulltext/worthies.

36. Thomas, *The Slave Trade*, p. 402.

37. Tobin's bid to become mayor was supported by the *Liverpool Courier*, one of whose owners was John Gladstone. A.J.H Latham, 'A trading alliance: John Tobin and Duke Ephraim', *History Today* 14/12 (1974), pp. 682–8.

38. Thomas, *The Slave Trade*, p. 563.

39. PP 1847–48, vol. XXII, *Slave Trade Committees* – Minutes of Evidence, Third Report, 30 May 1848, questions 5622–777.

Appendix 3

1. For details of the Bill and a brief mention of the Viscount's visit to the UK, see *Proceedings of the General Anti-Slavery Convention, held in London 1843* (1843), Miami: Mnemosyne Publishing, 1969, pp. 173–5.

2. *An exposition of the African Slave Trade, from the year 1840, to 1850, inclusive* (1851), Freeport: Books for Libraries Press, 1971, p. 90.

3. Ibid., p. 94.

4. Letter from Consul John Rendell, which was published by the government and reprinted in the *Anti-Slavery Reporter* on 7 October 1840, p. 264.

5. *Report of the Committee of the African Civilization Society, 21 June 1842, Exeter Hall*, London: John Murray, 1842, Appendix BB, p. lviii.

6. *Proceedings of the General Anti-Slavery Convention, held in London 1843*, p. 190, statement by G.W. Alexander.

7. *Anti-Slavery Reporter*, 14 December 1941, p. 198.

8. *Fifth Report of the British and Foreign Anti-Slavery Society*, London: BFSS, 1844, p. 151.

Index